Julian Robertson
A Tiger in the Land of Bulls and Bears

Daniel A. Strachman

WILEY

John Wiley & Sons, Inc.

Published by John Wiley & Sons, Inc., Hoboken, New Jersey.

Published simultaneously in Canada.

For general information on our other products and services, or technical support, please contact our Customer Care Department within the United States at 800-762-2974, outside the United States at 317-572-3993 or fax 317-572-4002.

Wiley also publishes its books in a variety of electronic formats. Some content that appears in print may not be available in electronic books.

For more information about Wiley products, visit our web site at www.wiley.com.

Library of Congress Cataloging-in-Publication Data:

Strachman, Daniel A., 1971–
   Julian Robertson : a tiger in the land of bulls and bears / Daniel A. Strachman.
      p.   cm.
      Includes bibliographical references (p.   ).
      ISBN 0-471-32363-2 (cloth) ISBN 978-1-119-08709-0 (paperback)
      1. Robertson, Julian.   2. Tiger Management (Firm)–History.   I. Title.
   HG928.5.R63877   2004
   332.64'5–dc22   2004013116

10 9 8 7 6 5 4 3 2 1

To my wife, Felice

"Genius is one percent inspiration,
ninety-nine percent perspiration."
—*Thomas A. Edison*

"The difference between a successful person and others
is not a lack of strength, not a lack of knowledge,
but rather, a lack of will."
—*Vince Lombardi*

ACKNOWLEDGMENTS

THIS PROJECT IS THE RESULT OF RESEARCH THAT REACHED across the globe in search of information about Julian H. Robertson Jr., his life, his family, his business, and his work in the community. Many people contributed to this effort, and I want to thank all the former Tigers, the current Cubs, and the many other individuals who subjected themselves to my interviews. To all of you I say thank you very much. Of course, without access to Julian Robertson, it would not have been possible to get the complete story, and I want to thank him for spending time with me.

Two individuals who were particularly helpful were Viki Goldman, the finest librarian I have ever met, and Sam Graff, a man who can make anyone look good in print. Without their effort, support, and guidance, this book would probably not be sitting on the book shelf. I also need to thank Erik Calonius, who truly knows his way around words and is someone for whom I have great respect and admiration. Joanna Ro is someone else who needs to get a nod. Her work on the manuscript and guidance through the editing process was insightful and incredibly useful.

Special thanks to my family for their understanding and support.

ACLNOWLEDGMENTS

To all of the people at John Wiley & Sons, especially Pamela van Giessen and Joan O'Neil, thanks again for the green light. I don't think I will ever find a place more supportive of my work. As I have said before, I hope this book is everything you intended it to be when you gave me the go-ahead to write it.

Daniel A. Strachman
New York City
July 2004

CONTENTS

INTRODUCTION

T HIS IS THE STORY OF HOW MONEY IS MANAGED AND HOW legends are made. This book is about one man's ability to continually exploit market inefficiencies and extract huge profits from his work. It is about how, by employing and utilizing some of Wall Street's best and brightest minds, he was able to continually beat the market and establish himself as one of the greatest money managers of all time. It is about how winning is not something but how it is everything. It is about how he sometimes pushed his employees to an extreme that caused them to deeply resent their boss. It is about how he expressed his thanks for their tireless efforts with nothing more than a pat on the back—and a bucketful of money. It is the story of how one individual with incredible drive and a will to win at whatever cost built one of the most successful hedge funds and money management organizations of all time. It is also the story of an individual who has forever impacted the way money is managed around the globe but whose success came with a streak of envy that many believed eventually led to his downfall.

This is the story of a money manager who became an overnight sensation by leading the growth of an organization from a group of under 20 people managing just around $8 million in assets to an organization with more than 100 people managing more than $21 billion in assets. It is about how the organization went from being a small family business with a culture based around mutual success and enjoyment to an investment management corporation with a culture laced with infighting and greed. It is about the growing pains, the frustrations, and the cultural problems that the company experienced on its rise and its fall in the wake of the technology bubble that rocked the equity markets at the dawn of the millennium.

It is the story of Julian Robertson and Tiger Management.

Julian Hart Robertson Jr. has been called everything from arrogant and mean to gruff and stubborn. He is considered by some to be extremely kind, and his southern charm is legendary. And while many of his contemporaries, former colleagues, and some his friends say nice things about him, one thing is quite clear: He is a complex man.

Talking to people on the Street about him yields comments like, "His is the finest hindsight of anybody around," and "You never know quite where you stand with him," along with, "He built a better mousetrap," and "Julian is in a class by himself." The comments are littered with praise, envy, and—in some cases—fear.

It is hard to find anyone who will not praise him for his work, both in and out of the markets, but it is also not uncommon to have some people praise Robertson on the record and then quickly ask to go off the record and augment their comments with a different flavor—a mean flavor, even a vicious flavor.

This is a man who can add a column of numbers in his head and know to the penny how much up or down is the portfolio (remember the way Dustin Hoffman counted the matchsticks in the movie *Rain Man*)—but he also has trouble remembering people's names.

He is a man who has a competitive streak that runs deep in his veins, and he unleashes it not only when he is trading or investing but also in his everyday life, including when he is relaxing on the golf course. He has taken this *hobby* so far that he has been building golf courses designed by the world's leading course architects. Although his skills on the course are something to be desired due to his lack of natural talent, he has been known to turn a simple round of golf into a hellish experience. Some friends and former colleagues say that they can't stand playing with him because he is so competitive that he hates to lose even a hole, let alone a round.

Julian Robertson is clearly a man who aims to be the best at whatever he does. He is willing to stomp, squash, and push anyone out of his way to be the best and to come out on top.

But to understand Robertson and the significance of Tiger Management on the hedge fund industry and the controlled mayhem that is Wall Street, one needs to first look at where hedge funds came from and how the industry evolved into its current state.

Over the last 60 years, the hedge fund revolution has made its way from Wall Street to almost every corner of the globe. While it is clearly not the most important financial development of the 20th century, the concept and the investment vehicle have forever changed the money management landscape, both here and abroad.

Hedge funds are the great equalizer. Anyone, regardless of education, experience, talent, or know-how, can launch a hedge fund and have the opportunity to earn millions of dollars. Started in 1949 by sociologist-turned-journalist Alfred Winslow Jones, hedge funds offer their managers an ability to earn significantly more than traditional investment managers. Simply because of the fee structure, which normally consists of a management fee of 1 percent and an incentive of 20 percent of the profits, the pot of gold is truly in front of the manager who performs well.

Because of this unlimited opportunity, hedge funds have grown exponentially over the last 50 years. As of mid-2004, there were approximately 6,000 hedge funds managing hundreds of billions of dollars, according to the Securities and Exchange Commission. It hasn't always been this way, though. In the beginning (the first 40-odd years of the industry), just a handful of managers, keeping their cards close to their vests, were running these obscure and profitable investment vehicles.

Many believe that hedge funds are able to beat the averages because they attract the best and the brightest people and because of the get-rich-quick aspect of the business. They believe that the mutual fund industry is always going to lose its best talent because it does not offer the financial reward that is offered by hedge funds. In hedge funds, profits are shared with the managers and their team, while mutual fund managers simply get paid based on the assets under management, not necessarily on how well they perform.

In recent years, as some of Wall Street's great trading partnerships have gone public and are no longer able to provide the liquidity and risk capital to the markets that once did, hedge funds have stepped in to fill this void. Historically, liquidity was provided by firms like Goldman Sachs, Morgan Stanley, Salomon Brothers and Lehman Brothers (Wall Street's greatest and most important firms), but now that they have to answer to individual investors from all walks of life, they no longer have the tolerance for risk that they did when they were private partnerships. This has left a gaping hole in markets: No longer can these firms run their once-great proprietary trading desks, and no longer can they take significant, albeit controlled, risks in order to extract huge profits and potentially post significant losses. Instead, they have been regulated to less interesting, more simplified businesses involving pure brokerage and clearing functions that, while extremely profitable, are quite boring.

Today, hedge funds have become a critical component of the capital markets because they provide a major portion of liquidity and risk capital to every global capital and derivative market. Some may claim that they wreak havoc on the global financial markets, but ultimately they provide important fodder to the market ecosystem and are good for everyone—managers, investors, and service providers alike.

Throughout most of the 1960s and much of the 1970s, the Jones partnership and a handful of others dominated the hedge fund scene. However, as Jones slowed down in the late 1970s and early 1980s, three wise men took the torch from his hand and passed it to thousands of others who, in the process, have made sure that the hedge fund flame will never go out.

The three wise men are George Soros, Michael Steinhardt, and Julian Robertson, the true founding fathers of the modern hedge fund industry. In their heyday, these men and their organizations were the envy of money managers around the world. They continue to be, even years after their retirement or return of capital to investors, the standard by which most hedge fund managers are judged.

Although Soros, Steinhardt, and Robertson have publicly moved away from the hedge fund limelight, it is clear to all who know them that once an investor, always an investor. The press and the public might think that they have retired because they have shuttered their funds, returned capital to investors, and now play the role of elder statesmen, but a visit to their offices tells something different.

These people are still quite active in the market. They have not simply returned their investors' capital and folded the tent and gone home. These people are all still involved in the markets around the globe. They are trading or managing money in some way, shape, or form.

It is believed that by the early spring of 2004, former Tiger Management employees were managing or overseeing more than 10 percent of all of the assets that were invested in hedge funds. Although his own funds had closed down in 2000, Robertson's presence was still being felt in the hedge fund industry some four years later.

And although Soros and Steinhardt have worked very hard to move from the image of swashbuckling hedge fund manager to hands-on philanthropist in an effort to preserve their place in history, Robertson has continued to remain quite active in the markets and, in turn, the hedge fund industry. The torch of the industry, so to speak, has been passed to another group of rising managers, people like John Griffin of Blue Ridge Capital, Steven Mandel of Lone Pine Capital, and Lee Ainslie of Maverick Capital Management. And while all of these managers are extraordinary in their own right, they all have one thing in common—they were born as cubs at a firm called Tiger Management.

The true success of Robertson and Tiger extends beyond the stellar performance numbers and mind-boggling assets under management. Ultimately, the success of the firm can be measured in the legacy of his cubs. Their success truly sets Robertson apart from Steinhardt and Soros. Both built successful organizations, but neither of them created a machine that literally spit out new successful manager after new successful manager, as Tiger has done.

"Julian's impact will be felt on the hedge fund industry for years to come," said Hunt Taylor, an industry observer and director of investments at private fund of funds. "He created a factory of sorts that, instead of making widgets, made great money managers. There are literally 30 to 40 people who run successful hedge funds who got their start at Tiger. It is truly an incredible thing that he has done."

This book is the story of the person who took Jones's torch and built one of the most successful and feared hedge fund organizations of all times and, in the process, created a legacy that continues to breed successful managers and will most likely impact the way money is managed for many years to come. Robertson is not only one of the greatest traders and money managers of the century, but he is also one of Wall Street's greatest teachers and inspirers. But great trading and inspiration does not come cheap or easy. This is the story of Julian Robertson's Tiger Management, and its impact on the hedge fund industry.

1

MAKING MONEY IN METALS

ON A CHILLY SPRING MORNING IN 1994, JULIAN Robertson, head of the Tiger Management, and his analysts were closeted in the firm's offices in midtown Manhattan, poring over reports and information from various commodities producers and users looking for the diamond in the rough. For Robertson, who had launched Tiger 14 years earlier as a hedge fund that used long/short equity strategies to extract profits from the market, the time had come to expand into bigger markets that offered greater profits. That year things had started off slowly for the firm, but as it rolled into the second half of 1994, the firm and its funds became a force in the market. Investors clawed their way for access to the hedge fund and the trading powerhouse, dumping nearly $4 billion into its coffers. It was clear by now that the 1990s was going to be the decade of the big cats.

Still, Robertson was troubled. There was a dark shadow around his consciousness, and the name of the shadow was George Soros. Soros had started his firm in the 1960s and was now a legend in international financial circles. He was the envy of money managers. Robertson felt that he could pick stocks and play the hedge fund game as well as Soros, but he had not yet had the big break that would take him from being a success-

1

ful name on Wall Street to an icon known around the world. That was the hunger that kept him searching for information from the reports that his associates brought to their weekly investment meetings.

But now something caught Robertson's eye that just might make a difference. He picked up a feeling of sorts from reading some information on the copper markets. He noticed that in the last few weeks, the prices of copper were increasing while demand had remained constant and showed signs it was decreasing. After discussing the market at length with his commodities analysts and talking to people he thought were in the know, he came to the conclusion that demand was, in fact, decreasing and that increases in demand did not seem to be on the horizon. In order for the trade to prove, Robertson needed more information—data from people on the ground. Mentally flipping through the massive Rolodex in his head, he began to assemble a list of people who would know what was going on in the copper markets and would be able to confirm that his hunch was right. He called a number of commodities brokers and spoke with some producers and was able to use the information to confirm his suspicions. Their data showed that mines were producing at normal levels and that producers seemed to be in the groove—production was humming along at a nice clip. Demand seemed to be weakening, and it looked like it was just a matter of time before prices would fall.

According to the research that his analysts had found from poring over reports from various sources, including brokerage firms, central banks, commodities merchants and the like, the price of the commodity contracts was overvalued. It was clear that the price was based on the current supply and demand of the commodity, and that if the demand decreased the price would fall. It was a basic supply-and-demand scenario. This told Robertson's analysts that they had what looked to be a very good short on their hands. The idea behind shorting is simple:

You believe that the price of a security is too high and that the price has to come down. Therefore, you enter into an agreement with an owner of the security to borrow it from them for a fee, and you sell it into the market. When the price falls, you buy back the security and give it back to the person you borrowed it from. The difference between what you sold and bought the security for, minus any costs associated with the transaction, is your profit.

Shorting was not something new to the folks at Tiger; it was the cornerstone of their operation and a significant portion of their success. They were comfortable with executing shorts and believed in their ability to spot good opportunities. Tiger was not the only group of investors who thought something was amiss in the copper markets, however. Other industry observers and participants, as well as some other hedge funds, could not understand why prices were increasing. They expected prices to level out.

Investor interest at Tiger was sparked by a spate of excellent performance. The firm had crossed a number of assets-under-management thresholds and was fast becoming one of the largest hedge funds in the industry. Robertson and his team knew that in order to maintain their position in the industry, they would need to maintain their performance. In order for a hedge fund to sustain its in flows of assets, it needs to continually put up solid performance numbers as well as prove to its existing and potential investors that it can maintain its performance as it attracts new assets. Therefore, Robertson and his team needed to continue to prove not only that they could manage money effectively but also that their skill set was scalable to handle the billions of dollars they were attracting from investors.

There was no room for error, and there was significant room for good ideas and good opportunities. Robertson drove the team hard, forcing them to look for and find opportunities that were worthy of the portfolio. Tiger had to be number one–it needed to be the best and the biggest, and Robertson needed his team to make it happen. He was no longer content to be thought of as a small shop or caught behind the shadow of the Soros organization. Robertson wanted to be known in his own right for his own successes. He needed a good trade to get them to the top–and the research on copper looked to be that trade.

The key behind all of the firm's investments was the *story*. If the story made sense, then the investment made sense. If there was no story or it was not easily understood, then it had no place in the portfolio. When the story changed, the investment had to change as well–it was and is all about the story.

Robertson's mantra was, as long as the story around the investment remained the same, the position should get bigger. As soon as the story changed, it was time to get out. His traders and analysts all knew this was the way that Tiger operated, and knew that this is what made Robertson and the firm such a huge beast in the hedge fund industry. It was a simple and smart way to do business.

To understand the concept of *story*, consider this example. Say you are interested in a solid oak wooden table. The analyst could tell you that he had checked out the market for tables, evaluated the information, and come to the conclusion that the table was a good buy at $100 because it was well made, solidly built, and would not fall apart. This is the story. So you go to the shop, prepared to buy the table. And then, just as you are running your hand over the table, a corner falls off. Well, now the seller is desperate to get rid of the broken table and is willing to sell it for $20. To the analyst, this seems like a steal. He sees an incredible opportunity to buy something for $20 that is really worth $100 and needs just a bit of fixing to get it there. But in Robertson's eyes, the *story* is now flawed, and now he would say that you should want no part of the deal. How could something so well built, made of the finest oak, break? Robertson would say that more than the table is broken. The credibility of the research is now called into question. The story is broken; it is time to move on to something else.

Robertson's uncanny ability to believe in himself and others was and continues to remain a characteristic that sets him apart from most other hedge fund managers. He understands his strengths and his weaknesses and understands how to compensate for both. He has the ability to stick to something when everyone else has bailed out, and has the ability to make incredibly important decisions almost in an instant. Most people do not possess this trait. It has proved successful for him time and again throughout Tiger's unique run.

This uncanny ability to stick to his belief is what led him and his team in 1995 to an unbelievable opportunity in the copper markets.

When Robertson and his team started looking at copper, they had no idea of the riches that the opportunity offered. They thought it was going to be a good trade for them, because they understood the story, the opportunity, and how profitable the trade could be, but they had no idea of the recognition that they would receive from their peers for sticking with the trade during copper's wild ride. At the time, all they knew was that the story made sense and, as such, it was a trade that was worthy of being in the portfolio. For Robertson, getting into copper was no different than any other investment the hedge fund made—at the end it was more than just any other trade. It was Tiger's sterling trade.

This was, however, *not* the case during 1994 as prices increased dramatically. By early 1995, prices started to level off a bit; by the end of the year, prices were back in line with expectations at around $1.10 a pound. The ride was a rough one for many investors, and a number of people lost significantly as prices seesawed for the better part of the year. But Robertson believed in the story, believed that it had not changed, and, more importantly, believed that he was right.

The price of the commodity remained in this range for the first few months of the year 1995, but the spring brought new price hikes. This caused many people to cover their shorts and get out of the trade. They believed that the market was going to run higher, leaving them with significant losses. This early spring rally wreaked havoc on many hedge fund managers, who saw their profits plummet.

Copper increased to more than $1.25 a pound, and it looked like it could have gone higher. Nobody seemed to understand where the rally was coming from or what was sustaining it, but it seemed like it was real. Real, that is, until some very interesting information about one of the largest copper traders in the world made its way onto the tape. It seemed that one of Sumitomo's traders had been involved in some nefarious dealings in the copper market and that the Japanese investment conglomerate had amassed significant losses from trades that went awry. The losses and the potential for loss led Sumitomo's management to order its traders to dump the firm's positions in an attempt to get completely out of the market and wash their hands of the whole affair. At the time, Sumitomo was one of the largest owners and buyers of the metal. This action by the firm to dump its stake in copper was the catalyst for the price to fall dramatically. For Robertson and his team, who understood the market, and understood that the price had to fall, this was the action they needed to see their trade through successfully. The news of Sumitomo's massive and increasing losses caused all hell to break loose in the copper market, and by May 1996 the price had fallen more than 30 percent. By July, copper futures for September were trading at about 87.80 cents per pound.

What caused the gyration in the market? The answer was simple: A scandal rocked the copper market, causing investors/speculators to run for cover and dump as much of the metal as possible. It was a going out of business sale–literally. Robertson and his team were attracted to copper because their research told them that the price of the metal was too high. While their research proved that the prices had to come down, they did not know when this would happen. They just knew it would happen at some point. The folks at Tiger liked the copper story, it offered them an opportunity to go short a market that they knew was overpriced and was destined to correct itself like a markets eventually do. However, what they did not know was that something was amiss in the copper market. They did not know of Sumitomo's problem and that the large Japanese conglomerate's trader was artificially propping up the price of the metal.

The crisis in copper reached its boiling point when Sumitomo Corporation fired Yasuo Hamanaka. This star copper trader, who was often called "Mr. Five Percent" by those who participated in the markets because of the huge positions he amassed, was found to have been improperly trading the copper markets, resulting in a scandal that cost his employer more than $2.6 billion in losses. This, as any trader who has ever held a short position will tell you, was music to Robertson's ears. It is one thing to make an assumption that the price of something is overvalued and see the price fall because it is truly overvalued by the market, and the market corrects itself. It is something completely different to make the assumption that something is overvalued and find out that the route of the overpricing is fraud. That just makes the trade even that much more enjoyable and, of course, profitable.[1]

In order to understand why Robertson and the folks at Tiger profited so handsomely from the copper trades, one first needs to understand the story behind the scandal that ended up rocking the market.

For the decade leading up to his firing in June of 1996,

Hamanaka had an iron grip on a significant portion of the copper market. His trading prowess was legendary, and he was a force to be reckoned with when it came to this metal. He had an uncanny ability to time the market and reap what were thought to be enormous profits for his employer.

And while many believe that the company uncovered his problems in the spring and early summer of 1996 when it first made its accusations of wrongdoing, a number of metal traders and speculators that were involved with the copper during this time said that they had suspected something was not quite right with the way Hamanaka was operating. Some people close with the organization say that in 1990, Hamanaka was responsible for significant losses at the company because of some bad trades and that during an investigation of sorts, the powers that be at Sumitomo had all the right answers and satisfied various regulatory inquiries, which allowed the trader to keep his job and the company to save face, and it set the markets up for what was to come a few years later. The losses in 1990 were much less than the estimated $2.6 billion the company got hit with in 1996, and this time management was left with no alternative but to go public with its rogue trader.

Like another rogue trader, Nick Leeson of Baring's fame, Hamanaka believed that he could trade his way out of the losses and win back all of the profits that vanished when the bets he made went against him. His problem, it turned out, was that the drawer where he was hiding his trading tickets was only so big, and when there was no more room in which to stuff the tickets, the whole scheme fell apart—literally.

Some information suggests that early on in his efforts, Sumitomo officials worked with Hamanaka to help him cover his losses by orchestrating a number of off-the-book transactions that were shielded from anyone on the outside. But as the losses grew, so did the off-the-book trades—he was able to hide his efforts because he falsified documents, forged signatures, and destroyed business records. He pled guilty to these crimes in December 1996, and the company was left with no alternative but to go public with the scandal.[2]

In the end, what caused the house of cards to fall was Hamanaka's inability to manage his huge physical position in the market, coupled with having huge long positions causing him to be extremely vulnerable to short sales. Many believe that what got Hamanaka into such a bind was his belief that his physical position was so big that he was able to drive prices up at will. Having this belief led him to sell over-the-counter put options to producers and cash in on the premiums. Put options give producers the right to sell copper at a set price in the future. If prices continue to move upward, the seller of the put makes money because the buyer does not exercise the option. Unfortunately, as traders and speculators started to learn about the size and scope of Hamanaka's positions, they forced the price of the metal lower, which meant that the puts he had sold would be exercised, resulting in massive losses.

The vulnerability was brought on by Hamanaka's effort to buy physical copper in order to boost world copper prices. This effort, coupled with Sumitomo's inability to get rid of short sellers by desperately dumping long positions on the market, forced down the price of copper. Sumitomo's lack of internal controls, poor management, and bad oversight was the root of the problem, but exposing the misdeeds was the work of hedge funds.

During the months and weeks before Sumitomo's announcement of Hamanaka's misdeeds, its massive positions, and soon-to-be massive losses, many in the hedge fund world had believed that something in the markets was amiss. Nobody could put their finger on what was going on in the market, but everyone who had looked at the price of copper knew the metal was priced inappropriately. They also knew that when something is priced inappropriately on the high side, the only thing to do is short the hell out of it.

Even before the hint of problems at Sumitomo, it is estimated that in 1995 through mid-1996 shortsellers collectively
borrowed as much as a million tons of copper to dump on the
market in hopes of driving the price down. Many believed
that while fundamentally the trade made sense, forces beyond
their control could have allowed Hamanaka to get out of the
mess and force prices is higher. To their delight, no such forces
existed.

To the folks at Tiger, this trade was fast becoming a once-in-a-
lifetime opportunity. It seemed that all their data showed the
prices had to fall and that they just had to hold on in order to
reap the benefits from their research. In early May, the team realized they were really going to make a windfall when a strike
at a large Chilean copper mine was averted, and the stores of
copper at the London Metal Exchange warehouse failed to fall.
The analysts knew that the bet was the right one, and Robertson
saw the profits adding up in his head. The team worked the
numbers out through the night and decided they should increase the short—prices were going to fall, and fall hard. It was
clear now, more than ever, that because prices remained strong,
there was too much capacity in the market. It was simple economics and a good opportunity. Just how good the opportunity
was would take close to 18 months to realize—but in the end, the
heartache and pain were clearly worth it.

Throughout the summer and fall, Tiger began to add to its
existing copper positions. Eventually, this led to the hedge
fund amassing a position of more than a billion dollars in the
metal by June 1995. Throughout the year, the team continued
to research the markets and furthered their conviction that they
were right and that prices were going to fall. Although the idea
had come to them from various sources, including a number of
hedge fund friends, Robertson did not operate on tips. In order
for him to commit capital, the team would have to see and
touch the industry first hand. It was dirt-under-your-fingernails

type of work. Robertson sent his analysts on planes and trains to get as much information as possible on the global state of copper, its uses, and its expected uses. In the early 1990s before information was readily available online, the only way to research something was to get out there and kick the tires. And while times have clearly changed, and information and data are just a click away, all serious investors continue to go into the field to gather their data on whether to go long or short a position.

The team met with metals producers and saw first hand the charts and diagrams that outlined production from new and existing mines. They met with users and saw their stock rooms full to the brim. They held meetings on the side of road and in boardrooms and continued to get the same answers–there was too much capacity. The metal was being pulled out of the ground faster than it could be used. It was clear that things did not add up–in fact, they added down. Robertson and his team knew there was no place for the price to go *but* down. Even though the price was remaining steady and, in fact, rising a bit, which meant that they were losing money on their shorts, they were confident in their research and that in time it would prove out. For the folks at Tiger, it was time to short the metal in a very big way. They knew their research had been right and they were ready to reap the benefits of their work.

Robertson instructed his traders to put on a series of short positions that were completely against everything that seemed to be going on in the market. The market was moving higher, and Robertson did not understand why. His analysts told him that the market was overvalued, and the supply was greater than the demand–the story had not changed–the market had it wrong.

Robertson believed in his team. He believed that they understood what was going on in the market, and he believed that price of copper would eventually fall. More importantly, he believed that Tiger as a result of his conviction in his research and in his positions would reap enormous profits from sticking to its knitting so to speak and held onto its short positions. It was clear that Robertson saw something that others who were trading the market missed. He did not buy into the prices that were being printed on the tape. He believed something was wrong with the way the market was trading, and he was not willing to miss an opportunity.

His conviction in the trade and, more importantly, the people who worked for him led him to great results. In the spring of 1996, in the wake of a copper hording scandal that was led by discovery of Hamanaka's misdeeds, the price of the commodity fell significantly. In one day in the end of May 1996 the firm saw its position in copper move to the tune of a profit of $300 million. This was probably the single biggest day of profits in the firm's history, and it solidified Robertson's place as one of the greatest money managers of all time. It was his conviction and belief that he was right while everyone else was wrong that led him to rack up these profits.

Robertson enjoyed the profits, but what he enjoyed more was a call he got from Stan Druckenmiller, the trader who made George Soros the world's greatest investor when the fund broke Great Britain's Central Bank (see Chapter 9). During the call, which came a few days after Tiger's profits were realized, Druckenmiller praised Robertson's ability to stick with the position and ride it all the way down. The Soros organization had gotten squeezed out of its copper position in April 1996 and did not reap any of the benefits that the folks at Tiger did by sticking with their trade; in fact, they lost money in copper. To Robertson, it was not simply about the money, it was about being right. It was the idea that his research worked and that he had the ability to stick with what he knew was right, regardless of what was going on in the markets and what his contemporaries were doing. He had the information, he had the conviction, and now he had the profits—which together got him a title.[3]

Now more than ever, Robertson and Tiger were clearly a force to be reckoned with. His copper trade was one of a few macro trades that put him on the map–the map outside of the hedge fund industry–the map of the greatest traders/speculators/money managers of all time.

2

THE BIRTH OF A TIGER

THE ROAD TO WALL STREET RICHES IS PAVED BY DECADES of people with drive, ambition, and good and bad ideas, and while there are many very successful people who travel this road, only a few make it to the gateway of money management success. As the book closed on the twentieth century, one could count the number of star managers and traders on two hands: JP Morgan and Charlie Merrill, the infamous Jesse Livermore, and more recently George Soros, Warren Buffett, Michael Steinhardt, and, of course, Julian Robertson. Analysts and writers, reporters, and psychologists have expended reams of paper and surely hundreds, if not thousands, of man hours identifying and analyzing the successes of the greats so as to present us with a recipe for success with which we might mix our own cocktail of fame and fortune.

When you ask people about what makes Julian Robertson different than other successful hedge fund managers, the answer always seems to be his competitive nature and his ability to truly enjoy what he does. It is clear that when Robertson wins, he has fun, and when he has fun, he is able to increase his winning percentage, causing him to have more fun and be a better trader, investor, and money manager. Winning, you see, is everything to Robertson. Robertson is all about keeping score. To the victor goes the spoils, and he always wants to be the victor.

So where does one gain a competitive nature? How does one tie it to that sense of humor and of fun that Robertson has become known for? These characteristics may be learned but are often acquired at an early age. Which leads us to the North Carolina of the 1930s.

Julian Hart Robertson Jr. was born in 1932, just two weeks before the Dow Jones Industrial Average dropped to its all-time of low of 41.22[1] and in the midst of the Great Depression. Salisbury, North Carolina, his birthplace, was a town of 27,000 located between Charlotte and Greensboro in the Piedmont region of the state. A typical Southern small town of yesteryear, Salisbury housed a Confederate prison during the Civil War. In the 1930s and through Robertson's formative years up to the 1950s, the town looked a lot like Mayberry, complete with its diners, hardware stores, drugstores, and the like. Besides Robertson and his sisters (Blanche Robertson Bacon, who lives in Raleigh, North Carolina, and Wyndham Robertson, who lives in Chapel Hill, North Carolina), Salisbury's other famous residents, past and present, include President Andrew Jackson and Senator Elizabeth Dole. President Jackson, who was born in Waxham, spent a fair amount of his childhood in Salisbury. Elizabeth Dole was born in Salisbury just four years after Julian.

The town was built on hard work and community. It was and is a place where townspeople gathered together on weekend afternoons for parties and get togethers. Where friends were made that last a lifetime, even after one moves away. It is a place where people care about their neighbors and work hard to make sure those who need help get it. It is a place that people envision when they picture a simple small town in America.

Salisbury was built on a foundation of community involvement. For longer than anyone in the town cares to remember, its residents have taken an active role in its development, its maintenance, and its survival. It is a place of great architecture, parks, and an aura of friendliness that has made the South what the South is.

Unlike other cities and towns that have seen their downtowns evaporate as shopping malls and the suburbs take over, Salisbury's downtown has remained a vibrant and active place, partly because of the town's fight to keep its downtown alive and partly due to many of its residents who have worked hard to ensure its buildings are not demolished and simply sold to the highest bidder. This effort to save the downtown is not something new. In fact, Blanche Robertson, Julian's mother, played an instrumental role in preserving some of the town's historic buildings. Her legacy has led Historic Salisbury, the town's historical society, to develop a program called the revolving fund. Through this effort, Historic Salisbury buys buildings from people who are going to demolish them, maintains the property, and then puts it back on the market, selling it to those who are willing to renovate and find uses for the old buildings. Most of the buildings date to the 1870s, with some going back to the 1850s. Today, there is very little vacant retail and residential space in the downtown. And while the town has all the modern amenities including, art galleries, coffee shops, and a copy shop, it has retained its old-time roots with a local barber shop and pharmacy.

Salisbury has remained vibrant due to the townspeople's commitment to seeing it through good and bad times. There has been very little flight to the suburbs, and over the years the downtown area has been redeveloped to meet residential, retail, and commercial needs. Former Mayor Margaret Klutz said, "After 20 years, we are an overnight success." The downtown area is often called one of the most "successful mid-sized" downtowns in North Carolina due to its maintenance of a first-floor occupancy rate of between 95 percent and 97 percent and a residential rate of close to 100 percent over the last five years.

Part of the success is due to the efforts of Julian and Blanche Robertson and their family. Julian Robertson Sr. was a businessman who knew that hard work not only paid off but it allowed you to do things that others could not. And while working to the make the community better was something he enjoyed, business was his passion. Over the course of his life he was involved heavily in the textile industry, serving as the president and treasurer of Erlanger Mills. He made a mark on the banking industry first as a director of the American Trust Company of Charlotte and as a founder of the North Carolina National Bank, the predecessor to NationsBank in 1976. (This deal was consummated in the Holiday Inn in Salisbury.) Robertson was thought of as a man of action and ability and someone who acted and thought for himself. He was able to express his opinions in terms that people could clearly understand.

He was an impeccably dressed individual who took enormous pride in his appearance and his clothes. There were many times when he would enter a room and talk to women about the fabric of their clothes. He made an impression when he entered a room. He lived life as full and varied and intense as it was long.[2] He was at times a Southern Amateur Champion in tennis, and he had an interest in flying and education. He had a keen interest in genealogy that led him to coauthor the book *The Family of William and Elizabeth Boling Robertson of Richard Va.* (He was a tenth-generation descendant of Pocahontas.)

His life was also shaped by his military service. In July 1918 he enlisted in the Army, serving as second lieutenant in the infantry after qualifying as an expert rifleman and small arms firing instructor. He served for a number years before returning to Salisbury to work at Erlanger Textile Enterprises. With the outbreak of World War II, Robertson took leave from his position at the firm and served his country again, this time from 1942 to 1945 as a lieutenant colonel with the 8th Infantry Division seeing combat in Europe. For his efforts he was awarded four bronze stars.[3]

Robertson's father was not only a successful businessman operating in the textile industry but also a savvy investor and quite a philanthropist. (Philanthropy, along with competition, continues to plays a very large role in Robertson's world, and it is something that he has worked hard to instill in all his Tigers. See Chapter 13.)

By all accounts, Robertson and his father had a relatively normal and healthy relationship. Robertson learned how to read the stock tables from his father, and together they spent a fair amount of time looking at companies trying to figure out which was better than the next while relaxing in the family home. He learned the importance of research and understanding how things worked from his father. Julian Jr. also learned the importance of dressing the part and enjoying the finer things in life from his father. Throughout his career he has worn finely tailored suits and Italian leather shoes. His adult height of over six feet tall and his robust figure made him a particularly imposing figure in custom-tailored clothing. Like his father, he uses his elegant image to make an impression.[4]

Julian Sr. instilled the value of being important in his only son and worked hard to ensure that his family was provided for and that his family could provide for others. He was a true Southern gentleman—exquisitely dressed on the outside and fiercely competitive on the inside. It is his competitiveness that led young Julian to greatness—it is a quality that his father prided himself on.

According to his sister, Blanche Bacon, father and son were alike to some degree, but the father was a bit more serious and the son had a better sense of humor.[5] However, if seriousness is something Julian Jr. is lacking, it is hard to tell from talking to him or observing him in action. Julian Robertson Jr. is one serious individual who prides himself on hard work and being right. These character traits were instilled in Robertson as he observed his father in professional, social, and family settings. It is this work ethic and beliefs system—combined with the research skills learned at his father's side—that many observers believe provided him with the foundation to be so successful throughout his career on Wall Street.

Certainly Julian Sr.'s work ethic never faltered. Well into his nineties, the elder Robertson would travel to his office in downtown Salisbury, where he managed a "right good portfolio of stocks." He died at the age of 95 on February 22, 1995. His obituary, which ran on page one of *The Salisbury Post*, called his death "a great loss to Salisbury." His son was quoted as saying; "[He was a] wonderful man. He may not agree with you but he agrees with the premise that you have the right to have your opinion."[6]

It seems that in conversations with many of Robertson's former Tigers, the same will be said of him when he passes. Former colleagues say that Robertson is not one to always agree with people, but he understands that people have the right to have a view. The problem is that he likes people to understand why they are wrong. Robertson has been known to get into very heated discussions with people in order to explain why they are wrong. Of course, he is always willing to let them have their opinion, however wrong it may be.

Competition is only one of the key attributes to the success of Julian Robertson and Tiger Management. Others include conviction in his research, a head for numbers, and the belief and the understanding that he could not go at it alone. This he learned from his mother.

Julian's mother, Blanche Spencer Robertson, is recalled by community leaders as a wonderful woman who was clearly involved in the community. She moved to Salisbury from Martinsville, Virginia, in the early 1930s after marrying Julian Hart Robertson.

"She was one of the prettiest girls in the South," recalled her niece Mary "Holtie" Woodsen. "She had many suitors, and there were a lot of disappointed gentlemen when she got married to Julian."[7]

Besides being kind to her fellow citizens and the envy of many of her contemporaries, she was active in the cultural and social scenes of Salisbury, a patron of the arts, and someone who loved flowers. Like her husband, she enjoyed the finer things in life. She filled the family home on 220 Confederate Avenue with fine china and porcelain figurines, period furniture and lamps, and a collection of dolls that her son brought her from his stint in the Navy. Each of the dolls was from a different port that he had visited—it was a collection that she truly treasured and appreciated. She also filled it with an enormous collection of rabbits. There were cloth ones, felt ones, stone ones, and wooden ones all over the house. When she died, one of her friends sent an extremely large pink rabbit made of chrysanthemums framed in carnations with a very happy smile to the funeral home. It was a moving tribute to woman that was loved by nearly all who knew her. She loved fine silk and linens, and things that we would now call antique.

The Robertson home was constantly filled with fresh-cut flowers from the family's rose garden, and it was often the place to be, as Julian and Blanche were famous for their entertaining. Blanche spent hours tending to her gardens and relied heavily on the help of her children to ensure that the garden was full year round. In the spring, she and the children would crawl over the dark black earth to plant the phlox, candy tuft, bleeding heart, and petunias, while in the fall the children and their mother would plant tulips and daffodils. Regardless of the season, both the inside and outside of the family home were full of flowers.

The family was known for their extremely tasteful dinners and parties. The Robertson home was the center of many important events and more often than not was the place to be. It was a large, distinct Southern-style home with deep wood floors and crown moldings that made it not only charming but stylish as well.

Just off the back of the main hall of the house was a small room that served as the flower room. In it, Blanche would spend hours arranging flowers, and when the family would entertain, the room would be turned into a bar—making it one of the sweetest-smelling bars in the South.

Blanche was also generous with her time. She was an active volunteer in many areas of the community, but preservation and restoration of Salisbury were two things she was probably most interested in and most active in. While giving financially was something the Robertsons were known for, Mrs. Robertson was said to have put her shoulder into working for the community to preserve the downtown and restore it to its glory.

There was one time while she was on her annual vacation to Myrtle Beach that she was in the grocery store and overheard a couple asking how to get to Brook Green Garden. Realizing that the people probably would not be able to find it on their own, she took them to their destination. She was said to have never met a stranger, and was known to treat everybody as if they were family.

Robertson attributes his sense of commitment to community and helping others to his mother, who taught him not only in words but with her actions. It has been a long time since the Robertson children have left Salisbury, yet they continue to support the place of their birth. The children set up and continue to fund The Blanche and Julian Robertson Family Foundation, which contributes money to many local Salisbury organizations, including book programs for young children and parents, fencing for a new baseball field at the local high schools, a veterans building expansion program, a bone-marrow testing project, and a community care clinic.[8] In 1986, *The*

Salisbury Post named her one of the town's most "watchable women," calling her, "the grande dame of Salisbury society" and "the former chairman of about every major social event in Salisbury for the past quarter century."[9]

Julian's mother is also clearly responsible for his sense of humor and his ability to poke fun with others. She taught him to use humor as a tool to build relationships and to handle social and business functions.

Blanche Robertson died at the age 87 in December 1993. Her obituary in *The Salisbury Post* was headlined, "City loses an 'angel.'" The story included laudatory quotes from local leaders, including the mayor, who called her Salisbury's biggest cheerleader.[10]

At her funeral, Julian recalled how his mother taught him never to care about the size of anyone's wallet or even how they looked or their level of intelligence. For these things did not and do not matter—what matters is one's feelings for other people. As a result, Julian recalled in his eulogy of his mother, some of the Salisbury's "blackest sheep" truly adored her and were people with which she had great fun.[11]

Julian and Blanche Robertson worked very hard to raise their children in what they believed to be the right way. And while the family was clearly one of privilege, the children were taught to respect all, regardless of their standing in society or place in the community. Blanche was famous for trying to help others less fortunate than her, and the children clearly learned by her example. Julian Sr. thought his son to be "terrifically competitive," a characteristic that Robertson showed at a very young age. When the children were younger, they would all sit on the living room floor and compare statements from Esso [now ExxonMobil] and Texaco [ChevronTexaco Corporation] to see who got the most sales per dollar of investment.

For young Julian, sports and activities with friends played an active role in his childhood; he was a good athlete and was an extremely competitive player of baseball and football. He, like most boys, preferred winning to losing and worked hard to hone his skills on the ball fields of Salisbury. During his formative years he was quite an athlete. His skills and abilities clearly separated him from the pack when it came time to be picked for teams or participate in games. His competitive nature drove him to success, from the ball fields of Salisbury to the hallowed canyons of Wall Street. Competition—and the rewards of winning—set him apart from the rest of the boys in town and on the Street.

One particular ball field was on a lot next to the family's home. The property had been purchased by his father and was used as a playground of sorts for the Robertson children and the children in town. Unfortunately, the home run lanes were a little short, which meant that baseball had to be all but abandoned at the age of 11, but the area was big enough to play football and Robertson enjoyed playing in the lot well into his teens. During football season one year, when Robertson was 10, a new boy came to the field to join in the fun. Unfortunately for Robertson and his friends, the boy was quite a bit better than the rest of them. Robertson, full of his competitive nature, felt that it was his duty to tell the boy that it was *his* field and that the boy had to leave. The boy, who was not one to be pushed around, replied with the famous childhood response, "Make me." Robertson's response was, "Maybe I can't, but my momma will," and with that ran into the house in a tizzy, upset that this stranger had taken control of his field. Although Robertson does not recall his mother's verbal response to his request to remove the boy from the field, he does clearly recall the shame he felt from the licking he took for having the audacity to make such a request. The event is something he did not talk about for more than 50 years—in fact, the first time (according to him) that he ever spoke about it was at his mother's funeral. It is clear that it is something that he never forgot, and it impacted him greatly.

This was just one of the many lessons of small-town living that were keenly important to Robertson, and they remained critical aspects to the success of his operation for many years.

Although competition on the fields was something he enjoyed, he had no interest in competition in the classroom. Throughout his schooling, studies were not really his cup of tea. Of his studies at the University of North Carolina, Robertson said he had a good time but did not do well academically in his subjects other than business. Math in particular was a subject he excelled in–something that he liked and was extremely good at. While he enjoyed the concept of school, he did not necessarily enjoy the rigor that goes along with higher education. He didn't like studying for classes and tests, so he didn't spend a lot of time doing it. As can be expected, business courses were extremely enjoyable to him. He liked learning how to read a balance sheet and how to understand the numbers and evaluate economic trends and their impacts on companies. He worked hard in these areas. In those nonbusiness courses, settling into the middle of the pack was something that he was willing to do; however, when it came to business courses and later in running Tiger, being number two was not something he was interested in being known for, or something he was willing to accept.

In 1955, when he was 23, Robertson entered the Navy as an ensign through the Reserve Officers Training Corps and served on a munitions ship. He was promoted to lieutenant, junior grade, by the time his two-year active duty obligation ended. On the ship and in the ports, Robertson learned the importance of taking responsibility for one's action, and that maturity goes a long way in the Navy and in life. It was also during this time that he was truly able to see the world outside of the United States. During his stint with the Navy he toured the Mediterranean and the Caribbean and was able to visit a number of countries and see first hand how people lived and worked outside of the United States.

Robertson said that in his naval service was the first time he had "any real responsibility" as an individual. He worked in various capacities on the ship and cited national security as a reason for not going into great detail about his responsibilities. But it is clear from talking to him about his experiences on board the ship that his time in the Navy had a lasting impact on him and helped shape his future. During his stint on the munitions ship at the height of the Cold War, he was charged with looking after weapons that, according to a number of Navy sources, had the ability to wreak enormous damage on major cities around the world. Robertson is believed to have been in charge of weapons maintenance and readiness. It was he to whom the captain would have turned had the orders to launch weapons been given. Neither the Navy nor Robertson would comment on his duties or responsibilities while in active duty. He was in charge of making sure the weapons did not fail and were ready at a moment's notice. It was quite a lot of responsibility for someone at such a young age. He truly enjoyed having such responsibility. It allowed him to understand leadership and taught him a great deal about what it takes to be in charge, earn respect, and respect others. The effect of having so much responsibility so young remains with him today and was evident during Tiger's 20-year run. When things were not good, he stood up and took the heat.

Robertston's childhood and early adult experiences shaped the man he would become. In the Navy, it was he whom his superiors relied on to ensure the ship was ready. They looked to him to make sure his men were doing what they were supposed to at all times. Robertson's run in the Navy taught him to accept responsibility for his actions and the actions of the men in his command. He learned the value of being a good leader and the importance of gaining the respect of those who reported to him. This affected him as he ran and built Tiger.

In 1957, after completing his stint in the Navy, Robertson decided, with some help from his father, to head north to find some money. The idea was for him to get involved in a Wall Street training program and get into the investment business. Robertson's father felt that New York was the only place where his son could truly learn the investment business. It was to New York that his father insisted he go in order to get his "formal" education in investing and the market. New York, after all, was "where the money was," and it was there that his son could find the opportunity to access some of it.

3

A SOUTHERNER ON
WALL STREET

IN 1957, ROBERTSON STARTED HIS CAREER ON WALL STREET as a sales trainee at Kidder Peabody & Co. He spent 22 years at the firm in various sales capacities, eventually running the firm's money management arm, Webster Management Corp.

"[I was] an honest slob they could count on," he has said many times in public of his rise and success at the venerable firm.[1] An honest slob who had gained the trust and admiration of many. He gained this trust and admiration not only because of his incredible people skills, but also because of his ability to make money for his clients and his peers, regardless of overall market conditions.

At Kidder, Robertson began as a trainee and moved through the firm, landing in many different areas of the firm's sell side. The sell side is the brokerage side of the business. It is here where the great salespeople of the Street work to push products—stocks and bonds in those days—to both retail and institutional investors. In the 1960s through much of the 1970s working on the sell side meant you were on the front line of the business—it was here that most of the money in the firm was made through commissions and trading activity. Although being an investment banker or analyst of sorts was seen as more glamorous, it was brokers and sales traders who made the real money on the Street.

Robertson earned the reputation as someone who could be trusted and someone who was willing to listen and learn from others at the firm. He was like a sponge, constantly soaking up as much information as he could from his colleagues, peers, and competitors. During his tenure at the firm, he spent a fair amount of time learning both the sell side and buy side of the business and understanding what made sense to do in the market and what needed to be avoided. His skill was learning from others and taking the knowledge and turning it into profits for the firm, his colleagues, his clients, and, of course, himself. Robertson was more than just a salesman; he worked hard to find opportunities to exploit while he was at Kidder. He did not simply try to push product, he tried to understand the products, why they worked, and how they would capture profits for his clients.

Over the years, he developed a unique network of friends and colleagues he called on for ideas and information on potential investment plays. Although his focus was primarily in the equity markets, he also spent a fair amount of time looking for value plays in the fixed income and commodity areas.

Throughout his career at the firm, Robertson earned a reputation from his colleagues and peers as the person to go to for financial advice or guidance. When colleagues had a little extra money or had no idea what to do with their bonus, they would ask Robertson to manage it for them. Slowly but surely he developed a reputation as a solid investor who could turn a profit, regardless of market conditions. Through these accounts of friends and colleagues, Robertson earned a reputation as someone who worked hard to find the nuggets that others missed. He earned a reputation as someone who could gather information, process it, and figure out ways to use for his advantage to make money for himself and his clients.

In the mid-1960s, Robert Burch was making "very little" money working as a banker at Kidder. He and his colleagues had heard stories of Julian's success in the market, and they all wanted to be part of it. When Burch got his bonus, which he recalls was about $5,000, he gave it to Julian to invest for him. Burch didn't ask where the idea came from or how long he had worked on it–he simply knew from his dealings with Julian that he knew how to find opportunities and extract profits. Burch said that he heard of Robertson's success for his clients and understood from his colleagues that he really had a talent for spotting value. He felt that Robertson could make better investment decisions than he could, so he decided that giving Robertson some money to manage was the right thing to do with his bonus. The faith that Burch showed in Robertson continued as Tiger grew and attracted more and more assets. Investors realized that Robertson knew how to manage money, believed in his skills, and trusted that he would do right by them.

As is typical, sometimes the investments went up and sometimes they went down, but for the next 10 years or so, regardless of performance, Burch and a number of the corporate finance folks at Kidder continued to give Julian money to manage. Thus they established quite a friendship and a network of sorts with the budding money manager. The relationships would prove fruitful when Robertson launched Tiger. (Throughout the years, their friendship has remained constant. Today Robertson still gives Burch ideas about new funds in which he should invest.) He had already established a track record of sorts and, more importantly, had established a following of potential investors who had witnessed first-hand how the man invested and how he found and took advantages of opportunities in the market.

Robertson developed a nose for research at Kidder, and he

enjoyed finding companies that he believed offered value plays. At Kidder, he was given the tools to go hunting for value. The first and most important tool for Robertson was grasping the basics of value investing. Value investing is simple to grasp, easy to understand, easy to deploy but incredibly difficult to master successfully because it takes patience and conviction.

To understand the development of Robertson's investment style and the methodology behind the investment strategy at Tiger, one first needs to understand the basics of value investing. Today when most people think of value investing they think of Warren Buffett and Charlie Munger, the greatest investors of all time according to some. However, both of these fine investors learned their game from Benjamin Graham and David L. Dodd.

Value investing is not a new concept and has probably been around for centuries, because there have always been people who have wanted to buy things on the cheap. However, as a discipline, value investing really came to light in the 1940s and 1950s after the 1934 publication of Graham and Dodd's book *Security Analysis*, a business book best seller, currently in its fifth edition. It lays out in a clear and concise format the theories of how to look at a company and determine how it might do in the future by evaluating a number of business and financial functions of its operation.

Graham and Dodd wrote, "An investment operation is one which, upon thorough analysis, promises safety of principal and an adequate return." And while there are number of things one needs to look at when evaluating or researching a potential investment, Graham outlines the following six items as essential factors to look at when analyzing a business:

1. Profitability
2. Stability
3. Growth in earnings

4. Financial position
5. Dividends
6. Price history

The idea behind Graham and Dodd's concept of security analysis provides the investor with information about the past and present and helps to quantify expectations for the future. The idea is to examine industries and securities of individual companies primarily to develop value and return expectations for securities and, in turn, to allow the investor to separate the overpriced securities from the under priced ones.[2]

Graham and Dodd wrote, "Investing, like medicine, law and economics, lies somewhere between an art and a science." The discipline that is investing is backed up by the use of security analysis to develop and present important facts regarding potential investments. The idea is to gather information in order to determine intrinsic value and risk characteristics of a specific security.

Today, as it has been for more than 50 years, security analysis as defined by Graham and Dodd is the backbone of all analytical analysis that goes on at Wall Street. Times have changed considerably, and the personal computer has, in some cases, made things a lot easier and more efficient, but the method to the madness is grounded in Graham and Dodd's seminal work.

For Robertson, certainly, Graham and Dodd laid out the principles of value investing. Throughout his career he knew of no substitute for careful and comprehensive analysis of investment situations. It was all about the research process, which included not only rigorous financial analysis, but interviews with senior members of a company's management team, and discussions with important customers, suppliers, and competitors in order to get a true handle on the business and it prospects. His skills as a value investor were learned in the trenches, where he worked as a salesman pitching ideas to clients. It was during his time at Kidder that he learned to appreciate the basic value philosophy and the opportunity that it offered.

The basics to any fundamental-based investment company comes from the text of Graham and Dodd, but what seems to separate some from others, and what seems to make others more successful than their peers is not only their ability to implement Graham and Dodd's theories and practices, but also how competitive they are and how they translate that competitive nature into the day-to-day activities of making investment decisions.

For Robertson the choice was clear: Use a system that works and is adaptable. Over the years, as he began to look for and search out investment opportunities, he would focus on finding something that was cheap or undervalued and offered the potential for value to be realized.

Working at Kidder and meeting with many of Wall Street's great minds shaped Robertson into a money manager who understood how to extract and exploit opportunities in stocks and other financial instruments. His father had shaped his drive and ambition, taught him the importance of winning, and given him a zeal for business. Kidder developed those attributes, giving Robertson the practical skills he needed to understand financial reports, do research, and build a valuable network of friends.

Robertson also learned that "the market," as many called it, didn't exist. There was no *market* as such, he decided—just a collection of companies that trade in one place or another. He came to believe that nobody really makes any money playing the markets. He came to believe that the only way to make money is to buy stocks that are cheap and watch them go up. The hunt for value was what he enjoyed most—the hunt for those opportunities is what drove him to be successful.

During his stint at Kidder, which lasted more than 20 years, Robertson spent a lot time trying to understand how things worked and why ideas failed. As he moved through various areas of the firm, he ended up heading the firm's money management arm. It was during this experience that he got a first-hand look at the marketing and sales side of the money management business. He realized he did not like it. To Robertson, selling was not doing; it was simply a way to do things for others. He did not like the marketing aspect of the business because it did not allow him to separate himself from the rest of the pack. On the Street, the marketers are considered the knuckle draggers, not the ones with any talent. They are looked at as simply the order takers, making money based on somebody else's work. For Julian, this was not acceptable. He wanted to be the producer, he wanted the respect, and he wanted to be the best. For Julian, the hedge fund business was the only place to achieve all three at once. But like all great plans, it needed to be refined, defined, and expanded before it could be put into motion. He needed to do his research, and for this he turned to his good friend at Kidder—Bob Burch.

In the fall of 1970, Robert Burch married Dale Jones, the daughter of Mary and Alfred Jones. Around that same time, Julian and Bob began to have lunch with Jones and spoke in depth about the concept of the hedge fund and its use in money management industry. Jones, who was famous for not having any interest in talking about money or markets, was more interested in talking about how the product worked and why it worked so well when it was applied the right way with the right people.[3]

Jones realized how powerful a portfolio of longs and shorts could be and, in turn, launched the first hedge fund some 21 years earlier. Started in 1949 by sociologist-turned-journalist-turned-money-manager Alfred Winslow Jones, hedge funds have swept around the world as the tool of choice by Wall Streeters searching for the last bastion of pure capitalism. There is no other job in which a skillful and lucky person can earn millions, if not tens of millions, of dollars year after year. Athletes might, but they have limited careers. Besides, how many people actually make it to the National Basketball Association or Major League Baseball?

The industry began when Jones, an underpaid journalist, was looking for a better way to provide for his family. In 1949, while researching an article for *Fortune* magazine, he began to look at the way the entire stock market moved and how individual stocks moved in relation to it. The article, titled "Fashion in Forecasting," taught Jones two things: First, although the market would definitely move both up and down, it was impossible to tell when; second, many market professionals didn't really know what they were doing.

"My father believed that he was as smart as many of the people he was writing about and realized very early on that working as a journalist would not allow him to provide for his family in the manner in which he was accustomed," said Jones's son, Tony. "So he set out on a path and somehow wound up creating the hedge fund industry."

Jones conducted research for the article that looked at how stock market behavior was interpreted by traders and how they developed ideas from looking at trading patterns. Jones's research for the *Fortune* piece laid the foundation, in part, for what we now know as the hedge fund industry Jones wrote:

> The standard, old fashioned method of predicting the course of the stock market is first to look at facts and figures external to the market itself, and then to examine stock prices to see whether they are too high or too low. Freight-car loadings, commodity prices, bank clearings, the outlook for tax legislation, political prospects, the danger of war and countless other factors determine corporations' earnings and dividend and these, combined with money rates, are supposed to (and in the long run do) determine the prices of common stocks. But in the

meantime awkward things get in the way and in the long run, as Keynes said, we are all dead.

In the late summer of 1946, for instance, the Dow Jones industrial stock average dropped in five weeks from 205 to 163, part of the move to a minor panic. In spite of the stock market, business was good before the break, remained good through it, and has been good ever since.

Nevertheless there are market analysts, whose concern is the internal character of the market, who could see the decline coming. To get these predictive powers they study the statistics that the stock market itself grinds out day after day. Refined, manipulated in various ways, and interpreted, these data are sold by probably as many as twenty stock-market services and are used independently by hundreds, perhaps thousands, of individuals. They are increasingly, used by brokerage firms, by some because the users believe in them and by others because their use brings in business.[4]

Jones used the research he collected to develop an investment strategy that allowed him to focus on picking stocks rather than timing the market. The idea was to create a portfolio that consisted of both long positions and short positions. The idea was that if you create a portfolio of some longs and some shorts, you are able to take out the volatility that is inherent in the market. The manager is thereby able to profit in good times when the market rises (the long positions will increase in value) and profit in bad times (the short positions will go down in value), which means that regardless of market conditions, the investor will profit.[5] By hedging bets with a series of longs and shorts, Jones realized that the investment manager could eliminate much of the market risk in a falling market and reduce exposure in a rising market. In a rising, or bull, market, the longs would go up in value and in a falling, or bear, market, the shorts would protect the portfolio from losses.

Putting together a portfolio like this seemed to make a lot of sense because it would limit volatility. But like all good ideas, there was still one significant problem: picking which stocks to go long and which stocks to go short. In the end, a theory is only as good as the person who can practice or implement it, and for Jones this was an issue. Although he understood the value of a portfolio of long and short positions, he did not necessarily know how to do the research to find which stocks to go long and which stocks to short.

Jones was a decent journalist and a better-than-decent researcher, but he was not a very good stock picker. He was not able to come up with the stocks to make the investments inside his hedged portfolio pay off. In the end, he found that he was a better salesman than stock picker and so put the money management in the hands of others. He developed an organization that consisted of a number of traders who were able to trade the firm's assets freely. Essentially, Jones ran a multistrategy fund, since all the traders at A.W. Jones & Company were able to move around the markets and take positions as if each operated his own fund.[6]

For the most part, the Jones model remains as the blueprint for today's hedge funds. A hedge fund, according to Jones, is a limited partnership so that the general partners–the managers– earn a share of the profits on the limited partners'–the investors'–assets. A hedge fund always uses leverage and must always carry some short positions. Jones believed that by using a series of shorts, the fund would be able to prosper in both good and bad times. Twenty percent of all profits went to the general partners and the rest to the limited partners. Jones did not believe in management fees, because he felt they distracted the manager from the portfolio's performance in the race to gather assets.

It is quite clear that Jones created the fee structure of the modern hedge fund, or *hedged fund*, as he called it. Yet clearly he didn't create the investment strategy that helped his firm be so successful. For this we need to recall the work of Benjamin Graham and David L. Dodd. They invented, developed, and used value investing and modern security analysis techniques.

While it is clear that the principles of the hedge fund were developed, created, and implemented by Jones, some of his investment strategies may have come from his discussions with other investors. He was the first to put the idea of a hedge fund on paper and put it to use, but he did not invent value investing. It is also clear that Alfred Winslow Jones's influence played a significant role in Robertson's decision to launch his hedge fund operation.

It was during his conversations with Burch and Jones that Robertson began to realize the power and rewards that came with running a hedge fund. After all, who better to learn about a business and all that it has to offer than from its creator. The meetings were as strange as they were important. Jones was not one who liked to talk business or shop—he was an intellectual trapped on Wall Street. Jones spent hours reading a book and then calling the author and inviting him or her to lunch to discuss it. He was interested in why water moved a certain way, and spent weeks and months trying to figure it out. Jones not only used the hedge fund business to provide him and his family with the finer things in life; he also used it to finance his pursuit of interests outside of investing.

The conversations between Robertson, Burch, and Jones took place when the market was breaking, in 1970, 1973, and 1975. These experiences taught Robertson the value of having some shorts. In fact, the value of short positions in a portfolio occupied a significant portion of their discussions. At the time, shorting was a rare thing on the Street. Most investors didn't understand how it worked or, more importantly, *why* it worked.

For that matter, they did not know what made a good short versus a bad one. Shorting was truly against almost everything everyone stood for in the investment world–after all, nobody wants to lose money, let alone see a company fail. But during the 1970s, the markets were in a constant state of losses. For Jones, shorting was critical to his success. Robertson learned that lesson well, not only in his discussions with Jones but in the real world.

By 1978, Robertson had had enough of Kidder and decided to take a sabbatical of sorts. He says he "got sort of tired of what he was doing." Toward the end of his career at the firm, the bulk of his work was focused on sales and marketing its money management products, rather than the actual money management side of the business. He was interested in getting paid for performance, instead of getting paid for merchandising. He did not like the merchandising aspect of the business and that goes with selling product and raising assets.

Robertson left New York and went to New Zealand with his wife Josie and their two boys. The goal of the sabbatical was to write the great American novel–which in this case was about a Southerner who makes his way up North and builds a successful career on Wall Street. Unfortunately, this book remains a work in progress. According to Josie, Robertson worked more on the book in Southampton in weeks leading up to the trip than he did while he was in New Zealand. "He got bored very quickly with the book in New Zealand," she said.

Two of the reasons that Robertson decided to go to New Zealand were because of his interest in the country's vast geographical resources and because their two sons, Spencer and Jay, would not have problems with the language. (Josie was pregnant with their youngest son Alex during the trip and gave birth to him upon the family's return to the United States.) Robertson thought that there was more geography per land mass than any other place in the world and thought it would be a good place to explore with his family. In a sense, he never totally left New Zealand. To him, New Zealand and New York would always be his two favorite places on earth. In New Zealand, he would later build a lodge and golf resort and buy a winery. In New Zealand, everyone was equal, Robertson recalled when talking about his sabbatical. He particularly enjoyed the fact that the pace was slower, and he spent considerable time playing tennis and other sports. He fondly recalled that new tennis balls were extremely hard to come by in New Zealand, and as such he and the family often would play with worn out, dead balls. This was par for the course in New Zealand; it was one of the things that he enjoyed about his experience there. This experience taught him a lesson about how good things were. It taught him to appreciate what he had achieved, and helped him put together his plans for the next phase of his life.

When he returned from New Zealand, Robertson decided it was time to end his career at Kidder.

4

THE TIGER FINDS NEW HUNTING GROUNDS

WALL STREET IS VERY MUCH LIKE PROFES-
sional sports in that scores are kept and averages are
watched on a daily basis. What makes a great Wall
Streeter, especially on the trading, brokerage, and money management sides of the business are *athletes*. Nonathletes are fine,
but the ones who really shine and become something on the
Street are those who were a part of a team, understand competition, and know the difference between winning and losing. On
the Street, the score is kept every day, and only people who
played or play sports competitively truly understand what that
means and how important it is to success.

For Robertson it just made sense to go out on his own, keep
his own score, and create his own average in order to truly get
the recognition he deserved for the work he was doing. One of
the true bastions of pure capitalism left in the world is the hedge
fund. It is without a doubt one of the only places left where a person is judged solely on his or her ability to manage money and is
truly rewarded for their efforts. Robertson believed there was no
alternative: He had to start a hedge fund because it was the only
way he could truly stand up and be counted on the Street.

Upon his return from his sabbatical in New Zealand, Robertson decided to start the Tiger Fund. He had seen the success that Jones had had with his fund, as well as a number of others who had successfully launched hedge funds. He liked the idea that investors either put up the money or they didn't; they either stay or they don't stay. To him it was a much simpler business. He also liked what he saw in the success that George Soros and Robert Wilson were having with their hedge funds and in the wake of this success, he realized he had no other choice.

Robertson liked the idea that in a hedge fund environment one is compensated based on performance. When you do well you are rewarded; when you don't do well, you get nothing. There was no quota and no salary so to speak. It is about the managers and all about their ability to make money for their investors. If they made money and the investors profited, then so did the managers—if they lost money and the investors lost money, well, then they did not get paid. Their fortunes were clearly aligned with their investors. It was a model he liked, and it was a model that worked for him.

Robertson and his then-partner Thorpe McKenzie launched Tiger in May 1980 with $8 million under management. McKenzie, who had been handling Robertson's customers while he was in New Zealand, left Tiger in 1982 for personal and professional reasons but also a far richer man than when he launched the firm with Julian.

Doing documents and getting investors are critical parts to launching a new hedge fund, but a name is also important. The pair tried a number of different names for the firm and its funds but could not find something they liked. It wasn't until Robertson's son Spencer, who was seven years old at the time, suggested that they call it Tiger that the pair found a name that would work. Spencer came up with the name because *Tiger* is what Robertson calls everyone whose name he can't remember.

When the pair launched the fund, they were very disappointed in the initial amount of capital that they raised. As is often the case with money managers, they believed that more money would simply come over the transom from relationships they had in the business. However, Robertson believed that the firm could probably grow to about $100 million in assets, based on their investor base. In just a few short years, that notion would be thrown out the window as he realized just how big the firm could become with good performance and strong marketing.

One of Tiger's first clients was Burch. In the early 1980s Jones had asked Burch to take over the day-to-day operation of A.W. Jones & Company. With Burch taking over, the firm made a dynamic shift, going from an organization that actually invested in the markets through in-house managers and traders to one that invested solely in other hedge funds.

The idea was to turn Jones into a fund of funds. By doing so, the firm was able to keep costs low and was able to have unlimited access to the best Jones-style hedge funds. Tiger was Burch's first choice. At this point, Tiger had been operating for a year or so. Burch spent a lot of time looking around for funds to invest in and found only five that fit his model; Jones's managers ran three. Burch liked Tiger; he kept his firm's money invested there year after year until the end of Tiger in 2000.

Launching a money management business in 1980 was not such a wonderful idea, many thought. The Dow was trading in the mid 800s having languished in this range off its high of 1000 in 1966. But after taking a significant dip, hitting about a 650 bottom, things started to rebound, and as the Reagan tax cuts kicked in 1982 and 1983, the bull entered lower Manhattan. The result was a solid five-year run to 2700.

Once he started Tiger, Robertson used the lessons he had learned at Kidder and from his experience on the Street to get the firm into the game. The key to success, he had learned, was in establishing contacts that he could go to for information. From the beginning of his career he had worked very hard at establishing a network of people around the world who he could turn to for information about potential investments and who he could use as a sounding board before he made investment decisions.

Early on in his career on the Street, Robertson learned to appreciate and subscribe to the old adage: once a salesman, always a salesman. It is extremely hard to refute for almost anyone who has ever been in sales—for those who have been in sales on Wall Street, is next to impossible to refute. While it's obvious from all outgoing appearance that the merchandising side of the money management business was not something Robertson was interested in when he set out to launch Tiger, it is undoubtedly a skill that he used to grow the business to levels beyond even his wildest imagination. In the early days of the firm, he realized the important role communication with investors and potential investors would play in the success of the firm. Thus, he was very keen on the use of performance to sell his products and to attract assets under management. The way he communicated was via letters to investors.

Communication was always a key element in Tiger's success. As a writer of sorts, Robertson was very keen on communicating his views on the markets, the economy, the White House, and the world to his investors. His willingness to communicate was one of the things that buoyed his success in marketing and selling his hedge funds, both domestically and abroad. But he also used his vast network of contacts to gather information faster than he disseminated it, making him an information superhighway of sorts years before the concept became a reality.

When he launched Tiger Management, Robertson's network was already so vast that all he had to do was pick up a phone and he could get pretty much in touch with anyone he wanted to. He prided himself on his connections, whether they were potential investments or potential investors. It was this skill and the constant refinement and expansion of his network that allowed him to build Tiger's foundation for the future.

His use of the phones to gather information is legendary. A reporter once commented after watching him in action that speed dial must have been invented for Robertson, in that he is constantly finishing up one call and dialing anther. At Tiger, Robertson spent most of his time either on the phone, looking at charts, or reviewing information. He constantly developed networks in order to make sure that when Tiger got information it had the right people available to process it.

Over the years, Robertson built a Rolodex of thousands of people he had met on his travels around the globe. He constantly gathered, processed, and spit out what he did not need. He was also known for his ability to store information for later use.

The launch of Tiger was more than a full-time job. It forced him to be in a constant state of motion. He was one of the first true multitaskers. During meetings, he rarely sat still. He constantly took calls from this person or that person in search of information. Some were friends, some were former colleagues, and some were people he just liked talking to.

Although processing numbers is clearly a talent, his ability to gather and process information about a company outside of its financial statements is also uncanny. Friends and colleagues call him the most gracious person in a social setting–gregarious, fun, and with a great sense of humor–but when he is focused on something he is intense, and he is very good at spotting people's weaknesses whatever they might be. When making investment decisions, he is not hesitant to exploit those weaknesses.

Initially the firm started off relatively small as most hedge funds do, with Robertson and McKenzie doing most if not all of the research and trading for the fund. Robertson told me that in order to make an educated decision, you need to know everything that is going on and must understand how each variable is going to affect the situation now and in the future. As the firm grew, however, handling so much information was not something he could do alone. So although for the better part of the firm's existence Robertson had the ultimate say about what did and did not get into the portfolio, he made good use of smart people from good schools who could be trained to ask lots of questions, find lots of answers, and never run out of a thirst for knowledge or information on which to base an idea.

As Tiger grew in assets under management it also increased its human assets. And while the firm grew in the number of people it had working for it, so did its assets under management. Throughout Tiger's existence, there was clearly one chief and an awful lot of Indians. And while Robertson prided himself on hiring a diverse group of very smart individuals, there were times when book smarts and brains clearly got in the way of the collegial atmosphere that was Tiger in its early days.

Like his mother, Julian was able to use joking and poking fun as a way to communicate. However, unlike his mother, Julian had been known to take the joking and ribbing to an extreme. Many of his Tiger colleagues pride themselves on having made it through one of his ribbings, albeit with a little less skin then when they first walked in the door at Tiger's offices. Because Robertson takes great pride in his appearance, he often pokes fun at those who do not. He is very complimentary and inquisitive about people's dress, and when he sees something he likes he inquires about where it was purchased and often times will go out and buy it. However, he will also poke endless fun when he sees something he does not approve of. One former colleague compared Robertson's jabs to that of the person who has a mosquito bite that just will not stop itching so that they scratch it until it bleeds.

As an ongoing operation in a constant state of growth, Tiger had a number of problems stemming from personality conflicts and the wrath of its leader. These types of issues are commonplace in most high-strung investment organizations and are often tolerated due to financial rewards that come with success. Throughout the firm's history, Tiger was a place where everyone was overpaid, knew they were overpaid, and were determined to continue to be overpaid. It was considered just compensation for withstanding the wrath of their leader. In the beginning, the profits were large and so were the paychecks; therefore it was worth it. As the firm grew and the profits increased, so did the payouts, and it became even more worth it for many. And while everyone seemed to enjoy the early part of the 1980s, it was truly only the beginning of what was to come for Robertson and the folks at Tiger.

At the end of 1980, the firm that began in early May had posted a return of 54.9 percent net of all fees, versus the S&P 500 and the Morgan Stanley Capital Index (MSCI), which finished the year up 28.9 percent and 21.8 percent, respectively. The fund had gotten off to a very good start. In 1981, the Tiger really showed its stripes; the fund posted a gain of 19.4 percent net of fees, versus the S&P and the MSCI, which both finished the years off negative 4.9 percent and negative 4.8 percent, respectively.

For Robertson, leaving Kidder had become the best decision he had ever made. Now he was not only being paid for bringing in the assets, but he was being paid for doing something successful with them. Tiger was on its way—it was he and his colleagues to run and now, after being in business for a year and a half, they all realized how important it was not to make mistakes.

5

THE TIGER BEGINS
TO GROWL

TIGER MAINTAINED ITS EDGE OVER THE INDEXES IN 1982 and 1983 up 42.4 percent net of fees and 46.7 percent net of fees respectively in those years. In the year of George Orwell, the fund continued to trounce the indexes. Investors earned just over 20 percent on their money net of fees in 1984, a return that beat the benchmark S&P and MSCI by 13.9 percent and 15.5 percent, respectively. In the fourth quarter of 1984 alone, Tiger earned almost 17 percent while the S&P 500 managed to eke out a gain of just 1.7 percent for the same period. The firm had entered its formative years and assets from existing and new investors flowed into its coffers.[1]

The idea behind a hedge fund is quite simple. Hedge funds, by their structure, offer investors a greater range of strategies and tools for their managers than traditional long-only funds. In theory, managers should be able to use this flexibility to put in place safeguards to dampen market volatility. One of the most common strategies is the equity long/short strategy. Most of the more famous fund managers start with this strategy and from there move into other strategies, including global macro trading, various arbitrage strategies, and, in some cases, fixed-income markets. Fund managers will change investment strategy if the amount of money they manage doesn't work with their existing strategy or if they believe that they can apply their skill sets to other areas of the investment management spectrum. Some managers also move into other areas as way of developing their business, in some cases, they view new strategies and new funds as the natural extensions of their investment management practice. As business develops, they are often requested to provide investors with more capacity. The problem is that many strategies have a limited amount of capacity, and a manager not interested in turning assets away might have to look to other strategies to employ to handle the influx of assets.

This was the dilemma facing Tiger Management. Robertson and his team, which by this time had grown to more than 30 people, were clearly masters of the investment game. But further review of the numbers revealed something even more impressive about the firm's investment prowess. During 1984, Tiger realized enormous profits from its shorts—over half of the year's performance numbers came from successful short trades. Robertson and his team were truly operating a hedge fund: The Tiger fund was making money regardless of market conditions and was proving to investors that not only could it find value in traditional long investments, but it could also find and exploit opportunities on the short side.

Investors were responding to Tiger's success by sending it more money. As more assets became available to invest, more investment options were needed. Finding opportunities was becoming harder, so Robertson hired more analysts to scour more markets in search of good trades. To paraphrase his words, the way to ameliorate the problem was to have more good people working together for the same cause. Robertson saw two possible paths to growth: the traditional markets and global macro investing.

In the traditional markets, his analysis of the current state of the economy and corporate America was leading him down a conservative road. He believed that there was too much optimism in the market, which caused him to not be terribly enthusiastic of things to come. The measure of Investment Advisory Sentiment showed that 59 percent of all those surveyed were bulls, while just 23 percent were bears (the remaining participants were undecided). He saw that margin-account buying (this is when investors borrow money against their portfolios to buy more stocks) on the American Stock Exchange (AMEX) and in the over-the-counter (OTC) market had been enormous in the first two weeks of the year, and that put–call ratios were low–which to most people indicated optimism.

The put–call ratio is the trading volume of put options to call options. Money managers use it as a gauge of investor sentiment. A high volume of calls compared to a low volume of puts means that investors are bullish. Robertson and the folks at Tiger only got really optimistic when the majority were pessimists. The data he reviewed showed that investors were borrowing at record levels to finance their investment portfolios. It was clear from this research that the investment public was bullish, which would push the market higher. At the same time, the smart money seemed to be shorting the heck out of the market. Professional investors believed that the euphoria was going to end, and it was only a matter of time before the market turned bearish.[2]

Money managers also perceived a lack of liquidity in the market–in other words, there was not enough cash to fuel a big advance. The assets entering the market were coming from speculators, as opposed to pension and profit-sharing plans, which meant a rally could not be sustained. Investments by pension and profit-sharing plans, then at an all-time low, usually provided more stability in the markets. Without such institutional investment, the safety net was looking ragged.

Robertson and his team were looking for ways to capitalize on this situation. They needed to find good places to put the money to work, and one area where they were lacking was *small cap* stocks. These are stocks of smaller, more speculative companies that are thinly traded and have little, if any, research coverage. They are emerging companies, not usually considered mainstream investments. These types of stocks had not been on his or his analysts' radar screens but now they sounded promising.

To explore this new territory, Robertson called on his investors to help. He requested their ideas for any companies that they thought would have been outside of his research scope but were worthy of being in the portfolio. In the past, many successful investment managers had exploited the use of smaller companies in their portfolios to provide them with returns. Robertson believed that the time was ripe again for these opportunities, and he wanted his investors to help him find his way to these companies. It was the first of many calls to arms that Robertson made to his investors.

In Robertson's view, 1985 was not shaping up to be a good year. As the flowers started to bloom, the firm had taken a defensive stance toward its investments. Its data showed that all was not right with the world. Two things in particular set off alarms in his head. The first was that the spread between earnings yield of the S&P 500 and the yield of S&P AA corporate bonds widened by more than 175 basis points in just a few short weeks. This made bonds a lot more attractive than stocks, and this was not good for an equity manager. The second was that the dollar was experiencing a sharp erosion in value, which Robertson believed would result in a negative reaction in the stock and bond markets. His research showed that foreign investors had weathered the other currency crises like the devaluation of the Mexican peso without losses because the loans were denominated in dollars. When the peso went from 28 to the dollar to 200, the borrowers suffered because they had to pay off the loan in dollars, but now that the dollar was falling, the lenders were getting hurt, and he believed that when the lenders got hurt, they would sell their positions in U.S.-based stocks and bonds.[3]

Even so, although Tiger saw significant opportunities in the equities markets, it was moving rather cautiously. Robertson had decided that the markets were too volatile and that he needed to pursue a rather conservative investment policy. We recall the three reasons that led him to implement this sort of investment strategy: bullish optimism on the Street; heavy speculation, especially in the OTC and AMEX issues, versus low investments by the more stable pension and profit-sharing plans; and a falling dollar.[4]

Nevertheless, Robertson still believed in March of 1985 that some stocks were "incredibly" cheap. He also had found hope in the form of the corporate raiders and takeover artists. A number of stocks were ripe for takeovers, and Robertson and his team believed it would be easy to identify which companies were poised for being taken out, and as such he would position them in the portfolio.

However, working on potential takeovers was not going to see Tiger through the volatility that was the market. The firm needed something more. It needed to expand its penetration into the global markets. So while exploring and finding new names for the portfolio, he was also focusing on expanding the firm's overall investment strategy and its move into other areas of the global markets to extract and exploit profits. Tiger had mastered the long/short game and was now looking for new, bigger, and more liquid markets to enter and extract profits. The answer was simple: global macro.

Global macro investing in it simplest definition is the search for returns regardless of borders, economies, and political environments. It is the ability to find investment opportunities in any area of the globe and exploit them for a profit. Most global macro investing takes advantage of investment opportunities by looking at a country's geopolitical situation, its economy, and its government to see if there is an opportunity to make a profit from investing in a local currency, a local fixed-income security, or a local company. Some managers operate through country-specific research, meaning that they look at one country at a time and make a decision based on various factors in and around the country. Others operate more broadly by investing in regions or areas of the world.

In global macro investing, the manager constructs a portfolio based on a top-down view of global economic trends, considering factors such as interest rates, economic policies, inflation, and government stability, among other things. The manager looks at the entire economic picture of a country or a region, rather than considering how individual stocks or bonds will perform. The idea is that the manager wants to profit from changes in the value of entire asset classes. For example, the manager may hold long positions in the U.S. dollar and Japanese equity indices while shorting the euro and U.S. treasury bills. The reality is that a global macro manager can go anywhere and do anything to extract profits from securities markets around the globe. The idea is that he or she can use basically unlimited resources to find opportunities and exploit them for profits. In these transactions, the reward is often quite substantial and the losses can be quite devastating. The idea is to not put all of your eggs in one basket. And although many are afraid of the potential for huge losses, what attracts most people to this strategy is the potential for enormous gains. Managers often move toward this side of the investment spectrum because it is in these transactions that they can put huge amounts of capital to work without taking unnecessary risks.

Slippage is a big factor in the equation and cannot be overlooked when a manager looks to accept new assets. The manager has to calculate how much money can be moved in and out of the position without causing the market to move. Taking too big of a position will cause the stock to rise too much when the trade is put on, thus reducing the potential for profit. The manager also needs to make sure he or she can get out of the position once the profit is realized or, more importantly, should the position begin to move against the investor. The position should not be so large that the investor cannot get out before the market falls. There is only so much money that can go into a long/short equity style, and once a manager passes a certain level of assets under management, the portfolio becomes un-wieldy because the firm becomes limited to the size and scope of the positions it can put on without adversely affecting the market. So it begins experimenting with strategies that can han-dle larger pools of assets and offer enormous liquidity. This is why managers like Robertson, Soros, and Steinhardt adopted the global macro strategy. Their funds grew so large that they needed to put vast sums of money to work, and the only way they could do it was to look to bigger, more liquid markets. Unfortunately, the stock market is only so liquid. Compared to the bond market and the currency markets, there is relatively little liquidity in all but the largest corporations. Finding mar-kets to move in and out of quickly and efficiently without mak-ing too much noise leads the biggest players to the most liquid markets: currency. The world markets in the dollar, euro, ster-ling, and the yen are by far the most liquid.

Robertson and Tiger's evolution from value-stock picking hedge fund manager to global macro manager began in the mid-1980s as the firm's assets began to grow rapidly. As money began to pour in from individual and institutional investors from around the globe, Robertson and his analysts needed to find trades where they could put a lot of money to work. In eq-uity markets, investors are faced with limits based on the size and depth of a company's stock. But in a global macro environ-ment, there are very few situations where size of assets truly matter. Robertson and his analysts realized that the bond markets and the currency markets were so big and so liquid that they could put huge amounts of capital to work in positions that were levered without running into liquidity problems.

Robertson and Tiger's global macro days began in earnest in 1985, when the firm entered into a dollar trade that yielded huge profits. The profits allowed Robertson to see first-hand that by entering this side of the business, he would be able to put great amounts of money to work and, in turn, be able to extract significant profits. It was this foray into dollar trading that caused the firm to change direction from focusing solely on the equity markets and equity-based products to focusing on anything that it could trade.

"I think, without actually realizing it, we put more and more into those types of trades because we realized that they were more liquid than anything else, so we became—sort of by osmosis—more involved in macro," he said. "It was a long-term kind of evolution that worked very well for us."[5]

Throughout the first quarter of 1985, Tiger had performance that was up and down. In the first two months of the year, the firm was beating the S&P 500 by just 50 basis points, and by the end of the quarter the firm had expanded the spread by about 4 percent. It was up 12.9 percent versus the S&P 500, which was up just 9.2 percent.[6]

The fund was beating the averages by almost 4 percent because it took advantage of the weakness of the dollar during that time. The dollar had lost almost 20 percent against the British pound and lost over 10 percent against a market basket of currencies. This was music to Robertson's ears. He believed that the dollars' strength was one of the biggest problems that the American economy was facing, and he was ready to take advantage of its fall.[7]

By the end of May, however, things had turned for Robertson. Tiger had experienced some heavy losses due to some shorts it had in the generic drug sector. This error shaved off nearly 5 percent from the fund's return. Robertson and his team had believed that the companies were grossly overvalued and that they were primed for a fall; unfortunately, the rest of the market believed that the companies were undervalued and pushed them significantly higher. And while Robertson did believe that the prices would eventually correct themselves and the positions that had hurt so badly would turn out OK, he decided to alert investors that he was, after all, human, and that he and his team were capable of mistakes. He told investors that he did not believe that Tiger could continue to perform as well as it did in its first five years of business—the firm's past growth was "unsustainable."[8] But that did not mean that he was about to throw in the towel. In fact, just the opposite—he called on his investors to give him more money to manage because he was, after all, doing something right. The fund had made up the losses it had suffered in the generic drug positions and was seeing nice returns from its short position in U.S. tobacco and the long position it held in Chrysler. Chrysler had resurrected itself from near bankruptcy and established itself as a low-cost producer that seemed to be headed on the right track. Tiger was also seeing profits from its position in Boeing. Airline traffic in 1985 was up 15 percent and that, coupled with the dollar being down against the British pound and the French franc, meant that the company would see its orders increase. It would be a stronger competitor to its British and French counterparts.[9]

And while the Seattle-based airplane manufacturer was on his mind, Robertson had also turned his attention to a company closer to home. The Pall Corporation, which was based in Long Island, New York, made filters for everything from beer to blood. The company's products had the capability to remove particles ranging from 40 pm in diameter—the smallest-size particle that the naked eye can see—to particles down to .04 pm in diameter. Because he lived near the company, he was aware of the fine reputation it had built as a corporate citizen. Upon meeting the company's chief executive officer, however, he learned first-hand how well the company was run and how solid an organization it was. And while the company's growth had slowed due to the weakening dollar, Robertson was a believer in the company and liked what he saw. Although he was interested in expanding his reach in the investment world, undervalued stocks would always play an important role in the Tiger portfolios.[10]

By mid-1985, the Tiger was back in form. The fund was beating the S&P 500 by more than 7 percent for the quarter and for the year by more than 12 percent. Robertson was pleased with the results, but was worried about the times ahead. His data said that the economy was being fueled by low interest rates that were intended to spur retail sales. The only problem was that consumers seemed to be spending on the wrong things. They were buying goods from Taiwan, Europe, and Japan, so he questioned if this increase in spending would really help the economy. The manufacturing sector was suffering with low-cost goods flooding the market, and producers were in dire shape. The only area that seemed to see growth was the services sector, and this was troubling to Robertson. His research showed that few, if any, were concerned about this issue, and few could give him a satisfactory answer to the question: Doesn't the country need to produce something? The solution was to see the dollar get weaker, which would make it more expensive to import items into the United States.[11]

Robertson did not like the pace at which the dollar was softening; he wanted it to fall faster. That being said, he and his team were finding extraordinary opportunities in the equities markets. Stocks, to put it bluntly, were cheap. At this time, the market was still undervalued enough that it was attractive for both speculators and companies to buy huge volumes of shares. The companies liked it because they could buy their stock cheap, while the speculators liked it because they knew that undervalued companies would become the targets of hostile takeovers and leveraged buyouts. The merger mania continued. As such, the price at which deals were getting done was far above market levels. If the mergers weren't enough, companies were buying stock back because the prices were so cheap, which meant that prices were rising and with that Tiger's performance was strong. However, Robertson was being cautious with his outlook. He wanted to make sure that the fund was protected against any sudden and serious market drops or fluctuations. To ensure the fund's profits and more importantly protect it from significant losses, he bought put options that in effect ensured the fund from losses of more than 3 percent. The options did not safeguard the fund against poor stock selection, but they did eliminate significant amounts of market risk.[12]

A mere 28 days later, Robertson had changed his tune and was cautiously optimistic. The dollar had fallen further, and this led him to be less sanguine about inflation and interest rates. He believed that the economy was indeed strengthening.[13] These feelings remained with Robertson well through the rest of the summer and into the fall. The dollar continued to fall, making it expensive for imports and cheaper for exports, which he believed would be the stimulus the economy needed. The cheaper dollar meant that nonservice areas of the economy such as farming, manufacturing, and mining would prosper. And while it was too early to tell how much the decline in the dollar would help the economy, he did believe that "every little bit helped."[14]

The summer of 1985 proved to be a good one for Tiger. Heading into the fall, the firm was up 34.7 percent for the year versus the S&P500, which was down 2.7 percent for the same time period in the middle of September. The fund continued to do well, although it was not having much luck in the stock selection part of its portfolio. Robertson thought the performance of the stock portfolio was directly related to the fact that the stocks did well in the previous quarter and were just experiencing a one-quarter lag. The decline in the dollar would continue to help the portfolio and stimulate the economy. If the weakening of the dollar was not enough to keep investors interested, he also explained why the current takeover activity was going to help them as well. Almost all the deals were being done at premiums to the market, and while Tiger did not participate in the acquisition game, it was not immune to this activity in the market. For example, the firm bought Aviall, Inc. in August at around $12.50 per share; it was tendered for at $25.00. The firm went long on Empire Airlines at $9.00 and was taken out at $15.00. And while he enjoyed the profits, Robertson thought it was interesting to see how much more the purchasers of the two companies thought of the companies than their own investors did.[15]

Heading into the final days of 1985, Robertson was excited about the possibilities for the upcoming year. He believed that a lot of money that had been sitting on the sidelines was getting ready to come into the market and that, coupled with the continued mania over mergers, meant that the stock market was due to rise. This, he believed, offered him and his investors a great opportunity for potential returns. He cautioned his investors in his letter of December 13, 1985, that if they had not planned on emeralds or diamonds as Christmas gifts, they better not show their wives the letter. It had been a good year for Tiger investors. Tiger had bet the right way when the dollar fell and posted a gain of 51.4 percent net of fees, versus Standard & Poor's 500 Stock Index, which was up 31.7 percent, and the Morgan Stanley Capital International indices, which climbed 40.6 percent.[16] He was expecting 1986 to be equally profitable. The stock market was experiencing a contraction as a significant amount of stock had been removed through takeovers and buyouts. For example, if an investor wanted to buy food stocks, there were few choices. Companies like General Foods, Nabisco, Iowa Beef Packers, and Carnation had been bought out, and the alternatives such as Ralston and Kellogg did not offer much promise as both companies had been in the midst of significant buy-back programs. Robertson believed that some 10 percent of the total shares available for purchase had been retired due to the leveraged buyouts and corporate repurchase programs. In his mind this was an astounding figure–where else could someone find something in which 10 percent of the supply had dried up in such a short period of time? The reality was that as supply shrank, demand was increasing, according to his research. Pensions were continuing to grow, profit-sharing plans were growing, there were more IRAs, and foreign investors were putting more and more capital into the United States. He believed that some $130 billion would be put to work over the next 12 months and that, coupled with demand from the retail investors, had the potential of heating up demand for stocks dramatically.[17]

In the early days of 1986, Robertson was in a good mood, Tiger was primed for continued growth. The business was growing faster and performing better than he could have ever dreamed when he launched the firm in 1980. And while the partnership was clearly thriving, Robertson was cautious to make sure his investors understood exactly the type of investment vehicle they had purchased with their money. He believed that some of the investors were confused as to how exactly Tiger was making money during this time. It seemed that some of the investors believed that simply because the firm went short, they would always make money. He went to great lengths to explain that while the shorts often provided a cushion against losses during down markets and provided some upside, these positions alone would not be the savior of the portfolio if the market dropped 30 or 40 percent. Robertson wanted his investors to know that should the market drop that much, the portfolio would probably lose about 15 to 20 percent of its value. After all, Tiger was an equity partnership, and as such, its overall performance was affected by overall equity trends. And while most investments were sold to investors on the basis of relative performance, Tiger was all about absolute performance. *Absolute performance* is the real return that is generated by the investment and is viewed in terms of actual dollars earned or lost. *Relative performance* is based on how one investment did versus another similar or equal investment. Hedge funds, for the most part, are looked at on an absolute basis while mutual funds are looked at for the most part on a relative basis. Tiger was all about the absolute return, and while it was good to beat the averages, the most important thing was to make money.

However, there was a problem of sorts brewing for Robertson and his team; it became apparent that while stock trading would always contribute significantly to the firm's bottom line, it was time to increase its global macro position. Just a few months earlier he had assured his investors that the portfolio's "finite" risk exposure would be limited to no more than 3 or 4 percent, but now he sought to alter the partnership agreement to allow it to "risk a maximum of 25 percent" of its assets in commodities positions.[18] The firm was dynamically shifting its focus, and for the manager and the investors this was going to be a very good thing.

Some of Robertson's investors and observers believe that he made a push into global macro strategies because of his "uncanny ability" to see and find trends before they became apparent to others. In the money management space, just because something is hot this year does not mean it is going to be hot next year, and one of Robertson's strengths is that he is able to see the proverbial forest through the trees when it comes to finding investment opportunities in the United States and abroad. There are many money managers who follow and act emotionally as they run to or from an investment opportunity. Robertson does not operate that way, according to many who have watched him make investment decisions. He is simply able to take emotion out of the equation and act in a clear and decisive manner.

"Our forte is picking stocks, good and bad, not dealing in commodities, which is a totally different business," he wrote to shareholders in February 1986. "Nevertheless, it is always a mistake to totally exclude yourself from any modality since that will result in missed opportunities." The point of the letter was to persuade investors to let the partnership add commodity-based trading to the firm's efforts. At the time, its Private Placement Memorandum stated that the general partner did not intend to trade in commodities and futures. To do so, the firm needed to win approval both from the Commodity Futures Trading Commission and its partners. To spell out his case, Robertson cited the success he found in the silver market during his days at Kidder. Below is an excerpt from the letter:

In the past, there have been times when it would have been a great mistake for me not to have taken advantage of certain special situations in the commodities field. Some of you knew me in the late sixties when a young analyst at Kidder Peabody discovered that the Treasury Department, which had effectively kept a ceiling on the price of silver by selling its hoard on the open market, was rapidly running out of silver. Silver became one of the most fabulous investments I have ever made, doubly so because there was no risk involved. Later on you may recall our delving into cattle futures when the herds diminished significantly.[19]

The firm had just made a significant amount of money in the currency markets. In 1985, currencies accounted for just about 28 percent of the firm's profits. Robertson and his team had limited its currency risk to about 5 percent. He had seen the opportunity, and he wanted to be able to take advantage of it.

While the Tiger documents allowed him to take some positions in the currency markets, the documents put a limit on how much of this exposure was allowed. In order to exploit the opportunities to the potential he believed existed, he needed to change the documents. Hedge funds are governed by an offering memorandum—a prospectus of sorts that thoroughly describes and puts forth how the investors' assets are going to be managed and what strategies are allowed to be used by the manager to seek return. At the time, the Tiger documents had a prohibition that said that the general partner (manager) did not currently intend to trade in the commodities and futures contracts and if he was going to do so, he would have to register as a commodity pool operator with the Commodity Futures Trading Commission. He had wanted to buy aluminum futures but was prohibited from doing so by the abovementioned stipulation in the documents. Robertson believed that these words had cost him dearly. Now he saw opportunity to go short the oil stocks and go long the oil futures. The oil stocks, he believed were discounting the price of oil down to $20 to $22 a barrel, while the March futures price was about $16 a barrel. This was a huge disparity, and he wanted to exploit it. The problem was, he couldn't because the documents would not allow him to use these instruments. The documents needed to be changed. He decided to register with the Commodity Futures Trading Commission.[20]

He was making the case to investors that he needed more weapons in his arsenal. It was very simple: There were opportunities to exploit and markets to conquer, and he needed to be able to use all of the tools that markets offered to generate returns. Investors did not seem to doubt that Robertson had an uncanny ability to navigate the global markets and find places to invest and make money. His fundamental approach to the equity markets had proved incredibly successful, and his investors believed that what he did in the equity markets could be repeated in the currency and futures markets. They wanted their manager to be successful and they wanted to make sure he had all the tools he needed to be successful. As such, the investors approved the changes to the private placement memorandum that allowed him to trade futures.

Global macro investing takes a fundamental approach to investing on a country level versus a company level. If unemployment is going up and consumer confidence is going down, the currency may be too strong versus the rest of the world so the country can't export. Money managers take all the information and draw a fundamental conclusion about the long-term pricing of that country and act accordingly.

The problem is that there are a lot more variables when it comes to global macro investing than there are in long/short equity investing. One of the greatest variables is political risk and one's ability to truly assess it.

If you are looking at country and can't figure out how stable or unstable its political situation is, then it is a pretty good idea to avoid that place. The thing that is different is that if you have a company with an ineffectual management team, then you know you have a bad company and you avoid it. When you are looking at a global macro situation, you have to assess the strength of the government, its central bank, and how it will act or react to local and word events. Then you make investments accordingly.

Robertson was anxious and interested in getting the partners' approval to start trading commodities in his hedge fund, but he was also interested in hedging *himself* with the following paragraph in a letter to investors:

"I do not mean to indicate that all of our commodity dealings have been profitable," he wrote. "Nor will they be in the future. Further, I want to point out that we have no expertise in commodities and commodities are inherently risky because of the leverage employed in these transactions. Nevertheless, I feel strongly that we should not be precluded by fiat from taking advantage of certain situations when they arrive."[21]

He proposed to change the firm's documents so that Tiger would be able to risk at cost a maximum of 25 percent of the firm's net worth in commodities positions. This meant that should the firm expose 25 percent of its equity in commodities, the actual dollars initially put up would probably be less than 2 or 2.5 percent of its overall equity, because the normal commodity margin is less than 10 to 1. And while the actual cash at risk was quite low, theoretically, the firm could have lost 25 percent of the value of its portfolio should the positions go to zero. That being said, Robertson believed that even in a steep decline in the commodities markets of, say, 20 or 30 percent, the firm would only lose between 5 and 7 percent of its value. The idea he was trying to get across was that even though he had what was perceived to be significant exposure, it was quite limited in reality to the firm's overall market exposure.

Robertson and his lawyers went to great lengths to express the risks and the potential for both profit and loss that implementing these strategies offered to the fund. In doing so, he made it clear that the Tiger team would trade with caution.

He stated that the firm would not exercise its option to be in commodities all the time, but that he did think it should have the option in order to take advantage of special situations when they arose. He was clear to calm those who questioned a stock jockey's ability to find opportunity and avoid the unnecessary risks associated with commodities, at the same time explaining why he also thought the risk was worth it, considering the potential rewards.

He closed the letter with thoughts on the performance for early 1986. As it turned out, Tiger was up 8.4 percent, while the

S&P was up about 2 percent through the end of the first few weeks of the year and things looked pretty good—after all, it was the year of the Tiger according to the Chinese calendar. Through the end of the first quarter the firm was doing very well. It was up more than 25.7 percent for the first three months of the year versus the S&P 500, which was up just over 14 percent. But trouble was brewing. Most of the money managers on Wall Street and the folks in Washington seemed to be forecasting an economy that was going to explode, but Robertson's data indicated that the economy was contracting. Home sales were up, while auto, retail, and capital goods sales were down. This led to a tough six weeks for the firm in the second quarter of 1986. By the end of the first quarter the economy showed signs of significant weakness, many of the economic indicators that the firm followed showed that things did not look too promising. Robertson, who had just a few months earlier predicted that the markets were going to run, was now operating in a defensive mood—waiting in the calm before the storm. During this period, the firm lost more than 5 percent and things did not look like they were reversing, meaning that the losses would wipe out the previous quarter's gain.

By the end of the first six months of the year, things had gotten worse. Tiger was flat for the quarter ending June 30, 1986, versus the S&P 500, which was up 5.6 percent. Robertson blamed the performance on the over optimism that was sweeping the markets. In his view, the bond traders were too bullish, shorting was almost nonexistent, and margin buying was at an all-time high. He was approaching the markets with great caution. He also was looking for other opportunities. He was waiting for and expecting things to get better. Interest rates were heading lower, oil prices were going lower, and the economic situation in Europe was getting better. But in the short term, he thought there was too much optimism by traders in bonds, treasury bills, and stocks, which was enough to cause him to think that short term pressure was building. Robertson was betting that the market was due for a short-term dip that would be followed by continued strength.

Robertson again was looking for ways to extract profits from the market and for this he needed to make another significant change in the firm's investment strategy. This time he was telling them that he would now put "an emphasis" on venture capital and private placement investments.[22]

He believed the equity markets were losing their luster and those things that were once reasonably priced were becoming overvalued. Now that price/earnings multiples and even multiples of book value had increased sharply, he thought that the time was right and that there was more relative appeal in venture capital investing.

He had decided to make a significant but small commitment to this area of the market. Tiger's overall commitments to these opportunities were not to be terribly high on a percentage-wise basis, somewhere south of 15 percent of the firm's total assets, but nonetheless, he did expect these investments to make a meaningful contribution in the years ahead to the firm's bottom line.[23]

While Robertson was clearly excited about the prospects of the venture capital markets, it seems that some of his investors were more skeptical. Investors were concerned about liquidity issues at the fund based on venturing into a very illiquid side of Wall Street. In order to calm investor worries and fears that they would not be able to get their money out of Tiger, Robertson told them there would be no changes to the liquidity provisions of the firm's private placement memorandum and that they could continue to withdraw money on a quarterly basis and were guaranteed the right to withdraw funds semiannually.

In a private placement or venture capital investment, Tiger's lock-up period might be as long as 10 years. Assuming substantial appreciation in the value of the private placements and an increase in withdrawals, the percentage of the funds in liquid, freely traded equities might drop below an optimum level. Therefore, he agreed that it would be imprudent for anything more than a nominal percentage of the fund's assets to be put in this long-term lock-up situation.[24]

And while he was careful to not promise better results in the second half, he reminded investors that while the fund was flat for the quarter, in the past, "poor quarterly performances have been followed by excellent results" in his monthly letter to shareholders. The manager who had not been interested in merchandising was now employing the use of soft-sell sales techniques to solicit assets. With this in mind, he wrote, "We ask you to consider adding to your investment."

Later that summer, Robertson decided to expand his presence in the jungle and rolled out the Puma Fund. Puma required investors to lock up their investments for a period of four years, had a debt component from the outset of approximately two-thirds equity to one-third debt, and, as part of its overall investment strategy, would be pursuing an aggressive trading role.[25] The lockup meant that Robertson was now free to make investments in private placements that would not have been prudent for the Tiger portfolio because partners could have withdrawn money on a quarterly basis. In a private placement, the securities are illiquid, which means investors cannot get out of the security for some time.

In his letter to shareholders of July 25, 1986, he sighted the fact that Tiger was unable to invest in a Macy's private placement because the security, while attractively priced, offered little if any liquidity. This was important for him to point out because he believed that in a market with higher price/earnings ratios, there would be an almost "defacto" improvement in the relative value of the private placement securities. Along with the lockup, the other significant difference between Tiger and Puma was that Robertson had hired Morgan Stanley to raise debt for the fund. This caused the capital ratio of the fund to be about two-thirds equity to one-third debt, which meant that Puma would have about 30 percent more dollars working for it than the Tiger Fund. He was mindful that there was an increased risk from using the leverage and therefore was going to put in place certain hedging strategies to provide the fund with a less fluctuating rate of return than that which he was getting on the firm's normal equity portfolio. The strategies he used sounded familiar to those he had used in the past, going long good stocks and shorting bad stocks and using a combination of commodity and stock hedges. These strategies would allow him to hedge and manage the risk for what he believed would be a steady stream of profits.

With Puma, Robertson intended to pursue an "aggressive" trading strategy. Prior to the launch of Puma, Robertson believed that he did not have the right traders or trading expertise to implement this type of strategy. He hired Michael Bills as the firm's head trader. Bills, who had previously been at Goldman Sachs where he was in equity trading and arbitrage, was given the job to both turn the firm's trading department around and to give it a more professional look and feel. Prior to Bills's coming on board, trading was not a focus for Robertson but as the firm's asset grew and new opportunities were discovered, trading became an integral and important part of the Tiger organization. It was Robertson's faith in Bills's trading ability and prowess that allowed Robertson to put together and implement the trading strategy for Puma.

By being able to trade aggressively in the markets, Robertson could take advantage of overhanging by *overtrading*. Say, for example, he liked IBM and liked what he saw in the stock market, and his firm found out that there were a couple of million shares of IBM overhanging the market for several weeks and that position had been worked down to the last 50,000 or 100,000 shares. It would make good sense to buy the last block. This is what he called overtrading, which was the natural evolution of what he had been doing at Tiger and now was going to be able to do at Puma.[26]

Robertson rationalized the lockup to investors by explaining that Puma would be an outstanding investment vehicle for investors who were able to forgo any payout for four years. "It will have, primarily because of its long-term nature, more arrows in its quiver than Tiger," he wrote. "It will even have more money working for it because of its debt component."

During the 1980s, Tiger consisted of a small group of people, about 16 to 20, and then as assets grew, the company expanded to include around 50 people. While Robertson ultimately retained all authority over investment decisions, there were many people involved in the analytical side of the business. But no matter how good the information or story was, nothing got into the fund's portfolio without his approval.

Puma was launched at the end of the summer and the rest, as they say, is history. Still, 1986, was turning out to be a disappointing year. The firm experienced significant losses in the three months that ended September 30, 1986. It was down just over 7 percent for the period. The oil stocks had turned against them and the losses were mounting. It was the short positions that was the cause of the losses. Oil was down more than 50 percent from November 1985 to September 1986; nonetheless, the oil stocks continued to rise. Robertson did not understand this at all. To him, the oil business in the fall of 1986 was an unmitigated disaster and things were not going to get better. He was clearly in the minority, because everyone else on Wall Street seemed to believe oil was the place to be and was pushing stocks higher. Although these losses clearly placed a dark cloud over the firm during this time, there was some positive news. The generic drug companies had finally collapsed—he was redeemed! Robertson had believed that these companies were incredibly overvalued and had been short the stocks for some time. Even so, the profits from these positions were not enough to move them from the red to the black. Even with a home run in the short on Zenith Labs, which had fallen some 45 percent for the quarter and was the eighth-worst performing stock on the New York Stock Exchange for the period, the profits were not enough to cover the losses in oil. He was not about to give up. Robertson knew that his research on oil was right and that he had positioned the fund properly in oil stocks, and he was sticking with it. Refining margins were coming down, and he saw poor results ahead for these companies. He also rationalized his position in oil another way: He was having a hard time finding good things to short. The small-growth component of the market, which in the past had provided him with many good shorts, was now significantly undervalued. It was so bad that instead of going short these companies, he was going long a number of them because he believed that they would rally.

The funds had sustained significant losses, based on both its global macro and long/short equity plays. Scrooge had entered the jungle, and the Tiger and the Puma were not enjoying his lack of Christmas spirit. "Bah, humbug!" Robertson began his letter to investors on December 18, 1986. On an absolute basis, the Tiger fund was up 17.4 percent net of fees which was not too bad, but on a relative basis, he was disappointed that for the first time in Tiger's history, its Limited Partners would probably not outperform the S&P 500. However, in the final few weeks of the year, the firm did sprint a bit ahead of the equity benchmark. It ended up beating it by just a hair.[27]

Looking ahead, however, he saw real promise for 1987. He believed that there was going to be a significant influx of capital into the markets from Asia which would push the stock market higher. Japan was already playing a significant role in the U.S. bond market, and even Taiwan was running a $1 billion-per-month trade surplus and was pouring this money into the markets. Robertson believed that Japan was where the money was

74

and that if the Japanese simply diverted some of the money they were putting into treasuries and the real estate market into the stock market, the equities would run to never-before-seen heights.

As an example of the richness in the Japanese market, he pointed to Toyota. The automobile manufacturer was selling at 17 times its 1986 earnings and was trading at 22 times its 1987 forecast. This was amazing compared to Ford, which was trading at 5 times earnings and 7.5 times its forecast. Another example he cited was Tokyo Electric. The utility company was selling at 70 times 1986 earnings and had recently had a market capitalization equal to the entire Australian equity market. During this time, the Japanese had turned their attention to the real estate market and the art market, and prices had gone through the roof. Robertson was hoping Asian investors would turn their attention to the stock market, which would force prices higher. While he did not believe that he could forecast the market, he clearly thought he had a handle on what had been going on and a very definite view of how things seemed to be shaping up as the New Year approached.[28]

6

THE CRASH OF 1987

THROUGHOUT MOST OF THE 1980S, WALL STREET WAS the place of champagne wishes and caviar dreams. People on all levels of the organizational chart had the pleasure of experiencing a market like no other and reaping the benefits of the enormous amount of wealth that was created in the age of the hostile takeover and the junk bond. Money was being made in every area of Wall Street, and it flowed to every corner of the globe. With this new-found wealth came a life of excess that knew no bounds for the money makers, the deal brokers, and the investment bankers. It was a marvelous time to be working on the Street. The engines were firing on all cylinders, and it seemed like a flame-out was not possible.

However, for one small but growing pocket of the Street, things had not been going so well. A rising tide usually raises all boats, but when those boats are anchored to short positions, the price increases can be devastating. At Tiger, the boat was taking on water. The fund, its manager, and his minions were all in a funk. On an absolute basis, things were not so bad, but relatively speaking, the performance was terrible.

By this time, the strength of the Tiger organization rested in Robertson's ability to attract and maintain talented people. It was on the backs of these analysts and traders that the business

77

evolved and developed. Because the firm was growing at such a fast clip, it constantly was experiencing infrastructure problems. Not only did the firm need sharp minds to work on research, but it also needed strong back office people to insure the trades were to be executed and cleared appropriately. Both front and back office infrastructure became a big factor in the firm's success as assets continued to flow into its coffers. These growing pains aside, the portfolio and its construction was without a doubt the center of attention and all that the Tiger's held onto. It was not uncommon for Robertson and the folks at Tiger to use a significant amount of leverage to extract profits from the market. While there was no set formula for the firm's long and short positions, it often ran a book with equity positions of around 175 percent long and 75 percent short positions which meant that on exposure basis—the fund was net long.

By early 1987, the fund's performance had changed a little bit. Tiger ended up beating the S&P on a gross percentage basis by the narrow margin of just about 70 basis points. It was the beginning of what would turn out to be a very volatile time in the equity markets around the globe. While newspaper articles were proclaiming the exuberance of the individual investors and politicians on both sides of the aisle were speaking out against the speculative excesses in the market, Robertson believed that the individual investors were not taking part in this unmitigated speculation. He believed that the recent run-up in stocks did not pique the interest of the individual investor and in his belief was frightened by it. Robertson's information also caused him to believe that many of the professional investors were concerned with the recent run-up. And if that was not enough, the Japanese had yet to pour their money into the markets. The Japanese seemed to be waiting on the sidelines as the yen was trading erratically. So what did the people at Tiger do? Robertson and his team focused solely on trying to pick winners. What others were doing around them, in or out of the market, was not a factor or of interest to them. They needed to find opportunities to exploit.

The folks at Tiger were, to say the least, quite bullish with a dose of healthy skepticism during this time. Robertson and his analysts were operating with a tremendous amount of confidence, tempered only by the fact that they considered themselves stock pickers, not market judges, and had a certain healthy skepticism of any market prognostications, their own included.[1]

In March, Robertson and his team remained in a neck-and-neck battle with the S&P 500. They were returning about the same for the first three months of the year, approximately 20 percent, and while this was good on an absolute basis, relatively speaking it was not so hot. He told investors in his letter to limited partners that he was pleased with this fund's results. He further believed that Tiger was ready for the time when the market flattened out, as it "inevitably does during these types of environments." It was when this occurred that he believed the Tiger would pounce, because he had put on a series of shorts that would do extremely well as the market lost value.[2]

In his letter to investors on March 6, 1987, he commented on a new phenomenon that he saw gripping the market. He called it the "silly season" and said that it was fast approaching, and that this was the reason for the extreme amounts of momentum that the market was experiencing. The momentum in the market called for investors to buy stocks with increasing growth rates and to sell stocks with decreasing growth rates, regardless of a company's perceived or inherent growth rate or its price-to-earnings multiples. Investors, he believed, were selling companies like Marsh & McLennan, the insurance concern whose growth rate was 15 to 30 percent per year, in favor of buying a semiconductor company whose growth rate was going from negative to positive and was trading at something like 40 times 1988 earnings. This strategy, he wrote, holds that value "be damned," and he was not going to take part in that investment strategy.[3]

During this same time, Robertson also found evidence of the market's "silly season" when he saw stocks in a number of areas of the market that became "automatic winners," despite their having little if any intrinsic value. For example, he saw the market deemed any company an automatic winner simply because it had something to do with AIDS. He observed that some of his best brokers and smartest partners had called him to talk about condoms and the opportunities that could be exploited from owning condom manufacturing companies. Robertson ran into similar investment advice atop a mountain in Colorado when an "aging Icelandic" ski instructor in Aspen bugged him about the condom industry's investment merits.

However, Tiger's research saw it completely differently. First, the data showed that while the market was clearly improving, treating the disease and fighting it through prevention was still a relatively small ($150 million a year) business. Second, Robertson's research caused him to be concerned that while small companies like Mentor had risen 142 percent since the end of the year on news of a new condom designed to be attractive to women, the more established companies would see the same opportunities and push the smaller players out of the market. To those who had pushed him to get into the condom craze, Robertson said no. And while he did not short Mentor and any other condom stocks, he believed that the time would come when he would have to, based on the industry contracting.[4]

During this same period Robertson was also forced to deal with another mania that had gripped Wall Street—insider trading. His old firm, Kidder Peabody, had been implicated in the indictment of three of its employees, one of whom was Martin Siegel. Siegel, who was a managing director at the firm, pled guilty to securities fraud for colluding with famed arbitrageur

Ivan Boesky and investment banker Dennis Levine of Drexel Burnham Lambert to extract illegal profits from the markets through the use of inside information.

Robertson knew Siegel when he worked at Kidder, liked him, and was impressed with his abilities, but thought that he had become a *moneyic*, someone who was totally poisoned by money as those who abuse alcohol are. However, he believed that while there clearly is no other industry where money flows so freely that people become "inebriated" by its lure and its power, people should not give up on Wall Street.[5]

Robertson was amazed that Wall Street still operated on the spoken word. There was no other industry where tens of billions of dollars' worth of trades took place daily, backed up only by the spoken word. No contract, no nothing, just the spoken word. He believed that the fact that a few people break down did not mean that the entire industry had broken down. Robertson believed then and now that the ethics of Wall Street were in line with those of any industry. However, he did see what he called a "time of tremendous change on Wall Street."

Prior to the mid-1980s, the country's great industrial giants like Ford, IBM, and General Motors would get the best and brightest minds that came out of the nation's business schools. Now, however, these people were going to the Street. In 1986, Goldman Sachs hired 7 percent of the graduating class of Harvard Business School, and 32 percent of its graduates went into the investment banking industry. He believed that the caliber of young people on Wall Street dwarfed what it was when he started on the Street in the late 1950s. In his view, the brightest and most attractive people were going to the Street, and it was a mistake. So many smart young people were congregating in this segment of the economy that Wall Street was becoming cutthroat. There simply was not enough room for all of them to achieve and get paid for their abilities.[6] Meanwhile, the industries that fueled economic growth—manufacturing and technology—were missing out on some of the brightest minds in business.

Robertson's firm had not been involved in any of the equity trading scandals, but things did not seem to be going well for Tiger. The firm's performance was just not up to par. It was "mired in its worst slump ever," as gauged by relative and absolute performance data. Yet Robertson believed that he and his team had the tools to get through the slump and move forward, just like any manager thinks his star hitter will return to glory after getting into a batting slump at the plate. There, however, were enormous problems that were confronting him. He was concerned that consumer debt was at a record high, Brazil had abrogated its foreign debt, and the trade deficit was running out of control. Nevertheless, Robertson still believed the outlook for the stock market was not all that bad. Stocks, in his view, were the best game in town. Even though valuations were out of whack compared to other investment choices such as real estate or bonds, which both had dismal outlooks, stocks made sense. A number of economists that Robertson followed believed that the economy was set to "perform in a manner that was conducive to a strong stock market."[7]

One economist told him that the strength of America's economy will come from making all of the goods that it had formerly imported. The economist believed that this would be the direct result of the lower dollar and, in turn, would push a 6 percent growth in the gross national product for the second half of the year. Robertson believed that if this occurred, then interest rates would remain low and, in turn, would prime the stock market for significant growth. Another factor that Robertson was watching closely was the impending Japanese invasion. His data showed him that the Japanese were big net buyers of stock in December of 1986 and continued to buy as the New Year went on. And while the buying was going on, it was not at levels that Robertson had predicted and expected. His view was that when the dollar stabilized, the flood gates would open and the Japanese would buy at extremely large levels.

As the year progressed, the firm saw its performance number fall. By May, the firm was down 6.4 percent versus the S&P 500, which was down just 0.6 percent. He blamed the losses on the shift from a value market to a momentum market, and the fact that Tiger had owned too many small-capitalization stocks, which he believed offered solid values. The small caps had fallen out of favor, however, and the large caps had rallied, causing him to be on the wrong side of both trades.

One thing he was not going to do during this time was panic, he assured his investors. He believed that he had done too well over a long period of time to change in total the fund's modus operandi. He did, however, begin to change the investment focus a bit as the fund began to be focused on buying high-capitalization companies, and analysts did work to reduce its overall use of leverage (not exposure, but leverage) until the numbers started to come back and the firm's relative performance improved.

Robertson emphasized in his monthly letter that they (investors and tigers alike) were in the same boat, and they would all sink or sail together. The letter was sent to tell them that the funds were not doing as well on a relative basis as they should have been doing, and he wanted to communicate how they were going to right the ship. The key, he believed, was the strength of the organization. He said he had the right people, with the right experience, who would be able to correct the problems. And furthermore, he and his team had a record to show that they were able to fix problems and move on.[8]

Closing in on the midpoint of the year, Robertson and his team turned their attention once again to Japan. In June 1987, the Asia nation was the world's financial capital. Not only was the Japanese stock market bigger then those in the States, but the federal government relied on Japan to finance its ever-increasing deficit. The folks at Tiger saw a number of opportunities. First, they liked the prospects of Japanese investments into American equities, and second, they believed that the prices of some of its companies were completely and utterly overvalued. One example was Nippon Telephone and Telegraph. The Japanese phone company had a market value of more than $334 billion; this was larger than the entire public market of a number of countries, including Germany, France, and Italy, which had a market value of $236 billion, $192 billion, and $153 billion, respectively. If that was not enough for him to see a bubble evolving, Robertson found the actions of Japanese corporate treasurers rather interesting. His research showed that the treasurers of many large corporations were not satisfied like their American counterparts to simply put the companies' cash into certificates of deposit. They had decided to put the money to work in the stock market through funds set up just for this purpose. The problem was that many of the treasurers had not been satisfied with the 40 percent increase the market had achieved and therefore had borrowed money to put even more into the market. They were basically using their free cash as margin collateral in order to make money in the markets. And while some of the funds were successful with this effort, the idea of using free cash to fund margin trading in the stock market was unsettling to Robertson and his analysts. The problem as Robertson saw it was that the Japanese, who had been so successful in achieving cooperation between government, management, and labor to create a great economic power, was operating under the mindset that if the market went up, it would only go higher, and that because it is better for everyone if the market goes higher, they would find the money to make it go higher.[9]

This thinking, of course, is what led to the tulip mania in Holland in the 1600s and all of the subsequent market busts. In 1636, unseen tulip bulbs were bought and sold and resold dozens of times. One Amsterdam man was said to have made 60,000 gilders in four months, when his annual salary as a burgomaster [mayor] was only 500 gilders. The mania kept on getting wilder and wilder until suddenly at the beginning of 1637, the market cracked. In a few days, hundreds of speculators were ruined. The losses were such that the whole credit system, not merely for tulips, was endangered. The collapse of the tulip market was a national catastrophe for Holland and had its reverberations in London, Paris, and other parts of Europe as well. But more importantly, it was what primed Robertson and his team to get ready for the decline of the Japanese market and take advantages of the opportunities the decline would offer them.

In mid-July, Robertson announced to his investors that he was going to invest 4 percent of Tiger's assets into a fund managed by his longtime friend Gilchrist Berg. The Polar fund, which was a short fund managed by Berg, offered Robertson the ability to gain unique access to the short side of the market. Berg had built an impeccable reputation as someone who could spot and find great short opportunities and oftentimes traded ideas with Robertson on an informal basis. Now by investing in the fund, Robertson had solidified his relationship with the short manager. John Nicholson, Tiger's medical consultant, resigned his position at the firm to run the fund with Berg. Investing in the fund also gave Robertson the first right to use Polar's ideas once the fund had made its investment. Robertson's investment into the Polar was approximately $9.4 million and represented nearly 4 percent of Polar's assets at the time of investment.[10]

Going into the dog days of summer, the tide had turned, sort of, by August 1987, "The Tiger" he wrote, "was beginning to growl. Not a full-fledged snarl, but certainly more than a purr."[11] The fund, which had been negative since mid-March, had recovered nicely and was up over 23 percent through the end of

July. Robertson had rallied his troops, got them to plug the holes, and was fast on his way to putting up another year of great performance numbers.

Robertson saw that the lower dollar was working for manufacturing companies. Earnings in some industries such as papers and metals were up and results were better then had been expected. One stock that was working well for Robertson was the paper company Jefferson Smurfit, which at the time was the firm's second largest holding. The stock, up almost 7 times from the lowest purchase price at which the firm had started buying it, was selling at 10 times its 1988 earnings and in his mind was still extremely attractive.

A renaissance of sorts was building in the American manufacturing world, and he and his analysts liked what they saw. There was also plenty of liquidity in the market, which meant that prices would undoubtedly go higher once that money was put to work. And if this was not enough, he believed that there was plenty of money sitting on the sidelines waiting to be put to work. The dollar was stabilizing, meaning that the Japanese who had already come into the market would go in even further.

Robertson liked what he was seeing in corporate America in terms of its stock buyback programs and its effects on the supply and demand of stocks including Chrysler, Ford, National Distillers, and Loews. These companies fit nicely into Tiger's portfolio, and their market potential "could hardly be brighter." He also was encouraged because he thought there would be warning signs of an inevitable downturn. The signs, he believed, would come from the East in the form of a severe crack in the Japanese market. The firm had prepared and expected the worse and was working hard to find opportunities to exploit on the short side of the market.[12]

During this time Tiger was already short a number of Japanese stocks; putting it another way, they were already paying a premium on an insurance policy that, though they hoped would never be collected, almost certainly would be. At Tiger they were paying their dues, learning about the Japanese market, and getting prepared. And in the meantime, while everything seemed to remain calm, they were enjoying the ride.

And enjoy the ride they did. For the rest of the summer and through the end of September, the portfolio performed rather nicely. During the summer and early fall, the investment community was filled with cries from the professionals who believed that the stock prices had gone too high, and there was a feeling that things could not remain good forever. Robertson believed people were looking for a reason, any reason at all, to sell stocks or brace their portfolios against a market sell-off. The Tiger portfolio was also being prepared for the sell-off (it was short quite a bit through Polar and its own funds) and at the same time was filled with stocks that the team believed were reasonably valued. One company that he truly enjoyed owning was Metropolitan Financial, a North Dakota–based savings and loan that was selling at a 44.2 percent discount to book value and at less then four times earnings. If that was not enough to make it worthy of Tiger assets, management at the bank put in place a stock buyback program—up to 10 percent of the outstanding shares—making it even more attractive. Tiger also was long West Fraser Timber Company. The company, which was mainly in the lumber business, was throwing off enough free cash at the time to fund expansion into the pulp and liner board industries. With the expansion, the company was still able to earn $4.00 per share and have significant cash flow, making it a very attractive investment. It was companies like these that represented excellent values that were giving Robertson opportunities to earn profits in the summer of 1987.

By early October, the fund was up 13.9 percent, significantly beating the S&P by more than 600 basis points. At the time, Robertson wrote that what was "particularly pleasing was the fact that this performance was accomplished with an exposure to the market which averaged somewhere between 80 percent and 85 percent." Robertson saw foreign buying as an important factor in the strong market. He believed that the money, which he deemed "terribly fickle," would continue to flow into U.S. equities until the market crashed in Japan. These inflows, coupled with the significant pools of assets being held by leverage buyout firms, would stabilize the market and keep it primed for continued growth. Robertson liked what he saw going on and was ready willing and able to take full advantage of it.

It was clearly the calm before the storm.

His words to investors in his October 2, 1987, newsletter were quite interesting: "I do not see great danger of a drastic market decline until we all get a great deal more complacent," he wrote. "Putting this another way, the danger point will come when we start spending our profits instead of worrying about keeping them."

And while he seemed to be painting quite a "rosy scenario," he also wanted to hedge himself and offered his investors a note of caution. All investors, he said, should have a little doomsday fund composed of a package of U.S. government bonds and notes. Investors, he believed, regardless of experience or wealth, should have this sort of fund in order to protect them from a major market decline. He warned them that the fund should not comprise a large percentage of one's capital because in the normal course of events, it would be the worst investment anyone could make simply because yields at the time were quite low. The idea that the market could go to zero was unthinkable, but it is a reality that prices can fall off, and Robertson wanted his investors prepared for the worst. This investment was strictly for the worst-case scenario and while it might never come, he believed everyone should be prepared for it.[13]

Just two weeks later, the ride turned unexpectedly wild and

Robertson and his team were forced to deal with a market unlike any they had ever experienced before. On October 19, 1987, the stock market crashed. The Dow Jones Industrial Average fell 508 points, or 22.6 percent, to end the day at 1738.74. The drop was significantly higher than the 12.8 percent crash of October 28, 1929, which signaled the start of the Great Depression. In the final 30 minutes of the trading session on October 19, the market lost 130 points. The decline on Monday, coupled with the losses of the previous Friday, totaled 743.47 points, or a loss of 30 percent. By comparison, the total drop on October 28 and 29, 1929, was 68.90 points, or 23.1 percent. By the end of the trading day on Monday, the Dow had given back all of its gains for the year and stood at a loss of 8.3 percent. On August 25, the market reached a high of 2722.42; in just two short months, it lost 36.1 percent. All of the major market indexes suffered significant losses. The S&P 500 lost 57.86 points, ending October 19 at 224.84. The Nasdaq fell 46.12 points to close at 360.21.

The crash of 1987 was without a doubt the worst day that most investors had ever witnessed. It was as close to a financial meltdown as anyone could have ever envisioned. The reaction around the Street was a mostly stunned disbelief. Investors of all shapes and sizes were in a state of shock, not knowing what to do or how to do it. At the time, the crash was blamed on a number of factors, including the fact that the market had gone without a serious correction for five years, fears of inflation, rising interest rates, and an increase in volatility based on the use of derivatives.[14]

For Robertson, the crash of 1987 exemplified the perfect storm; the firm did not receive any margin calls as a direct result of its losses during this period; however it did suffer significantly. Robertson and his team had always thought that if they ever had a bad period relative to the market, it would be in a distinctly up market, but it just so happened they got hit this time.[15] The reason was that the portfolio was not hedged appropriately in order to take advantage of the losses that the market experienced during its rout.

Many believe that during the crash and its aftermath, Tiger performed better than Robertson's only true peers at the time— Soros and Steinhardt. Nonetheless, Tiger did lose money, and did worse than the market on both an absolute and relative basis in the wake of the 1987 crash. Still, this performance reinforced his belief that to do better than the market, you don't think of the market. Instead you need to focus on finding solid investments. Look for value and go long wherever you can find it. That was the past, present, and future rallying cry at the firm, and crash or no crash, the rallying cry would remain the same.

The market is not something Robertson was ever interested in understanding, it has never spoken to him, and he believes that it never will. Picking stocks is what Julian Robertson, was and is good at, and it is in this side of the investment business that he excelled. His experience in the wake of the 1987 crash reaffirmed this belief by investors and competitors alike.

In the post-1987 crash days, he told a reporter that from where he was sitting, "there are so few bulls that I can't imagine who's going to impregnate the cows."[16]

Robertson believed he was in the clear minority when it came to being bullish during this uncertain time, and he was happy with where he found himself. Seeing things differently than everyone else is what had given him his edge throughout his entire career and believed that this instinct was what was going to carry him through this difficult period.

He hoped that there would be a lot of bearish opinions, because the more bears there are, the better things would be for his strategy. Throughout his travels and his research, he had a hard time finding anybody who wasn't exceedingly bearish—investors, it seemed, believed that the sky had truly fallen. He found few, if any, investors who were fully invested during this time. It seemed that many of the professionals that he spoke with were simply sitting on the sidelines waiting to see how the market was going to react and waiting for some semblance of normalcy before getting back into the game.

But Robertson and his Tigers felt that an extraordinary opportunity existed now that prices had come back in line. The excess valuations were lost once the market bottomed. The team's research found that there were an awful lot of companies that seemed like they were going to do very well over the next couple of years. However, one thing did stand in their way–the threat of recession. Robertson believed that Japan would fall, and when it did, it would probably signal the beginning of the end of the current state of overvaluation. This would signal the beginning of a great buying opportunity.

He felt that only about 15 percent to 20 percent of the population realized that they were affected by the crash. But the reality was that many more people were affected through pension funds, profit sharing, and stock options. However, because their main store of value was their home, which–with lower rates brought on by the crash–increased in value, they were presumably worth *more* as a result of the crash. [17]

Robertson was concerned that a number of things in both the domestic economy and the international scene seemed to be out of sorts. Although there were a number of "compelling buys," he found that he was thinking more about trade and budget deficits and how the government was going to deal with them, rather than just which stocks to short and which ones to go long.

Robertson told investors that the crash hit the fund "far worse" than any of the people on the management team had expected. The illiquidity that gripped the market "inflicted severe monetary not to mention emotional damage" on everyone at the firm. At the time, Tiger had less than 20 people running its day-to-day operation.

The fund came out of the crash just under 30 percent below where it was at the end of September. The crash and its effects on the portfolio was something he had never experienced before in his life. Tiger lost so much money so fast that the members of the firm were left in a state of shock questioning what it should do and how to operate going forward.[18]

Robertson was quick to deliver the bad news to his investors, but he also delivered some good news through his letter. First, he reiterated the firm's success, explaining that since inception Tiger was up more than 700 percent, which meant that investors who had been with him since the launch of the fund seven years earlier still had more than $7 for every dollar they had put in through their initial investment. And while the fund had experienced significant losses in the crash, for the year they were off only about 10 percent. The marketer who had left the building, so to speak, upon his return from New Zealand was now back and running the show.

What people don't realize is that when it comes to managing money, the hardest part is not actually managing the money; the hardest part is raising the money to be managed. The key to any successful money management business is 35 percent sustained solid performance over a significant period of time and 65 percent client relationship management. Success is not measured necessarily in how well the fund does, but rather, how big it gets—more importantly, in the wake of serious disruptions in the fund's performance numbers, that the assets don't walk out the door. For Robertson, not only was it a critical time in terms of the real losses the portfolio felt due to the crash, but also it was a critical time for his business. Robertson's tone to his investors, while quite matter-of-fact, was littered with upbeat and reassuring comments about the strength and resolve of Tiger and its employees. He needed to make sure investors did not go scurrying for the exits as rats do on a sinking ship.

Street and how he thought this was a brain drain on the rest of the economy. The crash signaled the end of this phenomenon, as the big firms would undoubtedly lay off individuals and simply not make as many new hires.

He was still unsure of where the market was heading and again showed signs of not listening to the market but being confident in his search for specific value plays. One thing he did know was that Ford Motor Company was a good value with four times earnings and twice the cash flow and with half of its market value in cash—it was a good, solid company, and, just as important, had the wherewithal to weather a storm. He believed that every businessperson should have shown interest in Ford because it was in such good financial shape.

He also railed against those who showed little interest in creating what he called "a doomsday fund" composed entirely of U.S. government securities, something he told his investors to create prior to the crash of October 1987. It now looked like it came from divine intervention.

During this time, Robertson believed that many of his investors who, prior to the crash, did not believe in the need of a doomsday fund would now go to the opposite extreme and put too much of their money into these types of investments. He wanted to make sure that his investors understood the risks associated with a doomsday fund: It was not a hedge against inflation, which he believes is the biggest risk an investor is faced with. And while it most certainly did provide for a good night's sleep, it did not provide investors with access to undervalued companies that offered them significant upside. These companies offered investors real values, and he believed that if they were patient they would realize significant profits from these and other investments.[21]

Nine days later, Robertson sent another letter to investors, telling them that "during these volatile and emotional times," he wanted to keep them "closely apprised" of management's thinking. In the letter, he wrote that the fund was going to maintain a conservative approach for some time because its managers could not find stocks or bonds that were attractively priced. His research showed that because Congress did not appear to be willing to curb spending, the dollar would fall further from its lows, which would make exports cheaper but would also reduce buying power. Things were looking up in his world. The research showed that the market was getting ready to offer a unique buying opportunity because American industry had not been so competitive with the rest of the world for some time. In November 1987, the firm had about 65 percent exposure to the market, being 115 percent long and 50 percent short. Tiger was operating with extreme liquidity, with buying power of nearly $90 million. While he was upbeat about his feelings for the future, he ended the letter saying, "Nevertheless, for the time being we will keep a conservative posture."[22] And a conservative posture is what he had created.

During the post-crash days of 1987, Robertson went public in *Barron's* about his thoughts on the economy, the market, investing, and the future of the pending recession. It was the first of two times that Robertson came to the aid of the markets and their weary investors. The second was in the wake of the terrorist attacks on September 11, 2001, when he appeared in a CNBC television interview. In both instances, the Southerner used his charm, his wit, and his investment knowledge to allay fears, substantiate the positive, and restore confidence in the equity markets and investing. Unlike other talking heads, Robertson provided well-founded arguments as to why America needed to get investing again in order to regain its feet after both extremely difficult body blows.

In 1987, he questioned the deficits as well as the utter overvaluation of the Japanese market. Yet what worried Robertson most was the fact that in most periods that followed a crash, equity prices stayed low or fell further, making them considerably more attractive than bonds. Robertson was having a problem finding bargains, however, and was worried about the long-term effects of overvaluation on the market as more significant than "the twin deficits."

While he believed that the market and economy were doing OK, he did believe that over time something drastic had to happen to correct the problems that were appearing in the world's economies. He believed that these problems would have a much greater impact and much longer effect on the world than the crash would. Japan was a real problem for Robertson. He found the economy to be "absurdly" overvalued and felt that the Japanese government's recent sale of $36 billion of Nippon Telephone and Telegraph stock to the public in an effort to reduce the public deficit was ridiculous. This was an astronomical sum, and the biggest deal done. To put it in perspective, the largest U.S. deal at that time was about $1 billion.

Robertson believed that the consistent overvaluation in the Japanese market would inevitably lead to a crash that would be followed by a painfully slow recovery. And while he did not know when, he predicted that it would eventually happen—either slowly or dramatically (a 30 percent or 40 percent break). This outlook caused him to tell investors that he could not see how a crash in Japan could be anything but very bearish for markets all over the world. To Robertson, that would be the proverbial last straw in this fragile economic state. A concern for investors was that in a crash, Japanese investors would dump U.S. Treasury issues, devastating the bond market and hurting the market for stocks, as well.

He did not know if a crash would jerk Japan's assets out of Treasuries, but he did know that there would not be as many buyers at the next quarterly refunding. And if that happened, it would probably really hurt the bond market, and that trouble would undoubtedly carry over to the stock market. Still, Robertson saw a bright side. He believed that once the yen stopped climbing, and the dollar bottomed out, the Japanese would put a lot more money in the United States because the value of what one could get in the United States was just so much greater than what one could get in Japan.

Robertson's belief was that "rational" people with security analysis in their background would be able to quite clearly see significant values outside Japan, so investment dollars would continue to move into Hawaii and New York. That being the case, Japan was the only place were Tiger and its analysts could find shorts.

While he was bearish on Japan, Robertson was a bit bullish on the U.S. equity markets. He recalled that during this period the funds were probably 70 percent invested, or exposed to the market, in positions 110 percent long and 40 percent short. However, had he and the Tiger team been extremely bullish, he would have put on positions to the tune of 150 percent long and 50 percent short, or even 170 percent and 70 percent. For the most part, however, he preferred to stay under a 105 percent net long position because of the level of uncertainty. The portfolio consisted of companies that were cheap and those that he thought were recession proof.

In the equity market, he liked a number of companies that produced polyvinyl chloride. These companies were selling at six times next year's earnings, with earnings improvements almost guaranteed for the next three years. He also was long stocks that he believed were recession proof—one company in particular was the Ford Motor Company.

Robertson liked Ford even if car sales dropped during a recession. His research showed that if car sales plummeted 60 percent, all the leveraged buyout firms would be interested in taking the company out. If a deal emerged, he believed they would have to pay something like $77 a share and in the process get about $35 in cash. He also believed that earnings were somewhere between $18 and $20 a share, so that even if sales fell by 15 percent, the company would have earnings in the $12 range. This made the company an attractive target to the leverage buyout firms and something that he wanted to own in his portfolio. And as such, they were long Ford, not only because the numbers moved but because they also believed in the company's products. Julian and his wife, Josie, both drove Ford vehicles (a Mercury and a Lincoln, respectively).

What else was he buying and selling in the Tiger portfolios at this time? Well, the answer might surprise you. Although many portfolio managers had varied their investment style and strategy in the wake of the market break, Robertson and his analysts at Tiger kept on doing the same thing. They simply looked at good old fundamentals and used their research skills to find good longs and good shorts to exploit.

Tiger was shorting the Winn-Dixie supermarket chain in Florida because the research showed the competition was better. They were also short a number of Japanese companies, including Japan Airlines. Tiger analysts also liked the paper company Jefferson Smurfit, and Georgia Gulf and Vista Chemical.

The folks at Tiger were attracted to Georgia Gulf because the company had virtually no debt. The company was generating free cash and was operating a profitable business that they believed had good roots. Tiger's attraction to Vista, which had quite a bit of debt, came from Robertson's belief that over the course of 1988 and 1989, the company would be able to get the debt off its balance sheet. Once the debt was removed, the company should be quite attractive because it would continue to grow its business and generate free cash for expansions and acquisitions. However, there was one thing that kept him cautious and that was if the demand for plastic dried up. If that occurred, the company would have been in trouble—as they say, all bets would be off.

Robertson and his analysts also liked the money management and brokerage firm Dreyfus. Tiger owned the company because at $24 a share, it was selling at less than 10 times the next year's earnings, and it had little or no capital requirements. Tiger analysts believed the company was undervalued. They believed that even a "nasty and prolonged" recession would have little or no effect on Dreyfus, because it was so heavily involved in the money market business.

Another financial services stock that Tiger was buying was Marsh & McLennan, the insurance company. They liked it because the company offered something that everybody needs–insurance–and it took very little underwriting risk. Those factors, coupled with the fact that Robertson thought it was very cheap, at about 10 times next year's earnings, made it a solid addition to Tiger's portfolio.

Insurance and money management were not the only financial names he had been buying. He also liked a company that nobody else seemed to at the time–Morgan Stanley. Robertson believed that the Street's consensus about the firm was wrong because the broker-dealer had great diversification among its revenue streams. Buying the company, Robertson said, would enable Tiger to get "more brains for a buck than anything else he could have imagined."

The only problem with brains, of course, is that they can get up and leave. While Robertson said he preferred "smokestacks to brains," Morgan Stanley was his brain company during this period. A good portion of his interest in Morgan Stanley came from his belief and understanding of the abilities and depth of the organization. Robertson had been working closely with the folks at Morgan Stanley since the beginning of Tiger. The firm acted as its prime broker and was intimately involved in the launch of Puma. Robertson had bounced countless ideas off Morgan Stanley analysts as he developed the portfolio and the

Tiger organization. It was a natural for him to be bullish on Morgan Stanley simply because he witnessed their good work on a day-to-day basis.

While big names were making their way into Tiger's portfolio, Robertson and his analysts were was also buying some small savings and loan associations in places like Egg Harbor, New Jersey; Nashville, Tennessee; and Fargo, North Dakota. Robertson believed someone with deep pockets was going to come along and take these stocks out before they reached market value–buying these small names offered him the opportunity to get involved in the constant consolidation that is the banking industry. He told the financial community that he was hot on these stocks in the post-crash days. It was these names that would allow him to cover his losses and bring the fund back to par, erasing its poor performance results in the wake of the crash.

By December, Robertson and the folks at Tiger clearly seemed to regain some of their steam and were operating with all cylinders firing. The first evidence of this was in his letter to partners dated December 24, 1987. It was clear from the tone that he was back to his old form and once again willing to write to investors about the strength of Tiger's stock-picking abilities. He reiterated his belief that the Graham and Dodd way was the only way to view the markets, and that to fully make an educated decision, portfolio managers had to look at a company's financial documents. He wrote that Graham's overriding concern in picking a company would have first been its balance sheet and then its earnings, and there would be very little concern as regards to the market. The key is to find reasonable value *not* in consultation with so-called stock market gurus. He talked about the strength of the Ben Graham–Warren Buffett–John Templeton–Peter Lynch style of investing. He talked about how he believed that market technicians may have their day, but he wondered where they would be in five years.

Once again he told his investors that people worried too much about the overall market and, in turn, wasted time thinking about the wrong things. The market did not exist as anything more then a place to buy and sell companies. He wanted his investors to realize the importance of investing in specific companies that had reasonable valuations. It was this skill set that would allow him to pick the right companies, and as long as he was reasonably patient, Tiger would do just fine—because over time, the valuations and the prices would increase and profits would be realized.

Robertson believed that he was not the only investor to come to the conclusion that it is easier to find great values than to make market timing judgments as to when the market is going up and down. "Remember, the market timer must be right both when he buys and when he sells," he wrote.[23]

It was clear that Robertson was having fun again at the helm of his hedge fund. While, 1987 was not a good year for the firm, he was able to put the events behind him and move the organization along. He reminded his investors that just two years earlier he had told them to hide the year-end letter from their spouses to avoid having to provide an exceptional holiday gift. At the close of 1987, he suggested that investors show their spouses the current letter, which would explain away their receipt of such "a pathetic gift."[24]

Ending the year, the Tiger was very close to breakeven—so close that he did not want to jinx their efforts by printing the figures. Tiger finished 1987 flat for the year. It was the first year that the fund had not earned double-digit returns for investors since its firm's inception seven years earlier. But with the crash behind them, it was time to move on to bigger and better things.

7

THE DAWN OF A NEW ERA

LIKE MOST INVESTMENT ORGANIZATIONS, TIGER WEATHered the crash and took part in the rebound that swept the markets in waning days of the 1980s. In the light of the crash, however, one thing was quite clear: The firm would need to diversify its assets to ensure that it did not put all of its eggs in one basket. The days of a firm that was an equity-based shop that did a little global macro were over. From now on, global macro investing would play a greater role in the way that Robertson and his tigers managed the firm's assets. He realized that he would need to spread Tiger's capital to areas outside of the equity markets if he hoped to continue to trounce the averages, wreak his vengeance on the markets, and, more importantly, outperform his competitors.

By February 1988, the folks at Tiger were feeling a bit bullish, while it seemed that the rest of the world was feeling quite bearish. It seemed as though the commentators and newsmakers believed that the United States was on the brink of depression. Robertson, however, believed the economy was doing just fine and was worried that because it was an election year, the economy would experience some overheating. For example, his research in the automobile industry showed that many of the companies had been experiencing an inventory build-up that was directly correlated to the individual company's interest in expanding the export side of their businesses. The dollar was weak, which meant American goods were more attractive and cheaper than their European and Asian competitors. The car companies could not simply operate on a hand-to-hand basis; they needed inventories to be able to sell, which meant that they needed to put people to work.

He believed that the economy was somehow operating in a "best of both worlds" environment during the spring of 1988. On one hand, consumers were reducing their consumption levels, but there was also a boom occurring in industrial production area of the economy. This resulted in the negative (the reduction of consumer spending) to be cancelled out by the positive (the increase in industrial production), which meant that money was being put to work. Industrial America, his research indicated, had never been stronger. And as dollar-affected commodities remained in tight supply, he found it hard to ratchet up his earnings estimates quick enough to stay on track with what seemed to be an improving economic situation.

Robertson took advantage of this perceived opportunity to increase the firm's exposure to the market. He based his decision on a "better feeling" about the economy and the lack of bullishness on Wall Street. However, all that glitters is not necessarily gold, and one of the things that made Robertson keenly aware of the tenuous situation in the markets and in a number of the world's largest economies was the issue of America's inability to live within its means and the extraordinary rise in the Japanese stock market. Others were focusing on the strength and power of Japan—it was, after all, the richest nation in the world at this time, a nation that was lending money to America to pay her bills. It was the country/economy that many believed had built a better mousetrap with its ability to create a unique level of cooperation between government, industry, and work force—an arrangement that many believed would keep the

Japanese market continuously rising. Robertson was confused by all this. For him, it was a time either to be short the Japanese market or not be in it all. After all, these so-called great Japanese companies were the same ones that rated below the world average in returns on equity and assets and therefore had some "real explaining" to do in his mind.

Robertson sent a team of analysts to Tokyo to try to figure out what was going on and to find out if there were any names that were worthy of being in the Tiger portfolios. The report he got back proved that he was right all along. The rampant optimism was a sure sign that things were going to crash eventually–no different than they had in Holland during the tulip craze or more recently in the Middle East with the oil market. He knew that Japan would break; he just did not know when or how far down it would go.

The problem was that because Japan was so strong, and because it was so active in the U.S. markets, Robertson was concerned about what would happen to the U.S. economy when the Japanese economy crashed. If the Japanese were taken out of the market, then the treasury would have a hard time covering its debt, causing interest rates to rise and the stock market to fall.

Robertson's conclusion was that industrial America was booming, but because (1) U.S. consumers were such big spenders; (2) the U.S. economy had become dependent on Japan; and (3) Japan did not know the meaning of the word *sell*, or even believe that stocks *could* go down, Japan was setting itself up for a bust–a bust that would take the United States with it.

So what did Tiger do to protect itself from this predicted carnage? Robertson returned to his roots and looked for value plays in America's smokestacks. And he shorted the Japanese market.[1]

Robertson found value plays to be something that made the investment management business fascinating. He had always worked hard to avoid making investment in American smoke-stack companies, focusing instead on marketing and service-oriented companies. On top of that, he was short Japan, looking at currency plays and foreign bond opportunities. There were a lot of promising opportunities, and problems that he believed would be turned into opportunities. The key for Robertson during this time was the team behind him. The strength of Tiger was its analysts and traders, the people who helped him turn problems into opportunities. They were clearly not the only ones who believed that Japan was overvalued or the dollar was weak, but he believed that unlike some other investment management organizations, they could and would act on this information.

In April 1988, Robertson became more vocal with his concern over what was going on in Japan. Over the previous year or so he had told investors that he believed the Japanese market was overvalued and was headed for a crash, but he felt that investors were not listening—or at least were hearing something different than what he was saying.

Robertson and his team thought Japan's economy, though growing, was facing significant challenges. From a pure valuation standpoint, the yen was too strong, the companies' valuations were too high, and the economy was full of speculative excesses. He felt that the Japanese economy and, in turn, the companies in it were expanding too far too fast, and that most of the expansion was occurring in the face of lackluster earnings results. That, coupled with a significant deterioration in return on investments, were real causes for concern.[2]

In order to combat this problem, he set the firm's exposure to Japan through a series of long and short positions that he believed would be able to take advantage of the investment opportunities that had been created in the market over the previous few years. The firm was short the large-capitalization stocks because it believed that the prices had been bid up to level that were unsustainable. It was long the small- to medium-capitalization stocks where it was able to find value in relation to underlying growth.[3] Tiger operated by putting on a series of hedges to limit volatility. For example, during this time it was short Mitsukoshi and long Shimachu.

Mitsukoshi was the second largest department store in Japan, with almost $5 billion in sales. The firm had steadily lost market share, not only to newer, more innovative competitors, but also to discount and specialty stores that were carving a niche for themselves with Japanese consumers. The company had virtually no earnings in 1986 and 1987, yet it saw its share price rise from ¥580 in 1985 to more than ¥1980 in the summer of 1987. The firm's research showed that the company would generate a return on equity of 4.8 percent and have net margins of 0.7 percent on earnings per share of ¥9.7. When Tiger looked at the stock, it was trading at approximately ¥1490, which meant it was selling at 154 times estimated earnings.

Shimachu was a different story. The company, which operated furniture and home improvement centers, had a sales base of $360 million and was well positioned in its view for significant rapid growth. The company had a return on equity of 11 percent, net margins of 8 percent, and Tiger expected the earnings to grow at about a compounded rate of 15 percent annually. Shimachu was trading at ¥3440, which was about 26 times earnings. It was, in Tiger analysts' minds, a real steal in the Japanese market. The idea was simply to use a fundamental value-based approach to investing in the Japanese markets. Through that research, these and other ideas were found and the trades were executed.[4]

Right before Memorial Day 1988, Robertson sent a memo to his investors titled "Supply and Demand in the Stock Market." In the missive, he explained what was going on in the stock market and how he and his team were expecting to reap profits for their investors. It was clearly an awkward time in the economy. While some remnants of the crash remained, a calm of sorts had settled into the investment community. The memo outlined five characteristics of the Street that troubled Robertson and his team:

1. *Corporate stock repurchases and leveraged buyouts were eating up just under 10% percent of the total shares outstanding of American equities on an annual basis.* This was equal to about 16 percent of the floating supply of stock throughout the land, which meant that if the trend continued, Tiger and its funds, along with other large investment vehicles, would own just about all the stock that was available on the market by 1993.

2. *There was too much cash on the sidelines.* Mutual funds were sitting on hordes of cash. Investors had moved $12 billion out of equity-based products and into fixed-income products. And pension funds were seeing an increase in their cash positions. The money would have to be put to work eventually.

3. *The independent investors seemed to be all but out of the market.* The crash had scared them away. They were waiting for it to seem safe to enter the markets again. They would eventually come back, and when they did—well, this was a plus factor.

4. *Wall Street was bored.* The heydays of the 1980s were over, and pessimism and lethargy had set in. The phones had stopped ringing. There were fewer ideas being generated by brokers.

5. *The crash was still in peoples' minds.* This caused people to be extremely conservative with their investments.

So what were they to do, and how were things going to get better? The answers were in corporate America being smarter with its free cash. During this time, Robertson believed, that companies around the world were experiencing an economic boom of sorts which left them flush with cash. The question was where they would put the cash. In Robertson's mind, there was one place among the worthy–American industry. Since the dollar was down, American goods were the cheapest in the world, and America's competitiveness was extremely high. It seemed only natural that companies would put their cash into the United States. Robertson also believed companies needed to look long and hard at stock buybacks. Dow Chemical had more than $2 billion in free cash flow; he believed that it would be only natural for the company to buy its own stock. After all, where else could it earn 15 percent on its money, be knowledgeable about the company, and have confidence in its management? He also believed that Japanese firms would turn their sights on mainland U.S.A. and start buying properties, as they had done recently in Hawaii. It made sense to him that the Japanese could find value in the lower 48 if they had found value in Hawaii. Robertson's research showed him that industrial America was doing better than anytime since World War II, and the only thing that would stop the economy from coming out of its hole was a worldwide recession or a dramatic increase in the dollar, neither of which he expected. Therefore, in his mind the portfolio was primed for growth.[5]

By the early part of the summer, Tiger and its funds were doing well; Robertson was on a tear of sorts, outperforming the S&P 500 by about 12 percent through the end of the first half of the year. He believed that people were beginning to believe his view of the American industrial story. He was seeing significant movements in a number of names in the portfolio. Robertson understood that the economy would experience a series of fits and starts, and believed what he was witnessing was only the beginning of a rebound. His researched showed that the dollar had nearly bottomed or was very close to bottoming, and as such he took on a large long position in the currency. And while the threat of a market collapse due to problems in Japan were still weighing on his shoulders—and the portfolio—he turned to two issues at home that he thought would have a greater effect on the economy—defense spending and Social Security.

As the Soviet Union and the United States seemed to be getting along better and the Cold War was coming to an end, Robertson wondered what would happen to U.S. defense spending. How would a reduction in this major government expenditure affect the market and the economy? Also, what effect would a significant surplus in Social Security payments have on the economy? At the time, the government was forecasting a surplus of close to $185 billion by the year 2000, and it was expected that that money would be invested in government bonds. This could help fund the deficit over the next few years.

By July, Robertson had turned his attention to corporate governance issues and the realization of shareholder value. To his shock and dismay, one of the companies that he found to be lacking in these areas was the Ford Motor Company—one of his key picks after the 1987 crash for its upside potential. The problem was the management. Robertson believed that the company was wasting its profits by making acquisitions instead of repurchasing its stock. Robertson's research showed that the company was in a position to buy its stock back at about four times earnings. The company had repurchased some of its shares, but had decided to aggressively pursue other companies through acquisition instead of focusing solely on increasing the stock price and, in turn, shareholder value. To Robertson, this was ludicrous. Why would a company that had the opportunity to make a return on investment in the 20 percent to 25 percent range be willing to settle for an investment that would yield about 4 percent? Robertson and his analysts were not willing to put up with it. It was clear that Ford should be buying back the stock, continuing to clean up its defense and retail business. If Ford was going to focus on acquisitions, it should focus on ones that would add significant value, not just be purchases for purchases' sake.

"Make no mistake," he wrote to investors on July 1, 1988, "if they go ahead with the big acquisition program rather than [an] aggressive stock repurchase, they are giving up long-term investment opportunities in favor of building an empire, which will ultimately crumble. But we can and should do something about this. If not, the corporate chieftains, left to their own devices, may very well miss the opportunity of a life-time."

In order to get his message across, Robertson sent letters to Ford's directors and encouraged investors to reach out to members of the Ford organization on his behalf. Below is an excerpt from the letter sent to Mr. William Clay Ford, vice chairman of the board of the Ford Motor Company on July 1, 1988:

Dear Mr. Ford:

I want to offer sincere congratulations for Ford's dramatic turnaround over the last four years. This is one of the great success stories in the annals of American business and should evoke pride in every member of the management team. However, this turnaround has now made a new demand on Ford's management—how to invest the surplus cash generated by Ford's success?

So far, Ford's investment performance does not measure up to the company's operating performance. Management could repurchase its own shares, achieving an immediate return of over 18% (based upon trailing 12 months' earnings). Instead the company has made acquisitions that do not have the slightest chance of earning the same return as Ford's core businesses. It was hard enough to understand the purchase of First Nationwide, Sperry New Holland, U.S. Leasing, and Hertz. But the real shocker for me, and the impetus for this letter, was Ford's purchase of BDM International, an unknown quantity which provides a 4.6% return (425 million for a company which earned 19.7 million last year). The rationale seems to be that "the acquisition fills in a hole in our defense business." Why does Ford need to be in the defense business, considering that Ford Aerospace has consistently lost money over the last decade?

Successfully investing the fruits of management's operation is not easy, but the rewards are enormous. For example a $10,000 investment in ITT when Harold Geneen took control is worth $30,000 today. On the other hand, $10,000 invested with Henry Singleton of Teledyne is worth over $1,000,000. Geneen is strictly an acquirer, while Singleton bought companies with Teledyne stock when it was expensive and repurchased Teledyne stock when it was cheap.

Ford's shares are extremely cheap. They would be reasonably priced at twice the price. I hope that Ford's management will forget building an empire and instead fulfill their pledge in the 1987 Annual Report that "We work for our shareholders—the owner of our business—and we have a responsibility to maximize the value of your investment." I have to point out the example given supporting this pledge was that Ford was repurchasing its own stock. To accomplish the goal of maximizing value, I do not believe management can do better than to accelerate its share purchase.

We own less than one million shares of stock so I know the odds of influencing management are slight. Nevertheless, our firm is spending an enormous amount of time and effort trying to encourage sound investment of Ford's profits. I believe that I speak for many investors when I ask that future investments provide as good as a return as an investment in Ford. Manage our company like Singleton, not Geenen.

Sincerely
Julian H. Robertson Jr.[6]

His efforts did not fall on deaf ears. Ford's management began a dialogue with Robertson and his team about how free cash was being allocated and how Ford could increase shareholder value. The response he received from the company and its directors bolstered his confidence in the company, simply because they were willing to listen to a shareholders view.

He was still concerned about Japan and the threat it posed to the U.S. markets. Through the middle of May, the firm was running a semihedged position in Japan. It was four to one shorts versus longs. However, as the summer progressed, Tiger cut back on its longs and increased its shorts. It was now running a net short position in Japan that was equal to over 13 percent of the firm's assets. Robertson believed that the overall market risk had increased: Price-to-earnings multiples were at "ridiculous" levels at a time when further monetary tightening and a turn in dollar versus yen all pointed to a continued draw-down in liquidity and margin.[7]

As the summer moved on, Robertson continued to worry about a number of things that were going on both from a political and economic view. And while some fund managers seemed to take a pretty good hit as fears of a recession rocked the markets and whacked the cyclicals, he was more worried about the trade deficit. He did not like that Americans had gone crazy for imported items. He thought that this infatuation of sorts with imported goods was a real problem for the economy on the long turn. Robertson's second worry was President George Bush. Although he had been a supporter of President Bush for a long time, he was "shocked" over his appointment of

Nicholas Brady as Treasury Secretary. Robertson, who did not know Brady personally at the time, knew him professionally and was not fond of the work he did at Dillon Read. According to Robertson, during Brady's reign Dillon Read did not just slip from a contender to the bottom of the league, it slipped completely out of the league. Brady had a reputation for being a nice guy—ethical, honest, and intelligent—but President Bush should not have picked someone whose track record as head of a firm was so bad, in Robertson's view. He believed that President Bush had hired Brady because he was comfortable with him. Robertson had hoped that the president would hire the best people, people who would not hesitate to disagree with him when they thought he was wrong.[8]

By the early fall, the malaise of an election set in, and Wall Street all but shut down—or at least was on autopilot. In Robertson's mind, everyone was apathetic about everything! Everyone, it seemed, had a reason to do nothing, and he loved it. His data indicated that the public were selling their stocks and bonds, and the mood throughout the country was among the most bearish it had been in his history on Wall Street. That left Robertson with plenty of opportunities, and he was taking advantage of them. Robertson had once again turned to using puts as insurance against a major break in Japan. However, with all this optimism he still was acting cautiously and limited his exposure to the market to just about 85 percent of capital in order to have significant reserves for the opportunities that undoubtedly would present themselves as the year progressed.[9]

By the late fall, Tiger had stumbled a bit. The market had turned, and Tiger was on the wrong side. The dollar increased against other currencies, the Japanese market continued to rise, and because the firm had little exposure to leverage buyout deals, it took a hit. Robertson pared back the Japanese shorts, reduced Tiger's currency exposure excluding Japanese stocks to less than 1 percent of the fund's equity, and continued to maintain his put on the Japanese market. It was the first time in his career that he was excited about companies like Wal-Mart, Merck, and Johnson & Johnson because they showed that they could grow no matter what the state of the economy. Ford, Cleveland Cliffs, and United Airlines also impressed him because they were growing at rates higher than he had expected. Times were tough, but overall the year had been a positive one even though finding opportunities in the market had been difficult and discouraging.[10] As 1988 drew to a close, Robertson and his team fought on. They finished the year up 26.3 percent.

The tone of Robertson's comments to investors shifted significantly in the late 1980s and early 1990s while he continued to focus on explaining how he and the analysts were doing in finding stocks to go long and short and by communicating his thoughts on the equity markets, but he also began to comment extensively on the geopolitical situation and the role it played in the financial markets. In his January 6, 1989, letter to investors, he commented on the fact that in the first nine months of 1988, personal savings by U.S. citizens rose faster than at any time in the last 20 years. Premier Mikhail Gorbachev and the Russians gave real hope that arms accommodation between the East and West could occur. Together, an increase in personal savings and decreases in defense expenditures would be highly bullish for both the fixed-income and equity markets.[11] And while Robertson did see all sorts of opportunities in the markets, he was concerned about the American government's willingness to spend money it did not have and not take advantage of opportunities to pay down the deficit.

In 1988, Tiger Management increased its expertise in global markets by hiring Tim Schilt, who formerly ran the Japan Fund and Morgan Stanley's Japanese research effort. Arnold Snider, a pharmaceuticals analyst at Kidder Peabody, Peter Belton, and Patrick Duff joined the firm as well, rounding out the depth of the firm's investment and analytical talent. Assets continued to come in record amounts; not only did the firm increase its team in New York, but it also started to open offices around the world.

During this time, Tiger had a number of holdings that Robertson considered to be in monopolies and oligopolies. One such holding was DeBeers, the company that controlled more than 80 percent of the world's diamond market. During a trip to London to visit DeBeers, Robertson observed that while the company needed to make some definite steps to provide more financial and business disclosure to its investors in the near future and that sales could be improved, with a monopoly, "one rarely has to worry about profit margin."

The portfolios also had positions in United Airlines, American, and Delta, three firms that survived the airline crunch and in his view operated a virtual oligopoly. He also liked Tosco, an independent oil-refining company that was the only company operating in its market area. Wal-Mart, too, was considered attractive because of its significant cost advantage over its competitors, making it a position that was almost "unassailable."

Robertson saw good things ahead for the market because the laws of supply and demand were infallible. There was a tremendous amount of cash and a decreasing supply of stock (due to buyout mania), which caused him to look at the weeks and months ahead with confidence. The politicians, however, were still disappointing him with their lack of focus on the budget deficit and their lack of leadership.

The problems in Japan worried him, as did the lack of President Bush's ability to get the economy moving. He wanted something to be done about the problems in the United States and felt that the current administration had done little if anything to get things moving again. To him the answer was simple: Look at what others have done to fix their problems and do the same thing. Robertson's ideas during this time were based on the success that Great Britain had in solving its economic woes.

He spent a significant amount of ink on the subject in his communications with investors:

> At the beginning of the eighties, America's closest ally faced escalating socialism, causing a brain drain of its best entrepreneurs being forced by taxes to live abroad and a general malaise in the economy. Its currency was weak and getting weaker, its budget deficit was ever increasing. But that ally had something that stopped it from going into a bottomless pit–it had leadership which exerted itself.
>
> Now, that ally is running a budget surplus. As a matter of fact, if present trends continue, it will be completely out of debt by 1995. Its currency and its markets are strong and its people have a new entrepreneurial spirit. Even ultra high interest rates cannot slow down its powerful economy. The ally is, of course Great Britain and its leader, the Iron Lady, Mrs. Thatcher. Think of what could happen here if our leaders did what they are supposed to do, i.e., lead.[12]

A number of years later, Robertson retained the Baroness Thatcher as a Tiger advisor. He looked to her for advice on the global economic and political situation and as someone who added to the strength of the firm's knowledge base. He would also retain Senator Robert Dole as an advisor to help him better understand the geopolitical situation.

While Robertson was keen on writing letters to investors that were filled with information and commentary about the firm's portfolios, its positions and its strategy, he also included ideas on ways to lower the budget deficit–first a 25-cent tax on gasoline, then a sin tax for booze and cigarettes, and maybe even a health tax on ice cream and candy.[13]

The deficit was a constant theme in his communications. He

blamed it squarely on a lack of action in Washington. He felt that there were all sorts of opportunities available to reduce the budget deficit: Whether government officials would make these tough decisions was open to question. As he saw it, the country was living through an ever-increasing period of time where the government spent more than it took in, and doing so without calamity had made it easier for the politicians to postpone remedial action.

But problems in Washington and tax issues were just two of the subjects that he tackled in his newsletters and in the construction of the firm's portfolios. One of the main topics was greed. He was very focused during this time on the leveraged buyout trend that was sweeping the market, in particular the Kohlberg Kravis Roberts purchase of R.J. Reynolds. He pointed out that KKR's purchase price was almost 100 percent more than the market was willing to pay, and in purchasing the whole company, the firm gave up liquidity. Unlike Tiger, they could not get out of the position because they owned the whole thing and *were* the market.[14]

> Congress, the press and even the public all worry about the leveraged buyout phenomenon. We suspect that were it not for leveraged buyouts, these same people would be worried about foreign buying of American corporations, for surely the Japanese would be right there. The way to stop leveraged buyouts, and the foreign buying, of course, is for stock prices to go higher. And in a curious way, that is exactly what the leveraged buyouts will cause. For as Mr. Kravis's $20 billion for RJR and Phillip Morris's $6 billion for Kraft paid out, these billions will filter back to the Wal-Marts and UAL's of the world.[15]

At that time, Tiger owned significant positions in both Wal-Mart and United Airlines, and Robertson believed that there was nobody better to be running each of those companies than the current management, which included Sam Walton and Steve Wolf, respectively. He believed that his benefit in owning positions was that Tiger was getting the best management at a price of about four-and-half times earnings—multiples that he believed would "make Messrs. [Carl] Icahn and [Henry] Kravis drool."[16]

In the summer of 1989, Robertson was very much in need of new ideas and looked to his investors for their thoughts. Robertson always believed that one of the great resources of Tiger was the knowledge and experience of its partners—and Tiger Management really needed to utilize this resource. Robertson began his letter to investors of August 31, 1989, with the word "HELP!!!"

While acknowledging that the firm was working as hard as ever, the organization, particularly Puma, needed "new ideas right now as badly as it has at any time in its history."

Robertson believed that in order to function at maximum efficiency, the firm required a continuing flow of better, new ideas that could be used to replace existing good ideas in the portfolio. The firm's inability to find ideas not only slowed its positive momentum but increased the chances that some of its existing investments would remain in the portfolio for too long. He blamed the fund's need for ideas on a series of recent successes and a few mistakes. Robertson mentioned the fund's successful trades in Squibb, United Airlines, and American Airlines. He wrote that some investments had not worked out, like the fund's positions in refining, which it had reduced considerably.

Robertson believed that the best source of an investment idea would probably come from an industry that investors knew well. For example, a doctor who had seen research on a new drug or procedure might recommend a particular manufacturer as an investment opportunity. The second best place to find an idea would be from a friend who could alert them when their business were turning. However, this avenue was not as easily defined. If the friend was *too* well connected, the information would be tainted, and Robertson wanted clean information. "In light of the problems all of us are confronted with as regards 'inside information,' please be careful not to pass along or receive anything that could fall within the scope of this ruling," he wrote in August 1989. "Better safe than sorry."

Going into the fall of 1989, Robertson and his team decided to take a more conservative approach to their investment decisions. A number of events caused them to muster this posture, including the belief that the economy was weakening. They were not sure what was going on in the economy or how long the problems were going to last, but they were anticipating an economic downturn. The firm owned a number of counter-cyclical names during this time. It was long Wal- Mart, Toys R Us, Merck, and Johnson & Johnson and short a number of cyclical stocks.

Robertson believed that Tiger was appropriately hedged for the near future. He did not believe that the problems were insurmountable or that they would not pass. Rates were coming down, which meant the short end of the yield curve was less attractive than stocks were at the time. It also seemed as though retirement plans, which were the largest purchasers of securities, owned a very low percentage of stocks versus bonds. His research showed that over the last 30 years, the equity portion of retirement portfolios had ranged between a low of 42 percent versus a high of 67 percent, and at that time they were at approximately 45 percent. Along with those numbers, it seemed like the Japanese were continuing to buy U.S. equities. At the rate that they were buying, Robertson believed that it would take a doubling in the size of the U.S. market or a halving in the size of the Japanese market to get their market even a bit more competitive to the U.S. market. He found that the Europeans were buying as well, which meant there were three groups putting buying pressure on the markets.

Over the years, Robertson spent a lot of money on what he called his "Japanese Insurance Policy." The policy of sorts was in the form of two- and three-year puts on the Nikkei averages. For most of the time in which the policy was in effect, it proved to be completely unnecessary. The Nikkei did not crack. To Robertson, it was like owning life insurance: You know you need it, and you want your heirs to benefit from it, but you hope that the premiums will be wasted for some time to come.

He believed, however, that Japan's time would come and that the policy would pay off. Things that were going on in Japan made him believe that the policy's premium would not be wasted. The numbers he found about standard of living and costs of modest homes—and even memberships to golf clubs—suggested that the country's economy was ready to collapse. And while he saw signals that the economy was going to get hit, he was amazed with the culture and successes. He marveled at the country's ability to save and how it had developed a great school system that dwarfed those in the States.

In November, Robertson sent his investors a chart compiled by Tim Schilt. It showed the relative returns of Japanese companies versus American companies (see Table 7.1). The comparisons exposed as myth the belief that Japanese businesses are superior to their U.S. counterparts.[17]

Once again he found himself in the position of warning his limited partners to hide the year-end letter from their spouses in December 1989. The Tiger fund was up 49.9 percent net of fees versus the S&P 500, which was up 31.7 percent, and the MSCI, which was up 16.6 percent for the same period.[18] The portfolio had done extremely well, under somewhat different strategies from any time in the firm's history. Tiger had taken positions in junk bonds, taking advantage of the perception

Table 7.1   Comparison of Japan and the United States

Corporate Statistics	Japan	United States
Operating Margins	3.20%	10.40%
Pre-Tax Margins	3.20%	8.80%
Net Margins	1.60%	5.40%
Return on Equity	7.30%	15.40%
Return on Capital	4.90%	11.80%
Cash Flow / Equity	19.00%	28.90%
Equity / Capital	56.30%	64.20%
Interest Rates		
3 Month CD Rates	6.50%	8.00%
10 Year Government	5.40%	7.90%
Stock Market Ratios		
1989 (Estimates)		
Price / Earnings	55.4 times	13.4 times
Price / Book Value	4.2 times	2.4 times
Earnings Yield	1.80%	7.50%

Source: Memo to Investors from Julian H. Robertson Jr., November 3, 1989.

that the industry was totally corrupt. It found that even reasonably good junk bonds had been lumped in with the enormous majority of bad deals so that there were some excellent buys available. He felt comfortable owning names like RJR Nabisco and Hospital Corporation of America whose bonds were yielding around 30 percent, and the only risk was the solvency of the company. Robertson also found that instead of being involved in Japan, as he had been for quite some time, he was now focusing on Germany. Robertson wrote that while Germany was, "possibly the most fiscally sound nation in the world," it suffered from "the incongruity of having perhaps the world's cheapest stock market."

In the wake of the collapse of the Soviet Union and the crumbling of the Berlin Wall, the firm steadily increased its investment in Germany. And while Wall Street was experiencing its own "recession" and there was an overall feeling of bearishness, Tiger remained bullish during this time. Yet because the Tiger team was finding opportunities in "non-market situations" like Germany and junk bonds, there was a threat that Tiger would underperform the broad market if the market behaved quite strongly over the next few months.

Going into the 1990s, the firm was stronger then ever. The lion may be the king of the jungle, but Tiger was the king of Wall Street. Robertson's beast plowed its way through the Wall Street jungle, trouncing all the relevant indices time and time again. Not only was he better then anyone else at the time, he was also the envy of his peers and contemporaries. For years, the firm had been well known in and around Wall Street but had gathered little if any attention outside of the professional side of the business. Now Robertson wanted to change that. To increase its profile and exposure, Robertson began an earnest attempt to get media coverage.

8

THE TIGER TANGLES
WITH THE PRESS

THE FIRM'S FIRST BIG STORY (SOMETHING MORE THAN market or company comments) was in a short-lived publication called *BusinessWeek Assets*. It was the cover story in the November/December 1990 issue and was titled "The World's Best Money Manager–What You Can Learn from Julian Robertson." Gary Weiss wrote it, and it begins:

"Tiger . . . 47." So reads the lobby directory at 101 Park Avenue. The Manhattan white pages are more helpful–Tiger Management–and it gives a phone number as well as an address. The public manifestations of Julian Robertson are like that–sparse. An SEC filing here. A paragraph in the financial press there. Fame has not come to Julian Robertson. Fortune yes. But not fame. . . .

The Standard & Poor's 500 Stock Index was up a paltry 2.6 percent for the year. At this point his flagship Tiger limited partnership has gained by a figure resembling the S&P–except that the decimal point has been moved to the right. Unbeknownst to all but a handful of rather happy people, the money in Tiger has gained not

2.6 percent but 26.7 percent. Most money managers would burst a blood vessel from sheer joy if they had done half as well.

Robertson is proud of his record, all right, but it seems that something more important is gnawing at him. "Stocks have been good to us this year," he says in a slow, North Carolina drawl. He names a couple and then pauses, lost in thought. "Hey, Ed," he calls to an associate seated not far away. "We talked to a guy today who says that Chase is the thing we ought to be short. . . . It might be interesting to look at Chase." His colleague is noncommittal. Yes, he is familiar with Chase, and he begins to expound upon it. Robertson, amiably, cuts him short. "I want to tell you this: If you don't short some of those banks . . ." He grins mischievously.

The rest is (for want of a better word) history. On Aug. 9, Chase stock was changing hands at $19. The Street was cautious but hardly bearish. Two days earlier, one prominent analyst had reaffirmed the "attractive" rating of another prominent bank holding company, Chemical Bank. But in a matter of weeks, as news of the ill tidings afflicting banks in general and Chase in particular spread across the financial pages, money center bank stocks went into a free fall. And none fell further or faster than Chase—which collapsed to $11 a share, a loss of 42 percent of its market value, by the end of September.

As financial crises go, this one ran true to form from the investment standpoint: By the time the full dimensions of the banking fiasco became obvious, the stocks were already in the cellar. It was too late. For most investors, the decline and fall of the banks was a short-selling opportunity lost unless you had a crystal ball. Or were Julian Robertson.

Foresight. Flexibility. A global perspective—with the

ability to go short as well as long anywhere on the planet. For Robertson there is simply no other way..."[1]

Reprinted from November/December 1990 issue of BusinessWeek *by special permission, copyright © 2004 by The McGraw-Hill Companies, Inc.*

If that wasn't enough to get people thinking about the power and might of this manager and his ability to navigate the markets, Weiss continued to stroke the Tiger's ego:

> There is no more successful practitioner of adroit global investing than the occupant of the suite of offices with the view at 101 Park. No one can hold a candle to Robertson's recent track record. Moreover, Robertson's investment vehicles have defied the odds, and the "small is beautiful" conventional wisdom on Wall Street, by gaining spectacularly even while growing in size to almost $1 billion.[2]

After another thousand words or so the author concluded:

> Even if the public remains shut out of the Tiger partnerships by regulatory constraints, there is at least the solace that Robertson & Co. will be forging ahead, setting the example for the sheep like masses of money managers.[3]

It is clear from reading and examining this article and speaking with its author that in the opinion of Wall Street, there was no one better in the money management business in the late 1980s and early 1990s than Robertson and the team at Tiger Management, LLC. In the hedge fund space, he was better than Soros and he was better than Steinhardt. There was no one who could touch him in the mutual fund space either, not even the legendary Peter Lynch. He was even better than Warren Buffett.

But beyond the fact that the story played well into Robertson's ego and made his parents extremely proud, the piece helped spark an interest in Tiger from people and organizations that had not yet learned about the firm's market prowess. Many in and around the hedge fund business and Wall Street knew of Robertson and Tiger, but the article marked his debut in the wider world of sophisticated high net worth investors and institutions.

Putting Tiger on the map was probably not the idea behind the story for editor and writer at the publication. Sales in the magazine did not catch on, and according to Weiss, the magazine stopped publishing a short time after the issue with Robertson on the cover. Still, the article proved to be a very good marketing tool for Tiger for many years to come. A reprint of it was used in the firm's marketing material well into the 1990s.

This initial story was a spark for a flurry of Robertson and Tiger stories. Over the next few years, articles continued to appear in the major financial publications, including *Institutional Investor*, *Barron's*, and others. Most of the stories were profiles. A number were simple interviews about the equity markets and his thoughts on specific stocks. In most cases, Robertson spoke at length about his view on the geopolitical situation, how various country and regional economies were being affected by events around the globe, and how investors should be looking at investments in light of various newsmaking events. The stories brought attention to the firm, and that brought assets, larger management fees, the potential for even greater incentive fees—and a series of growing pains that all firms experience at one time or another as they build their business and cross significant asset-under-management thresholds.

In January 1991, Robertson celebrated yet another year of solid performance. While the fourth quarter was not as good as he hoped (Tiger underperformed on a relative basis versus the S&P 500), it did trounce the averages. Tiger was up 20.5 percent for the year versus the S&P 500, which was down 3.1 percent, and the MSCI, which was down 17 percent.[4]

Robertson was not satisfied with the fourth quarter performance, citing the fact that the firm was only 45 percent invested during the period. If it had hoped to keep pace with the broad market, it would have had to significantly outperform the index.

Unlike some of his colleagues in the money management industry, in the beginning of 1991, Robertson did not subscribe to their notion that a severe recession was on the way. His data showed that while the economy was clearly not out of the woods, things were getting a bit better. The Federal Reserve was in the middle of easing the money supply and interest rates, which he believed would spur the economy and impact the stock market. And while he thought the second and third quarters would be strong, he still positioned the portfolio with a conservative posture. Tiger owned companies like Smith Foods, Food Lion, Dairy Farm, Tesco, and Wal-Mart, all companies that he believed would be immune to a recession. He was, however, concerned about the firm's positions in the financial sector. Robertson believed that the banks were going to have trouble and as such, shorted a number of both domestic and foreign institutions. He was also expecting to see the Japanese market decline; he believed that if a recession hit the United States and Europe, Japan would be next. On the currency front, he was long the deutsche mark. To him it was the currency of choice. Amid the pressures of Russia and the reunification, Robertson had tremendous faith in the Bundesbank and its ability to control inflation and keep the currency strong. Tiger finished 1991 quite strong, earning 45.6 percent versus the S&P 500 and the MSCI, which finished the year up 30.5 percent and 18.3 percent, respectively.[5]

Robertson rode the public's interest in the stock market through the end of 1991 and well into 1992. He believed that individuals were fed up with earning 3.5 percent on their certificates of deposit and wanted more. In the past, investors looked elsewhere for their returns. They put money into commercial real estate ventures and second homes but during this time, they began to look to the stock market for their source of return. The question was, could the market rally continue, and, if so, how long would it go on?

Robertson believed that the market would continue to rally well into at least March and maybe April, but that eventually an increase in interest rates would send it back down. The price-to-earnings ratio of the S&P 500 was at 18.6, which was way above normal and on the verge of reaching an all-time high. Initial public offerings were coming out at a faster clip then ever before, meaning that new issues were flooding the market, and this was not a good thing. The market would need to correct itself before it could go up again. Robertson was willing to sit on the sidelines and wait for this to happen.

Robertson was also concerned by the public's lack of interest in fixed income securities and the government's inability to control the budget deficit. Although he did not have a solution for piquing the public's interest in bonds, he did have a suggestion for addressing the budget deficit—an increase in the gasoline tax.

He rationalized that gas was cheaper in the United States than anywhere else in the world, and that we could learn from countries like Britain and Norway, where gas was twice as expensive as in the United States and who were fuel self-sufficient. Robertson proposed that his investors with strong government connections make the case that the federal government impose a $0.35 per gallon tax. This, he believed, would accomplish two things: first, it would reduce the budget by nearly $35 billion a year and second, it would cause the United States to conserve fuel. He wrote that "cutting the budget deficit while at the same time improving the environment is a goal very much worth pursuing."[6]

Fortunately for Tiger, Robertson's financial picks were more successful than his political proposals. The gas tax idea went nowhere, but Tiger finished 1992 just under 27 percent for the year versus the S&P 500 and MSCI, which were up 7.6 percent and down 5.2 percent for the year, respectively.[7]

Earlier in this chapter it was noted that Tiger's continued success was causing growing pains. As the assets ballooned, and the firm attracted more investors, it went from being a small, friendly organization that operated in a collegial atmosphere to a sophisticated money management organization that relied on the strength of its back office to ensure that orders were executed and profit and losses were booked. Initially, Robertson looked for help in this side of the business from the people at his prime broker—Morgan Stanley. But as things began to progress, he realized he needed people in house who could be managed and, in turn, operate the other engine that drove the firm. In early 1993, Robertson reported to investors that the performance numbers for the funds for the period of June 30 through the end of November had been "seriously" overstated. It seemed that the monthly reports failed to include various financing costs of its macro trading operation, causing Tiger to overstate its performance for the period by just over 4 percent.[8] It was not the first time the firm had to restate its numbers and frankly, it is not rare in the investment community. Mistakes are made by the smallest and largest organizations on the Street and are the source of embarrassment to many. But for Robertson, it was not acceptable.

The firm had grown beyond his expectations, and he needed to make sure the infrastructure was in place to ensure that it continued to meet and exceed its investors' expectations, both in the front and back office. To help him establish the right sort of infrastructure in the firm's back office and trading departments,

Robertson looked to Lou Ricciardelli. Ricciardelli, legend on Wall Street in the prime brokerage operations area and named by Robertson as the Tiger of the year in 1991, joined the firm in mid-1992. (Tiger of the year was an honor that Robertson placed on people whom he believed contributed to the firm's success. As part of the honor, a large gift was made to a charity of the recipient's choice by Robertson.) When Ricciardelli got to the firm, he worked initially with the folks at Morgan Stanley who were being loaned to Tiger to develop systems and processes to not only handle Tigers increasing volume of trades in the equity markets but also handle the order flow and other administrational issues that the firm was experiencing in all the other areas it was operating. Eventually as the infrastructure took shape, Ricciardelli replaced the Morgan Stanley people with Tiger people and was charged with running all aspects of the firm's non–money management activities. Although Robertson was clearly in control of the organization as a whole and was intimately involved in the implementation of the money management side of the business, he was happy to have Ricciardelli run the administration and back-office side. Tiger needed to have Ricciardelli and his systems in place in order to quench its thirst in markets around the globe. For the first 10 years of the firm's existence, according to a number of former traders and analysts, it had exposure to investments in five or six countries. By the early 1990s, it was trading in the equities markets of more than 22 countries through an operation that literally ran around the clock five and half to six days a week.

One of the projects Ricciardelli developed was a shadow portfolio accounting system. Robertson asked him to put this kind of system in place so that if there was a situation where an analyst thought the firm should take a position in a stock of, say, 50,000 shares, and Robertson thought the firm should have 150,000 shares, the proper people would be credited for making the trading decision.

"Effectively, the analyst would be credited for whatever idea he came up with," said Ricciardelli. "And if he came up with the idea and nothing was ever changed in [the size of the position], he would get credited 100 percent of it. But if Julian wanted to double the bet, the analyst would get charged or credited with 50 percent of the bet and the rest would get credited to the house."

Using a shadow portfolio system allowed Robertson to keep score of how the analysts were doing in terms of what they were directly or indirectly contributing to the portfolio's profits. This helped establish an analyst's worth and, more importantly, the analyst's compensation.

At Tiger, remuneration was catch as catch can. Sure, everybody had a small salary or draw that allowed them to live during the year or at least keep their lights on, but the real money came from bonuses or points off of the firm's incentive fee. For the most part, Tiger charged its investors a 1 percent management fee and a 20 percent incentive fee throughout its existence. (A number of its offerings had different fee structures. See Appendix.) This meant that the firm collected 20 percent of the profits earned, which meant in some years the bonus pool was literally hundreds of millions of dollars.

Most managers allocate a portion of the firm's profits to all employees based on the merit system—you contributed this to the fund's performance, you receive that. At Tiger, this was the theory behind the compensation program, but it was not necessarily the practice: "The whole idea was to get his approval, which meant that you would be compensated extremely well," said one former analyst. "He never would tell you that you did a good job, but rather, he would give you representation in the portfolio. This meant he liked you and respected your work, but it did not necessarily mean you would be compensated for the work. It was not that simple."

At Tiger, it seems people were fighting for two things: respect from Robertson for their work and respect from

Robertson personally. "If he liked you, you would be compensated extremely well, regardless of how much or little you contributed to the portfolio," said a former analyst. "There was no set scale or compensation schedule, but somehow he made it work. How he determined who got what was something that I was not privy to, but I do know that if he liked you, you tended to get a lot of points."

People stayed with Tiger because even under these less-than-optimal conditions, they were making more money at the firm than they could anywhere else on the Street. And while it might not have been the greatest environment, there is something about it that made it work and that has caused these people to stick together. It seems that almost everybody who ever worked at the firm, regardless of their time there, is in contact with others in some way, shape, or form. While the relationships are not necessarily social in nature, they are all quite professional. It seems that when you talk to one former Tiger, especially the people who worked there in the early and mid-1990s, you talk to all of them. There is great camaraderie among these people that remains intact more than 10 years later.

Throughout most of the early and mid-1990s as the assets really began to balloon, Robertson looked to a number of people to help build a bigger and stronger investment team to ensure that the assets were being invested properly and efficiently. He first turned his attention on trading. Initially, the trading was done on sort of an ad hoc basis, but at the turn of the decade Robertson realized he needed to bring a new level of seriousness to this part of the firm's operation. It was relatively easy to move hundreds of millions of dollars around the markets, but when it came to billions, well, that was just another story. Not only did the firm now have to come up with the best and brightest ideas, but they also needed to be able to put the assets to work in a manner that would allow them to exploit the opportunities that they discovered. Tim Henney was given the task of getting the firm's trading operation into order.

If Robertson was the formula one race car driver, Henney was the mechanic. Every day he would get to the desk and have to find ways to create liquidity in stocks that sometimes had little volume. Henney worked to develop the firm's trading systems and procedures in order to handle the massive inflows of money. Tiger needed to build a machine that could put the money to work. He needed to move massive amounts of cash in and out of positions without causing the market to move or fluctuate. It was his job to put the money to work without the firm losing its edge over its competitors and, more importantly, losing an investment opportunity because the price moved so dramatically when the Street heard Tiger was getting into or out of a position.

Henney also played a significant psychological role at the firm. Robertson seemed to be in a constant state of fear that his traders and their brokers were going around him or doubling up on him. Henney had to constantly prove to Robertson that he and the people he worked with could be trusted to get things done and that nobody would violate the trust.

His job, among other things, was to take trading away from Robertson so that he could focus on making investment decisions. There was a tidal wave of assets during this period, and Robertson needed to be able to trust someone who could execute the orders. He put that trust in Henney and the people who worked with him on the desk, so that he could stay focused on finding places for the new assets that would maintain the firm's consistently high batting average.

As the firm grew and developed its trading and operational sides of the business, Robertson realized that he needed help on the business development and administration side of the business. Robertson looked to a young analyst at Morgan Stanley named John Griffin. Griffin had been working on a number of projects at the investment bank, one of which involved Tiger. It was the beginning of a great relationship, but it almost didn't happen at all.

Griffin had graduated from the University in Virginia in 1985, with a degree in Finance. He went to work at Morgan Stanley's merchant banking group as an analyst. During his stint there, he worked on a deal that raised subordinated debt for a hedge fund called Risk Arab Partners. The deal, which was pretty unique at the time, gained Robertson's attention, and he wanted to raise money for Tiger in the same way.

"Julian called his salesman at Morgan and asked him to bring someone who knew something about the deal over to Tiger to explain it to him," said Griffin. "On the day we were supposed to go over to Tiger, my boss was sick, and when I called to cancel the meeting, the salesman would not have it, so we went over together."

During the meeting, Robertson asked many questions about how the deal worked, the amount of money that could be raised, and the likelihood for success, to which Griffin replied, "We can try." The next day, Robertson called Griffin and gave Morgan Stanley the deal to raise money for Tiger's Puma fund. From the spring of 1986 to October 1986, Griffin and the people at Morgan Stanley worked on the deal and raised $30 million for the firm.

Griffin left Morgan Stanley in the early part of the summer of 1987, joining Tiger in July. He sort of talked his way into a job that really didn't exist at the firm–Julian's right-hand man. According to Robertson, Griffin got "all his friends" to join the firm as well. Prior to Griffin joining the firm, it was Julian and everybody else. Now it was Julian and Griffin and everybody else. The one snag that hit the relationship was that Griffin wanted to go to Stanford Business School. Julian did not want him to go to Stanford, but they agreed that he would work for

Tiger while he was in school and that he would return upon completing the program. In order to get Julian to agree to this plan, Griffin installed a fax machine in his room in order to be able to send and receive documents back and forth to New York. While today having a fax machine at home or even in the dorm is commonplace, in the mid-1980s it was quite an expensive and slow piece of technology. During this time, one was lucky to transmit a few pages clearly an hour and had to be careful not to run out of that thin, flimsy rolled paper that the machines used to receive the documents.

Griffin spent a year working in an administrative capacity. He entered Stanford business school in the fall of 1988, rejoining Tiger in the spring of 1990. As time went on, Griffin and Robertson's relationship grew. Griffin would eventually be made president of Tiger as Robertson's heir apparent. It all stemmed from a meeting that he did not really want to attend. Griffin stayed at Tiger until January 1996 when he left to go out on his own—a far wealthier and smarter man than when he entered the firm 11 years earlier.

While access to information was important, the ability to make good decisions about that information was the hallmark of Robertson's success. According to Gilchrist Berg, the manager who specializes in shorting and a longtime friend and associate of Robertson, one of things that set him apart from other money managers was his ability to listen to all sides of a discussion about the merits of a stock and then make a swift decision about it.

In an article in *Forbes* in September 1991, Berg talked about this ability, using as an example WTD Industries, a lumber company. In 1990, Tiger had a large position in the stock—one so large that the firm was required to report it to the Securities and Exchange Commission on Form 13D[9]. Robertson listened to a bearish report, checked with the analyst who recommended the company, then sold his entire position relatively quickly. When he explained his change of heart to the press, he simply said, "I was wrong." WTD filed for bankruptcy in 1991.[10]

In the same piece, Berg said that another thing setting Robertson apart from other managers was his ability to handle many investment opportunities at the same time and to trust his intuition. "Julian's got the best animal instincts in the jungle," Berg said.

Robertson's investment style was a study in "controlled aggression," wrote Richard Phalon in an article in *Forbes* in January 1990. He said Robertson was "one that might go for the bomb on first down, but never on fourth and short yardage." Using a hedge fund allowed Robertson to roam freely through securities and futures markets and to use shorting and leverage to take aggressively, but in a controlled style.

Many would try to emulate his organization and use a similar strategy, but it wasn't easy. Because Robertson didn't limit his approach to one discipline or one instrument, he was able to operate in all areas of the investment world. The key to his success was his openness to ideas and his ability to run the ideas through "the computer that is his mind."

Tiger was without a doubt "the hottest money manager" in the nation in the early and mid-1990s. After an 11-year run, the firm was managing just over $2 billion, with an annual return of 45.6 percent, net of fees, versus an S&P return of 30.5 percent and MSCI's 18.3 percent.

In 1993, Dr. Aaron Stern, a psychotherapist, joined the firm to help with the human capital side of the business. Robertson looked to Stern for guidance in the hiring process. Stern interviewed potential Tigers and developed and implemented a testing system that all applicants took before being offered a job at the firm. The tests helped Stern and Robertson determine if the person was a Tiger person or not.

A Tiger person came to mean many things over the years, but was and is a person with the following characteristics:

1. Smart, bright, and quick with functional intelligence
2. Strong sense of ethics
3. Background in sports and interest in physical fitness
4. Interest in charity and public welfare
5. Sense of humor and fun to be around
6. Good resume

According to Stern, during those years, Tiger operated in an informal manner with no ranked hierarchy. "People talked with each other," he said. "There were no walls between people."

Robertson himself still sits in an office that, by design, has no door. The idea was to create a place where there was a flow of ideas. "There was effort not to separate him from the team," said Stern.

Robertson was on a roll going into 1994, Tiger finished 1993 up nearly 80 percent versus the S&P 500 and the MSCI, which were up just over 10 percent and just under 21 percent, respectively, for the same period. The results were excellent, and Robertson was extremely satisfied with the way his money management machine performed. He counted among the few weaknesses of the year a problem with Tiger's foreign exchange positions and poor choices in shorting. The individual short positions had not worked out the way he had expected. His goal for 1994 was to get better at shorting and increase Tiger's ability in the foreign currency markets. Both would be accomplished by hiring experienced traders and analysts to the Tiger team.

Unfortunately, 1994 was not a good year for Tiger. Things did not work out as planned for the year. Tiger finished down just over 9 percent, while the S&P 500 was up 1.3 percent and the MSCI was up 3.3 percent. The losses came in the first four months of 1994, which Robertson attributed to "the normal regression" from the oversized profits in 1993. One of the interesting tax characteristics of hedge fund investing came out as a direct result of the losses of 1994. Some of the Tiger investors incurred a taxable gain in the year in which the fund had negative performance. Robertson attributed this to the fact that in many years, the fund's taxable gains had been significantly lower than its economic gains. This meant that some partners who had been investors for some time were forced to pay some taxes on the preceding year's unrealized gains. To illustrate the point he used the following example:

> A typical investor in Tiger had taxable gains in 1993 of about 30% while their economic gain was about 65%. In 1994, the investor had an economic loss of about nine percent and a taxable gain of about 10%.[11]

Things got better in 1995 and 1996, when the combined funds returned 50 percent to investors, and the firm saw its assets hit just under $8 billion.

During this time, the global macro manager style was going strong, and Tiger and its vast amount of assets were looking elsewhere for returns. The portfolios' holdings ranged from its traditional long and short positions in the equity markets, through Italian and Canadian short-term paper to New Zealand bonds, Russian debt and equity, to a number of Japanese and Mexican short positions.[12]

At the same time, Robertson was buying up palladium. He believed that both Russia and South Africa would eventually be unable to mine enough palladium to meet the surging demand for the metal in cell phones and automotive catalytic converters. Palladium was one of those trades that he just loved to make.[13]

Tiger had been investing in palladium for the better part of its existence. According to a number of sources, the fund initially got involved in the palladium market through an idea from Robertson's partner, Thorpe McKenzie, and even though Thorpe left the firm some years earlier, he did not take the position with him, so to speak. Robertson continued to have his analysts work on it for many years. However, in the mid-1990s, he went public with his success. In order to understand the market, Robertson and his team spent an enormous amount of time understanding not only the uses and expected uses of the commodity but also how it was mined and created, bought and sold. The firm talked to everyone from dentists in the United States to insurance companies in Japan to understand the market. They even went so far as to look at geological maps of mines around the globe to understand what could be mined and how it could be used.

Robertson and his analysts would not comment on exactly how large the firm's palladiums position was, but it is estimated by a number of former Tiger investors and observers that at one point Robertson controlled close to a year's worth of production of the commodity.

The one thing about palladium that made the market so attractive to Robertson was that his research showed no matter how high or low the price went, some companies were locked into buying vast quantities of the commodity due to regulatory requirements. Take, for example, the car companies. Car companies build massive assembly lines to create their products, one of which is a catalytic converter that uses palladium. The car companies build catalytic converters that meet and often exceed the specifications of the Environmental Protection Agency because changing the line is a costly and labor-intensive effort that could slow production. This means that regardless of the price of the commodity, the car companies are locked into buying the material in order to continue building their cars. Prices rise and fall based on factors that could take two years to change. Because Robertson and his analysts understood both sides of the market, the production and the uses, they were able to make significant profits trading the commodity.

So palladium was on his list of good investments during this

141

time, but he was still extremely bearish on Japan. In particular, he was shorting Japanese bank stocks. He believed that the Japanese banks were among the highest-cost producers in the world and that their costs per transaction were "dreadful." He thought that as a group they were the worst credit managers in the world. Wall Street in general was more sanguine, believing that the sector would rebound, much as U.S. banks had in the past. In 1995, things improved a bit as the firm returned 16.0 percent net of fees to investors while the S&P 500 and MSCI finished the year out up 37.6 percent and 20.75 percent, respectively. In the mid-1990s all that glittered was not gold for Tiger and its investors. Robertson's star began to fade.

In April 1996, the Tiger hit an extremely rough patch when a *BusinessWeek* cover story, "Fall of the Wizard; Julian Robertson was the best stock-picker on the Street. Has he lost his magic?" hit the newsstands. In the story, Gary Weiss wrote that Robertson was no longer visiting companies, had let his temper get out of control, was having problems allocating assets because the funds had grown too large, and that employees were having a hard time working with him. The article was significantly different from the one that had appeared six years earlier. Unlike the previous article, which had sparked a firestorm of interest in Tiger and its products, Robertson believed this story was likely to throw water on the flame. Below is an excerpt from the story:

> Robertson was the reigning titan of the world of hedge funds—the secretive, often highly leveraged private investment partnerships that are the piggy banks of trust funds, endowments and millionaires. Robertson assembled a team of the smartest and best-paid stock pickers on Wall Street.
>
> At his peak, no one could best him for sheer stock-picking acumen. Robertson was the Wizard of Wall Street. And he was paid well for it.

But something toppled him from that pinnacle. It all began with a disastrous first quarter in 1994. In contrast to a stunning 1993, when Tiger's funds gained 80 percent before fees, his funds declined 9 percent. Investors, who had poured money into Tiger in 1993, began to pull out. In 1995, as still more investors defected, he eked out a pre-fee gain of 17 percent, a humiliating 20 points below the Standard & Poor's 500 Stock Index. And even though Robertson began to do well again in 1996, climbing 17 percent in January, his gains soon were cut almost in half—and his revival has all the makings of a bump on a downward slope. On one horrible day, March 8, Tiger sustained a $200 million loss, as a bet on U.S. Treasuries turned sour.

. . . Assimilating and sifting vast quantities of information is the Robertson forte. Robertson's analysts give him ideas and data. He then makes the buy or sell decision—usually after checking and rechecking what they have to say. Other hedge fund operators, however, have found they can't run funds as one-man outfits, not when they grow to multibillion-dollar size. They are too large and complex—far more so than even the largest mutual funds. Some large hedge funds, such as Soros' and Odyssey Partners, the money-management machine run by Leon Levy and Jack Nash, delegate decision-making power. Soros even let one of his top analysts—London-based macro guru Nicholas Roditi—run an entire fund under his watchful eye. Under Roditi, Quota fund more than doubled in value in 1995, far outpacing Soros' flagship Quantum fund. Such independence is unheard-of at Tiger.

Size and centralization have clearly hurt Tiger. Another negative is that Robertson has pushed stock-picking even further into the background as macro bets on currencies and bonds have dominated Tiger. He no longer visits corporate managements, and most of his extensive travel during the year is spent educating himself about currency and interest-rate trends.[14]

Reprinted from November/December 1990 issue of BusinessWeek *by special permission, copyright © 2004 by The McGraw-Hill Companies, Inc.*

The article continues to explore what was wrong with the Tiger operation and its manager. It spoke of Robertson's lack of interest in stocks, his inability to follow analysts' recommendations, and his inability to keep employees. It also explores a number of personal issues that might have been affecting his ability to manage money effectively.

After a few paragraphs about Robertson's childhood in North Carolina, his relationship with his parents, and his advice discouraging his children from entering the fund business, Weiss concludes:

> "Perhaps that's for the best. But Robertson has another family—his once-glorious hedge fund empire. It is a dysfunctional family of brilliant analysts headed by a master stock-picker. If only it worked, it would be a monument to greatness—and not the fall of the Wizard of Wall Street."[15]

The article was all about what was wrong with Robertson, what was wrong with Tiger, and what was wrong with hedge funds. It was clear that Weiss had gained access not only to Robertson and some of his senior managers but to the inner sanctum of the hedge fund complex. He was privy to inside information about how the firm operated. Weiss was able to get under the surface of the firm and its operation—maybe too much access for Robertson and his investors. Because

Robertson for one did not like the story and wanted it retracted!

He complained bitterly to *Business Week* about what he believed were inaccuracies and half-truths. When that effort fell on deaf ears, he says, he filed a billion-dollar lawsuit against McGraw-Hill, the publisher of the magazine, Gary Weiss, and the magazine's editor, Stephen B. Shephard.

His lawyers filed the complaint in New York State Supreme Court on September 12, 1997. It charged that *Business Week* had published an article of "false innuendoes, and misleading half truths" about Robertson and Tiger Management that "ridicule and defame him as an individual and as a businessman."[16] Robertson asked for $500 million in punitive damages and $500 million in compensatory damages for the pain and suffering the article caused him and his company.

The complaint detailed how Weiss had written to Robertson asking for an interview. It included a portion of the letter requesting the interview, which is here excerpted:

> I'm contacting you today because I need your help. I'd like the opportunity to meet with you and your people again.
>
> I've followed, with great interest, how Tiger has achieved a significant rebound in just the past few weeks. As you know there was a story in the *Wall Street Journal* today that touched on this rebound superficially. We want to tell the full story, within the bounds of confidentiality of your business.
>
> I realize your sensitivity to this kind of publicity, and you have my promise that I will handle any access granted with the greatest sensitivity. I'd very much appreciate the opportunity to talk with you about this.[17]

The complaint details the plaintiff's view that the business and financial media "in pursuit of ever-higher circulation goals, have taken to publishing tabloid-style, colorful personality pieces" in an effort to reach more readers. The complaint alleges that the goals in publishing these stories in a "sensationalized style" are, first, to "increase and maintain" the publication's reputation for "aggressive inside stories," and, second, for editors and reporters to achieve "professional recognition," higher salaries, and "the potential for lucrative book contracts. . . . To accomplish these goals, Defendants increasingly publish articles designed to titillate more than inform," the complaint states.

Then the gloves really came off. Robertson and his lawyers alleged that *BusinessWeek* made up the negative comments and "were so unconcerned with factual accuracy that the article does not have a single attributed source for any of its false and defamatory statements." The defendants "chose to base their defamatory statements and inferences on the word of unidentified 'sources' who, if they exist at all will only carry out their character assassinations anonymously."[18]

The rest of the complaint details where the errors occurred and asks for relief with its demand of compensatory and punitive damages.

BusinessWeek responded literally point by point to the suit. Most significant was the response to Robertson's allegations in paragraph seven of the amended complaint calling into question Weiss's use of confidential sources. In response to this allegation, the defendants "deny the allegations of paragraph seven, except defendants admit that they based certain statements in the Article on interviews with confidential sources and aver that the Article as whole identifies and is based on numerous statements of on-the-record sources, including the plaintiff himself."[19]

Along with these statements, the defense listed nine reasons why the case should be dismissed, including constitutional and statutory grounds, the right of fair comment, and lack of proof of malice, falsehood, and injury.

Despite all the tough words, within two months Robertson dropped his suit and settled with the magazine. He received no financial consideration from the company. The settlement called for *BusinessWeek* to run an editor's note acknowledging an error in the story.

The magazine noted that its predication about Tiger's performance had been wrong. As part of the settlement, the parties agreed to disagree on a number of other issues in the story. Both sides were able to claim victory. Below is an excerpt from the joint statement about the settlement:

> *BusinessWeek* acknowledged that predications regarding Tiger's investment performance included in its cover story of April 1, 1996 . . . have not borne out by Tiger's subsequent investment performance, which included a 485 percent gain before fees in 1996 and a 67.1 percent gain before fees through December 11, 1997. These performances far exceed market averages and the performance of other leading hedge funds.
>
> In the article, *BusinessWeek* described how, after many years of stellar returns, including an 80 percent gain before fees in 1993, Robertson's Tiger management delivered below-market-average results in 1994 and 1995. While the article also noted that Tiger was beginning to do better in early 1996, *BusinessWeek* said that 'revival has all the makings of a bump on a downward slope.' *BusinessWeek* acknowledges today that Tiger's 1996 and year-to-date 1997 results, under Mr. Robertson's management, were superior performances by any measures. Among the article's statements with which Mr. Robertson took issue was the assertion that he no longer "visits corporate managements," and most of his extensive travel during the year" is spent educating himself about currency and interest rate trends." In objecting to the

article, Mr. Robertson provided *BusinessWeek* with a list of specific meetings with managements of more than 55 companies on three continents in the year immediately preceding the article. Robertson's list reflects meeting with corporate managements during Mr. Robertson's travels abroad and at Tiger's offices in New York. Based on that list, *BusinessWeek* acknowledges that Mr. Robertson had not stopped meeting with corporate managements."[20]

Although it appeared from reading the preceding paragraphs that Robertson had won a victory, except for the billion dollars, the second half of the joint statement made things a bit murky. The statement acknowledged that both sides agreed to disagree over *BusinessWeek*'s report that Robertson's temper around the time of 1987 crash had caused him to point at people randomly and to order them fired. It specifically quoted a former Tiger employee who said that the group that Robertson had ordered fired was consultants from Morgan Stanley, not Tiger employees.

Robertson continued to maintain that the incident had never happened. Moreover, he stated that everyone living who worked for Tiger at the time had specifically told to his lawyer that such an incident had never occurred. Both sides agreed to drop the matter and let it become history.[21]

At the time of the settlement, Robertson was quoted as saying that *BusinessWeek*'s admission of its errors "relegates the article to the trash heap it deserves. These people printed these facts even after it was clear there was no truth to what they were saying."[22]

In early 2003, Gary Weiss said that the experience had left him with a bad taste in his mouth. "I had no choice but to write the story the way I wrote it," he said. "I was just trying to do my job; I was not interested in treachery or a vendetta. Think about it, just a few years earlier I had just called him the world's greatest investor."

"I understand how he could be upset because the article was negative," he continued. "Although he did have a few good years after the article came out, it did prove to be correct because he did have to close."

Stephen Shepard, the editor-in-chief of *Business Week*, said that because of the settlement, he didn't feel comfortable talking about Robertson or Tiger. Still, he did say that he believed the stories stood on their own and had proved to be true.

"We agreed to disagree," said Shephard. "I am not really able to comment about the story, the settlement or what happened, that was part of the agreement, but in retrospect the story looked better than it did at the time."[23]

For Tiger, 1997 proved to be one of its most successful years. It seemed as if everything it did worked that year. The Tiger fund ended the year up just over 56 percent, compared to 33.4 percent for the S&P 500 and 15.8 percent for the MSCI. In the fourth quarter alone, the fund increased by more than 30 percent. The equity markets of United States, Japan and Hong Kong contributed significantly to the profits, along with the firm's macro trading efforts, which Robertson said contributed almost a third of the returns.[24]

"All of us at the management company are pleased with these results," he wrote to investors in January 1998. "You should be aware, however, that we continue to have exposure to a number of situations that probably entail greater than usual volatility and risk. We believe these investments offer potential well worth the risk and that the portfolio is set up to take advantage of significant opportunities and weather the challenges of 1998."

One of the areas of concern was South Korea. The firm's research showed that the country's economy was in shambles and its increasing interest rates and the decreasing value of its stock market was a bad sign. "The weakening won further imperil[ed] the already weak rupiah" and threatened the Chinese renminbi, according to Robertson. He believed "a significant drop in the renminbi could bring the world closer to international deflation and a concurrent 1930s-type depression."[25]

Robertson's concern about the Asian markets did not prevent him from ending his letter on a positive note: "We have all had a fantastic year," he wrote. "Let's enjoy it. Take my advice and give some of those profits away. It could be the most selfish thing you do all year, for they will be the dollars that give you greatest pleasure."[26]

At year-end 1998, Robertson, his family, and Tiger employees collectively were the single largest group of investors in the Tiger Funds. They always seemed to have the most to gain; it was not as readily apparent that they also had the most to lose.

That year, Robertson had another, albeit smaller, run-in with the press. This time the story took a different tone and focused more on his and his wife's work in the community. The story, which ran in *The New York Times* on September 29, 1998, was titled "Giving Out Millions While Losing Billions." Written by Elisabeth Bumiller, it concerned his recent gift of $25 million to Lincoln Center in honor of his wife. It noted that he made the gift while Tiger was experiencing heavy losses caused by the Asian financial crisis.

At the time, Robertson's wife, Josie, was extremely ill with cancer, and he had given a significant gift to Lincoln Center to honor her. The unveiling of the Josie Robertson Plaza was quite an event, attended by friends and family from across the country. The story that appeared in the *Times* was based on the thesis, 'How does this guy who lost a billion dollars endow the plaza?' Robertson said that the story, while "cute in a nice way," really annoyed and wronged him and his family and their good deed. And while Robertson retained much of his anger about the story for some time, about a year later, he wrote a letter to the writer apologizing for his actions. Elisabeth Bumiller did not respond to several messages seeking comment about the letter and the story.

Another situation with the press that irked Robertson around the same time had to do with one of the companies in its portfolio. Tiger had invested heavily in a company that turned out to have a board of directors that was "just a bad" group. As a result, Tiger put four of its people onto the board of the company to straighten things up and be more involved with the workings of the company.

Robertson thought it was a good thing for corporate governance around the country, so they let it out. Well, that turned out to be a serious mistake. Instead of getting a story that had some positive spin on the situation, a number of news services picked up the story about how a bunch of young guys at Tiger making all this money managed to throw out this old chief executive and his loyal team of executives. This experience, combined with the experiences with *BusinessWeek* and *The New York Times*, taught Robertson that when it came to the media, he needed some help. Dealing with the fourth estate was not one of his strengths.

In the beginning of the 1990s, the firm had reached $1 billion in assets under management, and by the end of 1998 and early 1999 it had almost $22 billion under management. At that time, it was clearly the largest and most powerful hedge fund complex in the world. Tiger was what it was called, and a Tiger was exactly what Robertson built and was running. His beast plowed its way through the Wall Street jungle, trouncing all the relevant indices time and time again, in a constant state of competition. Unfortunately, all of that was about to change. The market was once again entering its silly season, and this time the Tiger would not be able to roam free in the jungle.

9

THE PEAK AND THE FALL

GLOBAL MACRO INVESTING IS ONE OF THOSE WALL STREET terms that sounds more complicated than it is. The concept itself is not so difficult–successfully implementing the concept is the challenge. Global macro investing is a hedge-fund strategy that involves holding long and short positions in various equity, fixed income, currency, and futures markets. The holdings are based primarily on overall economic and political views of various countries (macroeconomic principles). If a manager believes that the United States is headed into recession, then they might short-sell stocks and futures contracts on major U.S. indexes or the U.S. dollar. However, the manager may also see big opportunity for growth in Japan, and therefore take long positions in Japan's assets, which would include stocks, bonds, or other financial instruments.

In global macro investing, the profit potential is huge because you are able to use very little capital to control enormous positions to set up huge trades. If you take the correct positions, you can gain significant profits. However, the risk of loss is quite significant. The idea that some people would put so much at risk is quite hard to grasp for many institutional, let alone individual, investors. In the hedge fund world, the reason long/short equity is so attractive is because it is relatively easy to understand, easy

153

to market, easy to execute, and has a track record. When Alfred Jones came up with the idea for hedge funds, he used a long/short equity model; today ,most of the "old-timers" in the industry believe that it is still the cleanest and simplest way to manage money. Today, there are more long/short equity hedge funds launched per year than any other strategy combined. The idea, simply put, is to find a basket of, say, 200 stocks and short half of them. The manager believes the long positions will rise in price and the shorts will fall; either way, he or she is protected.

In the 1990s at Tiger Management, LLC, assets were pouring in. In order to find a home for all of the money, Robertson's investment style began to evolve from focusing on value alone to more of a global macro style that employed many different strategies. Robertson believed that he had to change as he went along. As the firm developed its analytical staffs, its focus shifted from value stocks to growth stocks. For Robertson where the trade or investment fit in the strategy bucket did not necessarily matter. What mattered was whether the investment made sense and if it would add significantly to the portfolio's bottom line.

As the firm's assets swelled into the billions, Robertson realized that position liquidity was going to be a problem. The firm needed many more ideas to put its capital into as its coffers got increasingly bigger. He and his team began searching the world for not only undervalued stocks and bonds, but also currencies and commodities. Tiger was forced, like most large firms, to cast a wider net in hopes of snagging good liquid positions. It was hard to find good places for the money; in Asia, for example, the Tiger team was able to identify only ten companies outside of Japan that were worthy of the firm's investment.

From the beginning, the Tiger portfolio was in a constant state of reevaluation in an effort to find the best and freshest investments. This was a way of life for the investment team until the firm's last days. "Every day when we came in, it was a totally new portfolio," said one longtime Tiger employee. "He taught me that when you have conviction about something you go for it. If you believe in it, you have to go for it, no matter what."

Every day was indeed a new day, and Robertson was an extremely aggressive investor. Once he made up his mind about a position he went after it "the way a large-mouth bass strikes at a lure."[1] According to *Forbes* magazine, Robertson "did not delude himself or in any way [try to] rationalize a position." He understood why he owned a stock and also understood that if the story around the position changed, it was time to get out. In the same *Forbes* piece, Barton Biggs, the famed economist-turned-hedge-fund manager, said that Robertson, "had great" taste when it came to distilling massive amounts of information to make investment decisions.

To keep on top of the portfolios and their worldwide holdings, Robertson built a firm that could operate around the clock. He understood that it's very hard to keep a secret on Wall Street, so he needed to be able to make sure that once the firm found an investment idea, it would be able to bring it home. The firm's trading staff was able to carry out efficient and discreet execution of investment decisions in every major market around the world because of the efforts of people like traders Tim Henney and David Saunders–traders who knew how to keep brokers quiet and how to execute orders regardless of market conditions.

Managing risk was a significant aspect of the firm's success. It was an integral part of the investment selection process. Robertson spent enormous amounts of time understanding the risk of a trade, as well as the risk it could have to the portfolio, before a position was included in one of the funds.

A position was included in the portfolio only after Tiger analysts had examined a risk and decided very explicitly that it was worth taking, Robertson said when we met. In his mind, the objective of the investment selection process was and is to identify those individual investment situations in which the probability or cost of being wrong—the risk—is small compared to the gains.

Robertson believed that while the funds were built one position at a time, each holding had an effect on the collection of investments. To understand these risks better, the firm used a number of tools, including real-time profit-and-loss reports, liquidity stress testing, and daily exposure and performance reporting systems. These analyses were designed so that Robertson and his senior management team could understand and discuss all important aspects of the portfolio's behavior and risks.

Besides these analytical tools, Tiger used more traditional safeguards to minimize losses. There was a strict set of controls in all areas, including a clear and defined separation of the front and back offices and a series of internal and external audits to guard against "operational hazards."

Robertson told investors that the Tiger culture was driven by the investment returns to its investors. The growth of his, his colleagues, and his family's investment stake in the funds, their compensation, their professional pride, and their reputation—all were determined by how well they did for their investors. Therefore, risk monitoring and control commanded the highest priority throughout the entire organization. One trade was not going take down Tiger. But this also meant that one trade was not going to "make" the firm either.

Many people are familiar with how George Soros came to be known as the greatest investor of all time. It was the trade that broke the Bank of England. His trade shocked the world and set the stage for hedge funds to be forever blamed for whatever ails the financial markets.

It started in 1990, when Great Britain decided to join the new Western European monetary system. At the time, according to Robert Slater's biography *Soros: The Life, Times and Trading*

Secrets of the World's Greatest Investor, Soros did not believe that it was a good idea for Britain. Its economy was not as strong as the new united Germany's, he observed, at whose economic mercy it would be.

Under the European monetary agreement, Britain was to maintain an exchange rate of £2.95 to the German mark. As Britain's economy grew worse, the pound came under increasing pressure, but the monetary agreement tied the country's hands. Throughout the summer of 1992, John Major's Tory government assured the world that the pound would recover and that devaluation, thus breaking the agreement, was not an option.

Slater writes that Soros thought the economic situation was a lot worse than the government admitted. By mid-September, Italy, facing considerable economic pressure itself, devalued the lira. Although it did so within the guidelines of the agreement, it broke the system's back and set in motion the trade that made George Soros the most famous hedge fund manager ever.[2]

On September 15, 1992, Major's government announced that Britain was pulling out of the European rate mechanism and devaluing the pound. The news rocked the global currency markets. While most traders scrambled to stem losses, one hedge fund manager was laughing all the way to the bank. Soros and his team had sold $10 billion in sterling, and when the news broke, the hedge fund profited by close to a billion dollars. This trade made headlines not only because of its sheer size and the scope of the profits, but also because it was seen as one man doing one trade.

Once the news broke, nobody in the financial or political world ever looked at Soros and his fund—or any hedge fund—the same way again. Hedge funds became the place to be, and everyone wanted to get hold of the managers with a Midas touch.[3]

Many people had heard of hedge funds and some people actually understood what they did, but nobody had any clue a manager would go so far in one trade. The idea that somebody would put that much money at risk and be so sure of their abilities is extraordinary. It is something that very few individuals could comprehend.

Although leverage and position size played significantly into the day-to-day investment strategy at Tiger, diversification was also "a key element" in the firm's overall approach to investing. It led to significant personnel issues as the firm got more and more into implementing its global macro strategy.

During Tiger's existence, the funds invested in markets in some 25 countries and as many industries, with longs set against shorts in many of these sectors. Nothing, it seemed, was too far out there for the firm's assets, as long as the trade showed potential for profit. Over the years, about half of Tiger's equity investments were outside the United States, where the team was able to take advantage of pricing inefficiencies—Wall Street's way of saying investors have failed to know a good thing when they see it.

To gauge the currency and fixed-income markets, Tiger used the same fundamental approach as in the equity markets. In the currency plays, research focused on country economics, as opposed to company economics.

There was a close and mutually supportive relationship between Tiger's macro and equity analysts. Often the macro team's view would augment specific company research into equity investments. Likewise, information supplied by its equity analysts was frequently used to support macro investment decisions. However, this proved problematic because oftentimes, macro trades, which used significantly less of the firm's capital, brought in significantly more profits than a straight long or short equity play.

According to one former analyst, the problems arose because they were breaking their backs trying to find the best and brightest ideas for the portfolio, stocks that could move 20, 30–even 50 to 100–percent in a year. The guy next to them on the desk is talking about putting on a currency trade or bond trade because it uses so much less capital, and it might yield 20 or 30 percent in a *day* or a *week.* This sort of trading and profits made for a lot of unhappy people, especially around bonus time, when money was dispersed based on Robertson's belief of what the analyst had contributed to the overall performance of the portfolio.

Robertson liked the idea of being a global macro trader/manager because it offered him two things: significant returns with the use of less capital, and more respect from his peers because he was trading in the same markets as Soros. "People are in awe of global macro traders, and in the 1980s and 1990s, people were in awe of Soros. Julian was as well, and he wanted people to be in awe of him," said a former colleague. "Global macro was a natural extension of the empire he was building. It was a natural progression that served both in real terms by performance and perceived terms in the minds of people who watched Wall Street."

Macro investing provided Tiger with almost a quarter of its average returns from 1990 to 1998. The strategy Robertson believed added an important level of diversification to an otherwise equity-dominated portfolio and more importantly let him put massive amounts of capital to work with little or no trading effort.[4]

Robertson, however, was not necessarily interested in the quick bucks or fast returns but rather he was willing to wait for his profits. He believed that whether he was putting on equity or macro-based trades, the best investment usually takes a significant amount of time to achieve rational valuations. He always knew that neither he nor anyone who ever worked for him had a particular ability to forecast the timing or pattern of market or price movements. Therefore, the folks at Tiger put on trades and made investments that tended to have long time horizons—typically measured in years—and he was willing to wait until the potential was fulfilled.

As the organization grew and the assets in the portfolios began to swell into the billions, it became more and more apparent that global macro investing would play an increasing role in Tiger's ability to maintain its performance and find positions that offered liquidity.

"When it comes to equity investing, there is without a doubt a time when size does matter and there is a point when slippage factors come into play," said Hunt Taylor, a hedge fund industry expert. "However, when it comes to putting on trades in currencies, fixed income and even commodities because of the size and liquidity markets, size is rarely if ever an issue. There is always plenty to go around in these areas of the investment spectrum."[5]

To carry out a successful global macro strategy, Robertson relied on a continuously growing organization of people, whom he has often called some of the "brightest minds" on Wall Street. These were people who shared his competitive spirit, who enjoyed the rigor of working at Tiger and the energy that went into making an investment decision and allocation. The process was not an easy one. Once an analyst recommended an investment, Robertson and the rest of the investment team further scrutinized it to the point of what literally seemed like no return.

Robertson questioned ideas with rigor and discipline under conditions that could be described as nothing more than fierce. The firm's investment selection process was a brutal one that relied on incredible amounts of research and conviction, because when it came down to it, Robertson and the folks at Tiger knew that idea generation was the firm's competency. As such, competitive pressure was the key ingredient in selecting the very best investment ideas to make it to Tiger's portfolios.

While much has been made over the years of Robertson's temper, it seems that little has been made of his praise for individuals who worked for him. He was always willing to laud those whom he believed added to the funds' performance, although the ultimate decision was always up to him. And while tempers may have flared around the Friday lunch meeting—and every other day of the week during all hours of the day—in public and in press, Robertson has always been quick to praise the people who helped him build and maintain Tiger's success.

Simply put, Robertson wanted everyone to know that he was at the helm of the ship at all times, but also made it quite clear that he had the right people in the engine room and on deck to make sure the boat sailed straight ahead and could weather the storms. In the late 1990s, it was more important than ever to make sure this message came across loud and clear.

The Tiger earned its stripes in June of 1997 when the Thai government decided that it no longer was going to prop up its currency and let market forces take over. Almost overnight the currency fell 18 percent, which meant huge profits for Tiger which had been short currency. Through the rest of the summer, the currency continued to fall and, by early August, it had gone down nearly 30 percent from the time it was devalued. Robertson and his Tigers had made a fortune. This trade helped the firm rack up its best performance ever on absolute basis in the firm's history.

At its height in 1997, Tiger was up more than 70 percent versus the S&P 500 Index and the MSCI which were up 33.4 percent and 15.8 percent respectively. For the last quarter of 1997, Tiger was up 30.2 percent with every investment category contributing to the results. The firm's U.S., Japanese, and Hong Kong–based equities positions accounted for a majority of the profits. Tiger's macro positions led by their currency trades accounted for almost a third of the portfolio's return during the fourth quarter of 1997.[6]

The year 1998 started out fine for Robertson and his Tigers. It was not until the end of the spring and the early summer that the fund took any significant hits. In the past, the firm had been able to sustain blows and recover; however, this time it was different. This time the hit they took with the dollar/yen trade was a combination of both punches to the head and the body. The firm sustained significant losses when the trade turned against them, but Robertson believes that Tiger was hit even harder when the other hedge fund and institutional investors realized the situation they were in and squeezed them further. He believes that people knew that they were caught in the yen trade and that there would probably be redemptions, so other funds began to "shoot" at the firm. Robertson believes that Tiger was a victim of its size—it had a made a mistake in the yen trade, and other hedge fund managers smelled blood. The traders and analysts at Tiger were not happy when word got out about their positions or their trading intentions. It was difficult for them to watch since it appeared others were able to get in and out of positions faster than they could. They literally in some cases saw their trades slip through their fingers because the Tiger machine was too large and not nimble enough.

Many have said Robertson's success stems from his willingness to think outside the box, in broad strokes, and not just take things as they appear. When it comes to investing, most people follow a discipline: Here's the black box, here's the results it produced, and here is what they expect to produce. Therefore, they are going to simply follow that black box. Robertson's skill is that he knows that is *not* how the stock market works and is able work these misconceptions by others to his advantage.

By 1998, Tiger had more than 210 employees, 50 of them investment professionals, in offices in New York, London, and Tokyo. The trading staff consisted of 15 people in the New York office at 101 Park Avenue. At this point, 18 years into its existence, the original Tiger fund had an average annual compound return, net of all fees, of more than 29 percent. In comparison, the S&P 500 Stock Index returned 17.9 percent, and the MSCI returned 14.7 percent. According to records, one dollar invested in Tiger at its inception was worth $117 on December 31, 1998, versus $22 invested in the S&P 500 and $13 in the MSCI over the same period.[7]

During his reign, Robertson could, at any given time, know so much about so many different companies that an average person's head would spin. His ability to retain information about companies here in the states, in Europe, or Asia is said to be unbelievable. It is really a skill that many of his former colleagues tried to develop while working for him, but they have had very little success replicating it.

Because he knew so much about the markets, Robertson liked to look for value in places other people weren't looking. Anyone could pick up a *BusinessWeek* and decide to go long Wal-Mart and short its competitors. That would have been a decidedly boring play for Tiger. Robertson was looking for the unexpected plays–the diamonds in the rough.

For that reason, he sought out information wherever he could find it. In one of his letters to investors, he commented on "recently being reminded of the benefit of meeting with anyone smart" who wanted to meet him. At the time, one of his brokers had insisted that he meet with the chief executive and chief financial officer of a major financial institution, and while initially the meeting did not excite him, it turned out to be profitable and worthwhile. Below is an excerpt from his letter of May 9, 1989, to investors which illustrates one such instance:

> Because of a variety of prejudices, we really did not
> want to see these people but elected to because we had
> some thoughts on acquisitions they could make which

would help us. In effect, we were hoping to sell them something.

Our guests waited patiently while we made our sales presentation and then made their own. And what a presentation it was! We immediately tried to take a large position in the company, and although we were only partially successful in completing our position before the price ran away, it so far is proving a marvelous investment. Lesson learned—you never make a mistake by seeing people with brains.[8]

John Griffin said that he found Robertson's shareholder letters so informative that he read them with some regularity to find insight and guidance. Not only did Robertson apprise readers of the funds' current performances, he gave them political commentary. He also provided insight into his thoughts on places like Sun Valley, Idaho, and Aspen, Colorado, the importance of buying American, and the role of Japan in the global economy. He injected his letters and comments with a combination of Southern charm and Wall Street wit.

As Robertson developed Tiger's analytical staff, growth stocks became a very good investment. If the analyst was right on the growth, the growth stocks would be tremendous performers. There may have been a year or two when they suffered, but if they were true growth stocks, then they would continue to grow over time. This strategy worked well for much of the 1990s, but in 1998 and 1999, things did not go Tiger's way.

As the bull raged on and the technology bubble grew and grew, it became more and more apparent that good-value "old economy" stocks would not perform as well as the technology darlings. In fact, the hot money was dumping the old-time names like Gillette, Coca-Cola, and General Motors for Netscape, America Online, and Cisco Systems. These new-fangled companies with no earnings were seeing their stock prices triple and quadruple overnight, while good, solid companies with good, solid earnings were taking massive hits.

In the late 1990s, investors cared little or nothing at all about what a company did, what its prospects were, or who was involved in it. Mention the word *Internet* and–boom–you had a winner. As one fine business publication, writing about the demise of the value and growth managers, put it: "Those, whom the Internet does not make insufferably wealthy, it humbles." Never could a statement be truer about the folks at Tiger management.

In 1999, it was clear that Robertson was humbled. The things that had worked in the past no longer seemed to work in the technology-stimulated bull market. While Tiger owned names like Intel, Lucent, Motorola, and Microsoft, it stayed clear of some of the names that offered investors rocketship like returns. The end of Tiger was near, but just how near at year-end 1999, nobody but Robertson seemed to know.

Tiger and its analysts were getting bogged down in a number of bad investments. Things that were supposed to go up were going down, and things that were supposed to go down were going up. The hedge fund was not succeeding in the markets. Patience had grown thin among even some of Tiger's most loyal and faithful investors during this period–when it seemed like even a monkey could throw a dart at a list of stocks and see their investments rise, Tiger was losing ground. The idea of waiting for solid yet steady returns did not appeal to investors who had found they could make significant returns in insignificant amounts of time.

Equity markets around the globe were a wild place in the late 1990s. People were buying companies like eToys Inc., which went public at $20.00 and closed at $76.56 on its first day of trading, and FreeMarkets Inc., which went public at $48.00 and closed at $280.00 on its first day as well. *Investing* had taken on a whole new meaning. People were quitting their jobs to become day traders. Internet IPOs went through the roof, even though the companies had no assets, few clients, and little income. The folks at CNBC became minor celebrities, as people from all walks of life switched on the TV to find out what Neil Cavuto, Jim Cramer, and the guys on "Squawk Box" were saying about their stock picks. The Internet bubble seemed incapable of bursting, and everything seemed to go up regardless of the company, its management, or its ability to make money. If you did not make a fortune in the market overnight, you were a dummy! If a cab driver or hot dog vendor could make a fortune by investing in stocks, shouldn't one of the greatest investors of all time?

"Here you have one of the greatest investors of all time, someone who has more experience and more expertise making investments than almost anyone, and he seems to not be able to get anything right," said Dr. Ramie Tritt, an investor in Tiger's Ocelot fund. "It just did not add up. It seemed that no matter what he tried to do, he could get nothing right."

The thing about the euphoria of the technology craze was that nothing added up. It was not just that Robertson could not make good trades or the analysts could not find good investment opportunities—stocks that *should* have gone up went down, and stocks that should have been delisted or not even brought to market went up. The markets were like the wild, wild west shows. Everyone knows that there is going to be a good guy and a bad guy and that there is going to be some excitement—only in this case, it was unclear who was going to be wearing the black hats and who was going to be wearing the white hats.

After the disastrous 1999, the fund was down over 19 percent. The news of Tiger's impending demise in the early spring of 2000 surprised no one on Wall Street. For weeks before the formal announcement, many had predicted that Tiger and Robertson were done and that the ailing beast would have to be put down. The euphoria of the technology market had taken its toll on the value-investing strategist, and investors of all shapes and sizes had had enough. The reason for investing in hedge funds was to be able to profit in good and bad times. At Tiger, this was proving not to be the case.

In the months leading up to the decade's end, Robertson and a number of his most trusted advisors spent a significant amount of time looking for strategic partners who could come in and help him save the company, either by having the firm taken over by a larger, more traditional investment organization or by merger with another hedge fund complex. Robertson and his team worked extremely hard to avoid having the firm closed and seeing their beast put to sleep. He had a number of conversations with both traditional investment firms and some hedge fund complexes, but at the end of the day he could not get a deal done. In previous years, Robertson had looked to sell Tiger and rebuffed a number of offers from some of the leading investment management organizations because the price was not right. Now, price was not the issue. Robertson wanted to do right by his investors. There were many overtures from some of the most respected names in both traditional and alternative asset management, but as he saw it, the only thing these groups were interested in was the name or the franchise value–they had no interest in doing right by his investors.

According to a number of sources, during the summer and fall of 1999 and even in the beginning of 2000, Robertson was very close to getting a deal done a number of times. The problem was that when it came down to it, he wanted to make sure that his investors were taken care of, and nobody seemed to be willing to give him that guarantee. For Robertson that was the deal breaker. After all, a number of his investors had been with him since the beginning, and he felt a sense of loyalty to them for sticking with him during the good and bad times. He had reached a greater level of success in the investment business than he had ever dreamed. He had reached the point where he could say, I am at this age, the kids are this age, the wife is at this age, we have more money than we ever thought possible, and we are ready to move on. But without the investors, we would have had nothing. It's my responsibility to take care of them.

By March 2000, as the Nasdaq headed for the 5000 level, Robertson had decided it was better to close the fund than to sell it. It could not continue in its current inclination. Tiger as a hedge fund complex was over. The pain had grown too great; Robertson was no longer willing to try to navigate a market that he did not understand to fight for returns.

To many of the people on the trading desk at Tiger, it seemed like nothing was working. The team worked long and hard to find ways to salvage the portfolio and turn trades around, but for some reason, they just could not make it happen. The Tiger profit machine had stopped functioning. It was time to call it quits.

In a letter to investors dated March 30, 2000, he explained that since August 1998, the Tiger funds had "stumbled badly" and that investors had "voted strongly negatively with their pocketbooks" leading him to his decision to close the funds. During the 19-month period, investors had withdrawn more than $7.7 billion from the funds. This represented more than a third of the funds assets. It was a clear sign that investors had lost confidence in Robertson and the Tiger organization.[9]

In his letter to shareholders, he wrote of the firm's inability to find places to implement its value based investment strategy. And that coupled with the significant amounts of withdrawals, caused the firm and its employees a significant amount of stress. So much so that he decided to throw up his hand in disgust and close the funds down and return the remaining assets to investors.

Things had been tough before and in the past, the firm rode out the storms however, this time, it was different, Robertson did not see any end in sight for the euphoria that had gripped the markets. The "irrational exuberance" that Alan Greenspan had warned of in the late 1990s had gripped the markets for too long. Robertson was no longer able to navigate world markets and exploit them for profit. He knew that eventually things would change and that eventually his way of searching for profits would come back, but he did not see an end to the bull market in stocks. He believed he no longer could offer his investors any sort of value and that meant he needed to get out of the game. There was nothing left to do but fold the tents and go home. He could not know that even as he was writing the letter, the wall of euphoria was beginning to crumble at the foundations.

"It is the recognition that equities with cash-on-cash returns of 15 to 25 percent, regardless of their short-term market performance, are great investments," he wrote. " 'End' means a beginning by investors overall to put aside momentum and potential short-term gain in highly speculative stocks to take the more assured, yet still historically high returns available in out-of-favor equities."

By the time Robertson had decided to call it quits, the Tiger organization had grown to more than 2,500 times its original size 18 years earlier. Its assets had grown from $8.8 million to almost $25 billion, or 259,000 percent. The firm's compound rate of return to partners during its existence, net of all fees, was 31.7 percent.[10]

Robertson believed that the success of Tiger rested in his team's "steady commitment to buying the best stocks and shorting the worst." Now that the markets were "irrational," though, this skill set, it seemed, would no longer work. "In a rational environment [our] strategy functions well," he said. "But in an irrational market, where earnings and price considerations take a back seat to mouse clicks and momentum, such logic, as we have learned, does not count for much."

Robertson equated the then-current market environment to

that of a sophisticated pyramid scheme destined for ruin. He believed, like Buffett, that the euphoria surrounding technology stocks was the root of all that was wrong with investing. It was the tulip craze all over again, the only difference was, now it was about megabytes and mouse clicks.

"The current technology, Internet, and telecom craze fueled by performance desires of investors, money managers and even financial buyers is unwittingly creating a Ponzi pyramid destined for collapse," he wrote to investors. "The strategy is, however, that the only way to generate short-term performance in the current environment is to buy these stocks. That makes the process self-perpetuating until this pyramid eventually collapses under its own excess."

History was kind to Robertson in that his theories and beliefs on investing, the market, and the Nasdaq in particular, proved correct soon enough. As the technology sector fell apart a few weeks and months after he decided to close, investors suffered significant losses. The market entered into a prolonged period of decline. The Nasdaq, led by technology issues, fell flat on its face over the next few weeks, months, and even years. The carnage eventually led to losses in all areas of the market, causing investors of all shapes and sizes distress. The turmoil began in the spring of 2000 and had not completely ended at the time of this writing in the summer of 2004, even though there had been a significant rebound in the second quarter of the year, as a postwar optimism gripped the markets. The Nasdaq market had lost almost 80 percent of its value in less than three years; the Dow Jones Industrial Average, which hit an all-time high of 11722 in January 2000, closed 2003 at 10453 and was down to 10188 at the beginning of June 2004.

As the markets were beginning to unravel, Robertson was predicting that the technology craze would end. He believed that there would be a point when value investing came back in style. Robertson had seen manic periods like this before, and he remained confident that, despite the current disfavor in which it was held, value investing remained the best course. There is just too much reward in certain mundane, old-economy stocks to ignore, according to everything he knew. After all, this was not the first time in his storied career that value stocks had taken a licking. The losses that he was sustaining on the value side were similar to the situation that many of the great value investors experienced during the early and mid-1970s, in early 1980, and 1981 when they suffered terrible losses. As it had before, Robertson believed that things would change for the better. Value would come back.

The problem was that while Robertson believed in the value philosophy, his investors had given up hope. He knew that the strategy would eventually pay off, but he didn't know when, and their patience had grown increasingly thin as trade after trade turned out to be losers. As a result, he wrote, he had decided to liquidate the portfolios and return capital to investors. He closed the letter by thanking his investors for sticking with him and his colleagues throughout the years.

For him, the best part of running and operating Tiger was, by far, the opportunity to work closely with a unique cadre of coworkers and investors. "For every minute of it, the good times and the bad, the victories and the defeats, I speak for myself and the multitude of Tigers past and present who thank you from the bottom of our hearts."[11]

And with those parting words, the days of the Tiger organization as one of the world's largest hedge funds—and Julian Robertson as its head, heart, and soul—were over.

10

THE PRESS DISSECTS
THE TIGER

THE PRESS HAD A FIELD DAY WITH THE ANNOUNCEMENT and subsequent demise of the organization. Publications around the globe carried the story. It was clearly the end of a hedge fund era. The effect of Tiger's liquidation was felt in all corners of the globe.

Hedge fund industry followers seem to unanimously agree that the industry will never again have a singular force like Julian Robertson. Sure, there are big managers, but nobody will ever build an organization or spawn so many successful managers, probably, in my lifetime. He had an uncanny ability to find and exploit talent. That's made clear by the number of people who have left Tiger and set up successful hedge funds on their own.

To understand what went wrong, look at the state of the global debt and equity markets at the turn of the millennium. In 1999, while the Nasdaq Composite rose more than 80 percent, Tiger was down nearly 18 percent. During the first quarter of 2000, it lost an additional 13 percent. As the losses mounted, investors lost patience and starting taking money out of the funds. By the end of the March 2000 quarter, assets in the fund had fallen from almost $25 billion in August 1998 to less than $8 billion. The reason for the firm's demise was universally blamed on it inability to implement its value-based investment strategies.

Commenting on Tiger's demise for National Public Radio, Marc Reinganum, head of the finance department at Southern University's Cox School, said that the types of companies that he was investing in recently could be described as value companies, stocks that looked good from conventional valuation measures.[1] The problem was that the market performance of these companies over the last few years had been terrible relative to the performance of growth companies. Value was not in vogue.

Robertson and Tiger were not the only managers suffering during this unique period on the Street. They were in good company. Many other value investors, including Warren Buffett, saw their investment portfolios hit the dumps. Buffett saw his Berkshire Hathaway stock drop almost 32 percent in 1999 as he continued to focus on buying companies that offered investors real profits, not just a hope of success through the Internet or a new piece of technology.

It was not just the equity markets that caused Robertson grief. Some of Robertson's global macro trades went against him, as well. As the markets imploded in light of the Russian debt crisis and the near-collapse of Long-Term Capital Management, Tiger kneecapped itself. It made a particularly bad trade in the Japanese yen, losing 18 percent in October 1998. This trade alone caused the firm to end the year down 4 percent.

And 1999, of course, was worse. Tiger lost 19 percent, a firm 40 percent behind the S&P 500. During the preceding 18 months, Tiger lost a total of 43 percent, compared to a rise in the S&P 500 of 35 percent. All at once, it seemed that everything had stopped working.

In an article that appeared in the *New York Daily News* in April

2000, writer Peter Siris compared Robertson to great athletes who retire once their skills erode or when they simply get tired of playing the game.

Siris wrote that there were two possibilities why Robertson suddenly turned cold. One was that he, like many athletes, just got too old for his game, no different than the "star pitcher who losses a little zip from his fastball or the formerly great skater who can no longer land the triple-lutz." The second was that Robertson was still a great investor, but that his style was temporarily not working. "While he did have a rough period, great investors do not suddenly lose their touch," he wrote. Siris called him the Michael Jordan of hedge fund managers, stating that he believed almost no one had a more disciplined style or a better record. He analogized Robertson's fall from grace to when the New York Jets were losing every game in the fall of 1999. Fans were not calling Coach Bill Parcells to be fired; the fans knew he was a great coach, they realized he was just in the middle of a losing streak.[2]

Still, the stock market is not as easy to navigate as the gridiron. While the new kids on the block chased technology and biotechnology stocks, Robertson stuck to his game plan and went after what he always did, the undervalued old-economy stocks. Unfortunately, that wasn't the right play for that season.

Unlike a number of journalists who seemed to relish in his demise, Siris believed it was just a rough spot in a very smooth career path and should have been viewed by investors and critics that way. He believed that most investors could learn a lot from watching Robertson navigate the markets. Great investors are usually those who stick with a successful style, even when it may not be working for them. Robertson stubbornly stuck with his style, and, according to Siris, this is what would vindicate him over time.

While many believed that Robertson was a victim of the markets, a few journalists and a number of investors believed there was a completely different story behind the end of Tiger. In an article in *BusinessWeek*, Gary Weiss painted a very different story of the firm's demise. According to Weiss, in a story called "What Really Killed Tiger," the end came because the firm was hit by so many withdrawals that it had no choice but to liquidate its portfolios in order satisfy investor demand for cash. The incredibly high rate of withdrawals, not market forces, forced Robertson to close Tiger and to return whatever capital was left to investors, according to Weiss.

According to Weiss's story, Robertson didn't close his funds after months of agonizing because he was upset with irrational markets. He was forced to shut his funds down because the largest component of the fund complex, the Jaguar fund, was literally forced out of business by investors who made "the very rational" decision to get out of the investment. Jaguar was one of Tiger's offshore funds that was open to qualified U.S. tax-exempt investors and non-U.S. investors.[3]

Weiss based his story on a series of documents that the magazine had obtained from sources who were most likely investors or investor representatives. The documents, addressed to investors, indicated that redemptions at Jaguar had gotten so big that they would have reduced the number of shares outstanding to less then 20 percent of the authorized number, which caused an automatic liquidation according to the fund's offering memorandum. Although a Tiger spokesman said the firm could have paid out the shares, according to his documents, Weiss believed that Jaguar was in "a bind" that left it begging for cash in order to satisfy demand.

Some questioned Weiss's story. If he was right about the Jaguar problem, why didn't Robertson just close Jaguar and let the other funds continue to operate? The problem, according to Weiss and a number of investors, was that because Robertson managed all the funds in tandem, Jaguar could not have been liquidated without closing all of the funds.[4] "Such was the stark reality of the last days of Julian Robertson as a force in the world markets," wrote Weiss. "It was a sad, even squalid, end to an investment record that, throughout the 1980s and early 1990s, was among the finest on Wall Street."[5]

In early 2003, Weiss said that he stuck by the story and that he believed that the facts still hold up. A number of investors also echoed his comments in conversations. It seems that Robertson had got himself in a bind and that the only way was to get out of everything because demand for cash was so great. Both Robertson and Tiger's spokesperson would not comment on this matter–both cited the investor letter and news articles about the firm's demise. In plain English, they had their story, and they were sticking to it.

But Weiss took the demise of Tiger and Robertson a step farther then his investigative piece. In the same issue of the magazine, he wrote a commentary on the subject titled "The Buck Stops with Julian Robertson, Not the Market."

He wrote that the true cause of Tiger's demise wasn't Robertson's inability to manage an irrational market but his inability to manage redemptions. The irrational market story, in his view, was spin: "a salvage operation–an effort to rescue his reputation." The truth, Weiss believes, is that Robertson was faced with a crisis of confidence from his investors.

"Robertson's solution was a stroke of genius, and the press largely swallowed it whole," he wrote. "As a public relations strategy it was a dazzling success. Robertson made a persuasive case but was this a satisfactory explanation of the downfall of the widely hyped investment guru?"[6]

Weiss went to great lengths to lay out his argument that Robertson was really trying to deal with redemptions, not just the market. And although many journalistic purists may think it is odd to run both a news story and a commentary in the same publication by the same writer, it is commonplace in *BusinessWeek*. Many believed that Weiss's account of what happened looked like a vendetta stemming from Robertson's billion-dollar suit against the writer and the publishing company. The argument he laid out for what went wrong at Tiger Management differed significantly from the story being told by the folks at Tiger and Robertson himself.

However, it seems as if Weiss, like most reporters who cover hedge funds, missed the point of why people invest in them in the first place. Almost every story about hedge funds in the popular press has at least one of two themes: fees and secrecy. No matter who writes it, you'll find a comment about the "high fees" that managers charge or the "near secrecy" in which the investment managers operate. Weiss doesn't let the reader down, for he writes about the "egregious fees" that Robertson charged his investors.

In my opinion, Weiss loses his argument in this statement: "For years, wealthy investors paid Robertson a hefty 20 percent slice of profits." Why does it matter what Tiger or Robertson charged its investors, and why is that relevant to the story? If the fees were egregious, then no one would have paid them. Weiss did not address the veil of secrecy behind which the hedge fund industry operates, but he was rather blunt when he wrote, "Make no mistake, Julian Robertson didn't fail because he was a rational investor in an irrational world. He failed because he didn't do his job."[7]

The problem for some with Wall Street, as I have said before, is that it measures your performance on a quarterly, monthly, and often on a daily basis. Clearly, Robertson was measured by his performance, and as a result, hundreds of investors had given him billions of dollars to manage. Investors clearly believed in his money management skills. But, as Robertson now admits, Tiger grew too big too fast, and while his skills are extraordinary, he was unable to deal with the growth. As a result of his poor performance, investors withdrew significant sums of money, in effect, creating a run on the bank. He was left with no choice but to get out of the market altogether.

It seems pretty clear from speaking with former Tiger employees and investors that two things caused the demise of Tiger: the massive redemptions and the inability to navigate the markets.

"The press was extremely hard on Julian," said one longtime investor. "They made it seem like he wanted to fail, that he had to fail and that he was a pariah of sorts who wreaked havoc on the market at the expense of others."

In a letter to the editor of *Business Week*, Robertson and the folks at Tiger termed Weiss's story a work of fiction and called into question the statements about the forced liquidation. The letter said that Jaguar's liquidity, contrary to the story, was never a factor in the decision to close the funds.

BusinessWeek was not the only publication to write negatively about Tiger and Robertson, however. *The Times* of London offered its views in a piece that ran on March 31, 2000, called "No campaign to save the Tiger." It also attacked the firm's fee structure and Robertson's inability to handle the technology markets. It brought out its big guns on the havoc that Tiger wreaked on the economies of Asia with its huge trade against the Thai baht in 1997. Several other news organizations offered news stories about what went wrong at Tiger. In addition, *The New York Times* and *Barron's* published major opinion pieces.

In an op-ed piece titled "Reckonings; A Hedge Fund Pruned," that ran on April 2, 2000, columnist Paul Krugman, a Princeton economics professor, told *Times* readers that people should not feel bad for the humbled speculator whose reduced fortune is still a 10-digit number. But rather, he believed there were quite a few people who would have liked to see him suffer a bit more. Krugman said that while Robertson was famous for his temper and his deliberate coarseness, the firm's biggest successes involved profiting from economic distress, and, if you believe the complaints of some Asian governments, in some cases deliberately *creating* it. Krugman believes that it was "ironic" that Robertson blamed the firm's demise on irrational markets because he believed that Robertson could not have "thrived if markets were as rational as he complained they were not."[8]

He writes:

> The whole reason for a hedge fund's existence is the supposed ability of its managers to spot market errors—stocks, currencies, and so on that are priced either too high or too low given the fundamentals. The idea then is to engage in arbitrage—buying the underpriced assets, selling the overpriced. This strategy can make huge returns for the fund's investors, but it can't work if markets get the prices right in the first place.
>
> I don't want to say Mr. Robertson never knew what he was doing. In the early days of Tiger, when it was small enough to research and speculate in small companies, the story may have been different. But by the 90s, the inflow of money from eager investors who thought past success guaranteed future gains made Tiger too big to play that game. Mr. Robertson shifted his focus to "macro" bets—attempts to forecast the future of whole classes of stocks, even whole economies. And there are no consistently good macro economic forecasters—only bad forecasters who get lucky. (That includes me.) Fifteen years ago, Mr. Robertson may have known things about XYZ Inc. that the rest of us did not; but he's no more knowledgeable about Japan, or the future of tech stocks, than thousands of other people.
>
> And someone who repeatedly bets on what are, for all practical purposes, random coin tosses is bound to be

disappointed. He may win several times in a row–correctly guessing, for example, that Asian stocks are about to tumble–but if he comes to believe in his own prescience, and stakes his whole capital on each toss, sooner or later he is bound to come to grief. And so he did."[9]

Copyright © 2004 by The New York Times Co. *Reprinted with permission.*

Barron's famed editor, Alan Abelson, was also not so sympathetic to Tiger's demise. In his piece "Macro Trouble," which ran on April 3, 2000, he wrote that he believed that what led to Tiger's demise "was not that he stuck too rigidly to his investment last–but that he didn't." Abelson said that "macro" and "hubris" were the reasons for his downfall and that his "yearning for acclaim and celebrity" added significantly to his losses. He continued:

The hubris-driven macro strategy, meanwhile, also affected his micro, or stock picking, tactics, and not for the better. Selection undoubtedly hurt. But what really hurt was the elephantine size of his holdings. In seeking to deploy the billions it had accumulated, Tiger took huge positions in individual companies. That can cause great discomfort if a stock goes against you. But it can cause true pain for a hedge fund like Tiger.

If you're a megabuck investor who has attained a certain prominence and own too much of a stock and sell even a share, word quickly gets around, and you run the risk of killing the stock. But when you're a megabuck hedge fund investor in the same circumstances and the stock you own too much of is leveraged, the negative effect is vastly magnified. Size is the enemy of leverage, and a reasonable estimate is that Tiger was leveraged four to one.

Our point, again, is that what did Tiger in was not that Julian hewed to value investing. Quite the opposite. We contend that what did him in was that he strayed from the investment straight and narrow in pursuit of some grand agenda that had less to do, as it were, with fortune than with fame.[10]

While Abelson was harsh in his assessment of what went wrong and why, he did finish the piece with what many would consider the ultimate compliment. He wrote that after Robertson wound down Tiger and he settled into managing his own money, "if we were a well-heeled investor and Julian were disposed to do so, we'd be more than happy to have him manage our money along with his."[11]

Robertson would not comment on either *The New York Times* piece or the *Barron's* article, and he did not tell me if he was managing Abelson's money. What he did say, however, were comments very similar to those of Michael Steinhardt's and some other hedge fund managers that I have talked to over the years: The media always have the final say. They may not get it right, but they have the final say.

When it comes to what led to the demise of Tiger, it seems that while there are probably two sides to the story, the main issue was a crisis of confidence in his investors. It is clear that investors had lost their faith in his abilities, and this may have been caused by the market evolving into a beast he could not tame and, as a result, investors deciding they needed to focus on protecting their assets.

Three years after the liquidation, Robertson is still in the money management business. Today he manages his own money and works with up-and-coming managers to help them build successful operations.

In the summer of 2002, while we were sitting in his office at 101 Park Avenue discussing the closure of the funds, he still subscribed to the theory that the markets were the main cause of its demise, but something else had become apparent—size of assets under management.

Upon reflection of what went wrong, Robertson said that the firm just got to be too big. "The hedge fund business is about success breeding success," he said. "Over time as we continued to perform, many of our investors told their friends, their colleagues about what we were doing and that is how we grew."

He always thought that a firm could grow talent commensurate with the burgeoning assets under management but came to realize that while the idea was "theoretically sound, it was practically impossible." The bigger Tiger got, the bigger the amount of stock he would have to buy for it to affect the portfolio.

At the height, in order to take a meaningful position in a stock, he would need something like a $200 million position, which would have been 1 percent at the end. And during that time, there were not many stocks where you could get a $200 million position with liquidity, and so it was a real problem for the firm.

Liquidity, size, and withdrawals, among a number of additional factors, all played a role in the demise of Tiger. Although the glory days of the fund and its manager are clearly gone, one thing is for sure: Its legacy will live on for quite some time, especially in a group known as the Tiger Cubs—but more about them later.

Many people have theories about what went wrong at Tiger and the events that led to its downfall, but one of the critical issues has been widely overlooked. According to many former Tiger employees and a number of investors, their real problem with Tiger was not that Robertson and his team could not find investment opportunities because of irrational exuberance or that investors' demands for their assets caused the funds to be squeezed for cash, but rather that the organization itself had evolved. And that, combined with the failure of its leader to hire good people who had the same fire in their belly as those in the firm's early days, had led to its demise. No doubt, difficulty navigating the markets was the public reason for the firm's demise, but many believe they were not navigable because the crew at Tiger was not capable of handling the turbulent environment.

By all accounts, except for comments by Robertson and his spokesperson, it seems that personnel and the organization's culture played a far greater role in the firm's demise than that of the markets. The problem came from the fact that as Tiger grew and grew, and chased larger and larger pools of assets, the firm shifted from a collegial, informal atmosphere with a common goal and extremely serious place to work and manage money to a more corporate environment complete with bureaucratic issues and nightmares and internal fighting among its staff. The cultural change in the firm led to significant amounts of staff turmoil and turnover during its last years.

One analyst said that when he joined the firm, he worked with a group of people who were either fresh out of school or maybe had just completed their first job on Wall Street, and all were extremely hungry and extremely focused.

"None of us knew what we were doing so we took risks, not because we were gamblers but because we did not know any better. This led us to significant rewards—if I or any of us knew any better we would have been scared out of our minds, but back then it was simply par for the course," he said. "By the time I left, the firm was filled with Wall Street lifers who looked at going to Tiger as the last stop of the career. They were not hungry, they were not interested in taking risks, they were more interested in collecting a pay check than really working to build or maintain something that had some legs."

What went wrong with Tiger is similar to what goes wrong at many entrepreneurial shops that grow beyond their founder's expectations. The companies lose focus and go from being a place where ideas are generated to place where things are maintained rather than initiated. As Tiger grew, the firm became more and more corporate, it became bureaucratic, it went from being a place that people enjoyed freedoms to one in which the staff were forced to protect their fiefdoms.

It is clear that Tiger's evolution was based on Robertson chasing a dream and satisfying his competitive streak as being the best and most respected hedge fund manager of all time. But as the assets grew, the business model changed, and the bar kept being raised to new heights, and Robertson looked to gain recognition among his peers and contemporaries. Instead of hiring great young aggressive minds, who might not have a background in investing, he began hiring only senior experienced people, people who he believed had a perceived level of market and investment intelligence. During this same time, the firm stopped growing from within and started growing by the hiring of experienced talent from around the street. All-star analysts were hired, mutual fund managers were hired, and traders who had worked for years on many of the street's most important desks were hired. Without a doubt, Robertson had an ability to attract well-experienced people to Tiger; the problem was that the people were not necessarily able to add any significant value to the operation.

Many of the early employees said that when they joined the firm, if they wanted to talk to Julian, they could talk to him. By the time they left and as the firm grew, if they wanted to talk to Julian, they had to go through somebody else. It was not because Robertson did not like the analysts or traders or thought less of them or their ideas and abilities, but the firm had evolved from a place where ideas flowed and were generated in a collegial atmosphere to a place where people worked in their area and did not care about what anyone else did. All they wanted was to protect their area so that they could protect their paychecks.

Investment people lacked interest in new ideas or new areas

of the market. Many of the people the firm brought on in the late 1990s had been working in one or two specific areas of the markets and were true sector specialists. This posed a significant problem with the investment process. An analyst who was covering the automobile sector, for the most part, had little if any interest in anything else. This meant that at the Friday meetings, they didn't ask critical questions, and when *they* were asked critical questions, they took it as an affront to their abilities and not part of a sound investment process. In the end, this resulted in a number of very bad positions getting into the portfolio.

Some of these people were not interested in critiquing ideas and were put off by having so many young people around who they perceived did not have the level of knowledge that they professed to have about their industries or their segment of the market. The interaction between the people started to break down; people started focusing on what they knew and showed little if any interest in anything else. In the end, this hurt the firm because nobody seemed to care about anything other than what was going on in their area of the firm or their segment of the portfolio.

In the firm's early days, when one analyst left, someone from within would assume their role. However, as the firm grew, when an analyst left, instead of looking from within, Robertson went outside to find an analyst to fill the needs on the desk. He believed that hiring outside talent was a way to protect the franchise and that by going outside to find "the best" he could continue to maintain the firm's level of excellence in a particular market or sector.

According to a number of sources, in the early 1990s there were deal books—information packages about the firm—out on the Street for the purpose of selling Tiger or selling part of the organization, and everyone came up with the same thing: Without Julian, the model was not repeatable. Robertson's solution to this was to hire people who the Street would view as adding talent, which, in turn, created a platform and appearance of looking like Tiger was more than Julian.

Unfortunately, the firm's "experienced" people seemed to steer him to more and more wrong decisions. The firm made a series of bad macro bets, including losing significantly when Russia defaulted on its debt. (This occurred at the shock of many people as Robertson had looked to guidance on Russia from Margaret Thatcher and Bob Dole. Both had assured him a default was impossible.) The firm also began to fight positions. There were times when it would put on a position and see it go south and not believe that the research was wrong. Instead, analysts believed the *market* was wrong and that the position would eventually come out from under water.

And while bad decision making led to bad positions in the portfolio, many believe that another nail in the Tiger's coffin was Robertson's inability to continue working with those who left him. It is very clear that once you left Tiger, no matter how strong or tight your relationship with Julian was, it was significantly impacted when you decided to leave the firm. It did not matter if you went out to start a hedge fund or into a completely different business—leaving Tiger was a personal thing, and he did not like people to leave.

"I think that if you ask anyone if they talked to Julian in the first six months after they left the firm, you will get a resounding no. In some cases it took more than a year for him to be willing to talk to you," said one of the Tiger cubs. "It was a personal thing for all of us when we left, and he had a hard time handling it and really did not like it."

Robertson is like many of his peers: often viewed as a stubborn person who has a great ability to hold a grudge. This is something that clearly comes from his competitive nature and probably from his getting older. Toward the end, while he was willing to listen to those who questioned his ideas or comments, when it came down to it, his word was law, and if you did not like the decision you were free to leave. As he got older, he became more and more set in his ways and felt that his experience and expertise should not be questioned. It was this attitude that led him to fight positions rather than get out of them when they turned negative. Many have said that if Robertson had not been so stubborn and had not viewed the departures as personal attacks and as disloyal but rather as an opportunity, the firm would have been able to weather its problems.

Followers of the hedge fund and money management industry think that, in the end, the mistake Robertson made was not using the people who had worked so effectively for him to his advantage. "He should have gone to these guys and given them all a bunch of money and helped them get started—not banished them from the kingdom," said a former Tiger employee. If he had done that, he probably would be sitting on a $100 billion hedge fund complex today, and the whole dynamic of his existence in the industry would be different.

It is clear that he was willing to do whatever it took to win and be the best. He wanted the world to respect him as he perceived the world respected Soros. Robertson clearly wanted to be able to get a meeting with a central banker on a moment's notice and wanted to be looked to as the world's greatest investor. In the end however, he lost the investors' faith. They had come to expect profits from Tiger, and it was quite apparent that Robertson could no longer deliver.

11

THE TIGER CUBS

For more than three years, Julian Robertson has been retired from publicly managing other people's money. However, once an investor, always an investor, and as such, he still keeps his finger on the pulse of the world's economy. In this capacity, it is no different from when he was running Tiger, because he is in a constant state of looking for and finding the best and brightest investment ideas and exploiting them for his benefit.

Today, the Tiger money management machine has been dismantled. Robertson, however, still prides himself on using his vast network of sources to find out what is going on where and how he can profit from it. And while the phone is constantly ringing, one way he works today is through a group known as the Tiger Cubs. There is a group of 30 to 40 managers that Robertson invests with and counsels and seeks counsel from. At one point or another, all have worked with him or for him. Dubbed the Tiger Cubs by the press, the bulk of these individuals are former Tiger employees who, during the fund complex's reign, left to go out on their own. There is also another group of managers, the second generation of Tiger Cubs so to speak, that work in what used to be Tiger Management offices at 101 Park Avenue. Robertson is helping these managers along by providing them with back-office support and other tertiary money management services. He also is working with these managers to develop their organizations. These "Cubs" are the second generation of Tiger Management and have become the apparatus that Robertson uses to find value in the markets around the globe.

The second generation of Cubs–Cubs who run individual, independent funds–is being bred in the Tiger offices at 101 Park Avenue. When Tiger closed its funds it was not able to close its offices or get rid of its infrastructure, so Robertson turned the spacious facility into one of the city's hedge fund hotels.

"Julian realized that he did not really have any use for the facility and the capabilities and, more importantly, all the costs that go along with maintaining the infrastructure," said one ex-Tiger. "So he decided to do what any smart person would do: Find someone who could use the facilities and defray some of his costs while maintaining the infrastructure to handle his own needs."

"It was a very smart move," he continued. "By bringing these guys in, he not only covers some of his costs but he also gets a significant amount of idea generation without the costs of employing all the analysts."

Fifteen funds operated out of Tiger's offices in the spring of 2004. They were TigerShark Management LLC, run by Tom Facciola and Michael Sears; Tiger Asia, run by Bill Hwang; Tiger Technology, run by Chase Coleman; Tiger Consumer Partners, run by Patrick McCormack; and Emerging Sovereign Group, run by Kevin Kenny.

These funds have been able to step inside an organization and take advantage of 20 years of experience in the hedge fund business in about a second. There is no question that there is a lot of "Tiger magic" being spread around up there, and it is not a bad thing. The second generation of Cubs will probably prove, like the rest of the Cubs, to be some of the best managers in the industry. They're just earning their stripes differently than some of the other Cubs. Eventually, many believe that Julian's ideas about investing and making money will rub off on them. It's just a matter of time.

In each case, Robertson has invested in the funds and in some is a general partner, meaning that he shares in performance fees as well as investment profits. The group of managers meets with him regularly to go over ideas and talk about what is going on in the markets. It is not clear how their ideas affect his own trading, however, or how much influence he has over the positions that the funds take.

"When he closed Tiger, he still needed analysts and he still needed an idea factory," one ex-Tiger said. "By bringing these people in, he has been able to maintain his information flow. We don't know how much of the information he uses, but he must use some."

One of the successful spin-offs is TigerShark. Facciola and Sears run a "very boring" traditional long/short portfolio at TigerShark Management. They use a bottom-up strategy to identify sleepy stocks that they believe will add value to the fund. The pair basically scours documents and filings to look for investment ideas and once they find something they like, they hone in on it and dig as far as they can in order to make a good decision.

"We look at companies and try to figure out what is wrong or right with them," Facciola said. "We try to see if a company has a disease or a problem that the rest of the world has not yet found by doing as much research as we can on the company, its customers, its suppliers, and its competitors." By going as deep as possible, they try to get underneath the numbers and look beyond the management. It is a pure and simple boring strategy that never goes out of style. In the end, it is all about value.

Facciola and Sears worked together for at least six years at various Wall Street houses before launching the fund in February 2001. "We think most people don't really know what is going on in the market and that they look at the wrong things," Facciola said. "People invest on a lack of facts. Everybody is in the process of a witch hunt, but nobody knows what the witch looks like."

Facciola said the Tiger-Robertson relationship has enabled the partners to build their fund faster and to get better access to information and has banished a lot of the headaches of running a business. "We don't have to worry about accounting issues or other things that most managers who start out on their own do," he said. "We sort of just moved in and everything sort of worked."

Facciola said that managing a hedge fund is like "swimming upstream" every day. "Make no mistake, this is not a glamorous job," he said. "There are some days when I would rather bang my head against the wall because I am so bored with looking at information that I need to get out of the office and go home."

Their work has seemed to pay off. In 2003, the fund was down 5.5 percent versus the S&P 500 which was up over 26.3 percent, and the MSCI, which was up 30.8 percent for the year. In the first four months of 2004, TigerShark was up over 6 percent versus the S&P 500 which was down .42 percent and the MSCI which was up .064 percent for the same period.[1]

Chase Coleman may be one of the luckiest and smartest money managers alive. The twenty-something hedge fund manager has run Tiger Technology Fund since March 2001 with incredible success. The fund with more than $500 million in assets under management was up more than 50 percent in 2001 and 38 percent in 2002. It finished 2003 up over 14 percent, and in the first four months of 2004, it was up over 16 percent. A friend of Robertson's son, Coleman came to Tiger from school to do research and to learn how to manage money, and in a sense he has never left.[2]

"Our success is that we operate a hedge fund that is well hedged and takes a very long-term approach to making investment decisions," he said. "We take a fundamental approach to investing; remembering at all times that complacency is the enemy."

Coleman joined Tiger as a technology analyst right after graduation from Williams College in 1997 and has never looked back. "It is a good environment to run a truly hedged portfolio," he said. "We try to keep our finger on the pulse of the technology market, but because things change so quickly we have to be able to adapt and make adjustments as the market evolves."

"We realize that we don't know everything," he added, "but we know a lot about what we do."

Kevin Kenny thinks that he and his partners at Emerging Sovereign Group run the most liquid emerging market hedge fund on the planet. The fund, which was started in April 2002, had approximately $300 million under management when we spoke in the spring of 2004. Kenny, who works alongside partners Mete Tuncel and Yoon Chang, formerly ran the emerging market debt-trading business at Morgan Stanley. The group trades the debt of countries like Brazil, Turkey, Argentina, Mexico, Poland, and Russia.

"We only trade the government debt and currencies of these markets," he said. "These are the markets that time forgot, but now that the equity markets are under pressure, the dollar continues to be weak and the euro is getting stronger, people are looking for opportunities here and it is too late."

"We really try to speak to people on the ground and in the market to get a view of what is happening" both politically and economically, he said. "We take that information and apply fundamental analysis to make investment decisions."

Kenny, too, said working out of the Tiger complex is a big help. "Tiger is clearly one of the top 10 firms in the history of Wall Street," he said. "Working out of these offices, we have access to technology, accounting, and back-office systems and other things that have allowed us to stay focused on our main objective."

"There are a number of managers who I have invested with and that I believe in who I am introducing to old investors of ours who need managers," Robertson said. "Frankly, my set-up now is that I run most of my money and enjoy it and I don't have to run anybody else's so I don't have that conflict of interest when I am in New Zealand of, should I be here having a good time, or should I be in New York watching [the clients'] money."

Robertson said that he believes that one of the reasons that so many people look at him as one of the best money managers out there is because of the people who have left the firm and gone on to do great things in the hedge fund and money management industry. Many of the people that have walked through the firm's halls are now the leaders of the hedge fund industry. He relishes the success that his former employees have found with their funds and in the commitments these Tiger Cubs have made to other endeavors outside of simply making money.

His legacy continues to grow almost daily as former employees and colleagues launch funds and achieve great things in the industry. And in the three short years since the demise of the Tiger organization, Robertson is still the focus of newspaper articles, magazine profiles, and nightly business stories, not just because of his charitable work but because of his plays in such areas as the gold market and the equity markets and the success that his Cubs are having with their hedge funds. Not only are the Cubs successful at operating in the markets, but they are also successful at gathering assets—the hardest part of being a hedge fund manager.

In the fall of 2003, a number of market observers estimated that former Tiger employees managed close to 10 percent of all of the assets allocated to hedge funds and that the Tiger Cubs managed close to 20 percent of all of the assets allocated to long/short equity managers. The reality is that nobody really knows because unlike traditional funds, there is no single source or database of hedge fund data. However, if one were to do a quick back-of-the-envelope equation, it seems that the numbers would be rather close to being accurate. And even if the numbers are a bit off, what is accurate is the role that Robertson's Cubs play in the hedge fund industry. It has had an enormous impact on the way that money is managed, and most of these managers attribute their success directly to their experience working in the Tiger organization.

Robertson created a platform for success as Tiger Management evolved over the years that allowed for the cream to clearly rise to the top. He didn't give anyone a manual; he just let them watch, and as they watched they learned, and as they learned, they got better and better—to the point that they wanted to go out on their own. Many have said that the key to success at Tiger was their ability to pay attention to Robertson and what was going on in the portfolios. Simply put, if you paid attention, you could learn not only how to process and use information but how to build a business. It is clear that a significant number of people paid attention to what was going on and how things were getting done. But not all that glitters is gold, and one of the things that former Tigers talk about is that they learned what *not* to do as they built their fund complexes. They learned, in a sense, not to make the same mistakes twice.

Some hedge fund industry observers estimate that almost all of the 35 to 40 managers who have gone out on their own after leaving Tiger have hit the ball out of the park in terms of assets raised and performance numbers. Ex-Tigers have an uncanny ability to attract assets and build empires. When people read or hear stories of managers who go out on their own and find success, most of the time they are talking about Tiger Cubs or people who have left Tiger Cub shops. These are the people who raise $100 million dollars in the first week of existence, who by the end of the first quarter of operating have over $500 million in assets under management and by the end of the year have closed to new investors because they have all that they can manage and do not want any more.

Of all the former employees, only a handful have not been widely successful, according to a number of Cubs who keep track of each other. Many believe that the success rate Robertson has achieved during his 20-year reign will never be matched again—not in hedge funds, not on Wall Street, not anywhere in business. And nobody has a good reason why this is the case. It is like Tiger was, for a while, riding a continuous perfect storm, operating quicker, better, and faster than anyone else. It was getting the trades, making the profits, and gathering the assets. Unfortunately, the whole thing came crashing down like one big wave, but the aftermath has left a mark that has forever changed the way hedge funds operate and are looked at by people both in and outside of Wall Street.

The idea that one man or organization could have that great an impact on an industry is unbelievable. It really does not make any sense at all because things like this are not supposed to happen.

As Tiger grew over the years, so did Robertson's reputation as the manager to end all managers. People have called him the Wizard of Wall Street, and more than once the press has dubbed him the greatest manager of all time. He believes, though, that the real strength of Tiger was its people. The reality, of course, is that it's one thing to have a good team, but it's another to have a good team guided by a great coach.

"I liken him to Vince Lombardi," said one ex-Tiger. "Lombardi treated his people poorly, he made them work hard, and as a result, he got the best performance from his players at all times. Julian did the same thing."

Many people passed through the doors of 101 Park Avenue during the days of Tiger Management. Many of the folks went on to start new hedge funds, many left to go into other areas of the hedge fund business, and some retired to other industries altogether. Robertson believes that only one person who ever worked at Tiger left for a competitor. "About ten years later, this person came back to work for us and he told me that the reason he left was because he felt that we would really not amount to much," Robertson said. "But these people came in and sort of stimulated things and really drove me to make it better, and we did that throughout the 1990s."

Robert Burch, a former Tiger investor and lifelong friend, believes that Robertson's real strength and talent was his ability to pick people who have gone on to do such great things in the hedge funds. Burch is, of course, talking about the Tiger Cubs, the people who have come out of the organization and set up very successful hedge funds. Like Robertson, most of the Cubs are dedicated to the Julian–Alfred Jones model and style of investing.

Burch is speaking of people like Lee S. Ainslie III at Maverick, who runs about $7.5 billion; Griffin at Blue Ridge Capital, who runs more than $1.1 billion; O. Andreas Halvorsen at Viking Capital, with more than $3.5 billion; and Stephen Mandel Jr., who runs more than $4 billion at Lone Pine Capital. All of them have built extremely successful hedge funds, and all started at Tiger and served under Robertson in various capacities.

Robertson created an atmosphere where everyone wanted to work hard, where they wanted to please him. They knew that if you did not please him, he would become irate and lose his temper, and things would not be so pleasant. He got people to give him their best at all times. He made them work harder than they'd probably ever worked before and made them go further than they probably ever thought they could go. He led by

197

example as well as with fear. Over time, the genius of Tiger was that it was built as a platform for good managers—a place where talent could and did thrive. Robertson, like Alfred Winslow Jones, built an idea-generation and implementation machine. And like Jones, especially in the earlier years, Robertson kept very close tabs on his people to ensure they were doing what they were supposed be doing at all times and stayed focused on the task at hand—making money. Such personal investment in the firm and its analysts made it equally personal when someone decided to leave the firm. That's why it took several months for Robertson to cool off when someone decided to move on.

Many people have said that Robertson wasn't someone who just picked good people out of business schools or from other firms but that he was also able to get the best out of everyone who worked for him. He has an uncanny ability to find good people, get them to work for him, and make them work extremely hard—it does not matter if they went to the best schools or had the best pedigree—those things were fine—but he needed the people to pass his test.

"The people he hired were not natural-born hedge fund managers," said one former Tiger. "But, because he was so tough to work for, he forced us to be the best we could be at all times. He made us understand what was important, how to find it and process it, and make a decision based on it."

Robertson built a machine that churned out one idea after the next and operated on the premise that people needed to fight to get good names into the portfolio. Over time, it became clear that he expected that good names were to be replaced with better names and that the exercise would never end, as there was always room for improvement.

Robertson also believes that many of the Cubs share his commitment to the community. Many of them are involved in various charitable organizations, and some have even gone on to teach. It is questionable if these altruistic streaks in the Cubs character come from good upbringing or good on-the-job learning. Either way, Robertson prides himself on the work that his former employees have done in and outside of Wall Street.

As the years move on, the original Tiger Cubs are becoming bigger and bigger, and Robertson has relished his role in the development of the second generation of Tiger Cubs. This effort seems to be helping Robertson stay involved with the markets and also has allowed him to continue to use his skill at finding good people and helping them to build successful operations. He is proud of this second generation of Cubs working out of the office at 101 Park Avenue.

"Julian has surrounded himself with a bunch of young talents where he is seeding these new funds, who are independent but can use his office space, providing them with back office support, and letting them go," said Burch. "He makes himself available to these guys if they want, and so the drumbeat continues."

"He has some very attractive people, who I have invested in, because I see that they are the new hedge fund [managers]," he continued. "It is really wonderful, and both the Alfred legend and the Julian legend continue."

Hunt Taylor, an industry expert and manager of a fund of funds, likened Robertson's ability to find and teach good people to that of boarding schools that send their brightest students to the best universities. Taylor believes that while no one doubts that he was an extraordinary money manager, his real talent was his ability to attract the best and brightest minds, and, more important, really teach them how to manage money.

"If you look at the history of Wall Street, there are very few places that have spit out so many good people, but Tiger is truly a unique example of this," he said. "Over the years, people heard about this one or that one who came out of Soros, Moore, or Pequot," he continued, "but it was always one at a time, and was a whisper. When people came out of Tiger, they really stood apart from the rest, because investors knew the type of training and experience they got."

One of the things that many believed helped the Cubs was the rigor that Robertson put them through when it came to making investment decisions. There are many stories of his temper and of his sternness toward the people who worked at Tiger. While at the time it may have hurt, in the end it probably did the people more good than harm. In this business you have to be tough. You can't be a pussycat; a Tiger has to use teeth and claws to motivate people. It is a competitive business, and being nice isn't enough to be successful.

So along with building a successful money management organization in its own right, Robertson most likely—and probably completely inadvertently—built the most impressive hedge fund incubator of all time. Many have said that there will never be another manager like him. That he is truly one of a kind. He has a sixth sense for making money and driving people to be their best.

Taylor recalled a story that he was told by one of Robertson's analysts who had recommended shorting a Korean car company. The analyst had done some research and found that the company had a problem with one of its engines and that one model in particular was bad enough to do the company in. The analyst recommended that Tiger short the stock, and Robertson asked how the analyst had come to that conclusion. The analyst told him he had done the research and found the problem and wanted to exploit it. Robertson told him his idea wasn't good enough because the information was secondhand. So they both decided to buy two of the cars and have the engines tested independently. They found the problem and they shorted the stock.

"That is how high the bar was," Taylor said. "Today, many of the Tiger Cubs still perform at this level. It is truly remarkable."

The list of successful fund managers who left Tiger to run their own shops is quite long. It includes, besides those mentioned previously, Robert Karr at Joho Capital, Arnold Snider at Deerfield Capital, and Steven Shapiro at Intrepid Capital. Together, they manage about $17 billion as of the fall of 2003. K2's David Saunders runs more than a billion-dollar hedge fund-of-funds operation. The list goes on and on.

While the success of the Cubs' funds is not assured, their success in raising money just about is. Take, for example, Viking Capital. When the fund was launched in October 1999, it took in $500 million and immediately closed to new investors. Many have said that the firm's success came from investors' knowledge of its principals' experience working for Robertson at Tiger. Working for Robertson and at Tiger is like getting the *Good Housekeeping* Seal of Approval. It also does not hurt when he recommends or talks about a manager to former Tiger investors or friends in the industry. Once again the Robertson network comes into play.

Not only are the Cubs doing well in the United States, but former Tigers are also having success in Europe and in Asia. In 1999, Shigehiro Nakashin launched Crane Capital Management in Tokyo. At the time, Nakashin told a reporter that his style was to "focus strictly on liquidity," having seen what happened to Long-Term Capital Management. He planned to trade in highly liquid markets of the Group of Seven and Hong Kong.

The question still remains, however: Why did so many good managers come out of one organization? In a profile in the December 2002 issue of Institutional Investor, Robertson said that the people he hired were "highly intelligent, competitive and highly ethical." Besides being smart, Robertson also looked for people who were competitive and were jocks—in other words, people who liked to win.

In the 20-odd years of Tiger, most of the people who came through the door were people with athletic or near athletic backgrounds. Robertson shied away from hiring book smarts people—he looked for well-rounded people who excelled both in and outside of the classroom.

Robertson taught the Cubs his bottom-up stock-picking approach to the market. He emphasized the need for shorts and the need to get information at every level of an industry. Many of the Cubs say today they operate in much the same way.

"He taught us how to search for information and make decision on an investment only after exhausting all of our research capabilities," said one ex-Tiger. "The level of research that is performed on an investment idea is incredibly in depth. There are very few people who dig as deep as the Tiger people do."

One industry observer who has invested significantly with former Tiger managers said that the Cubs' organizations have a common denominator. The Cubs all realize the importance of having an infrastructure that handles operations and marketing and lets the analyst analyze and find ideas, and they all seem to spend more time working the shorts than they do their longs. They also share something else in common—they always seem to be fully invested. It seems that the Cubs like to have their money working for them at all times and are not interested in keeping it on the sidelines waiting to be put to work.

It seems the only time they make a move is when they find one thing they need to replace another thing with, and then sell a position, raise some cash, and make the investment. They do not keep cash on the side waiting for ideas to come along. They keep their money working constantly.

Robertson hired many people right out of the country's top business schools or from Wall Street's best training programs. For example, you will recall that Griffin, who was Robertson's right hand for almost 10 years, joined after working on a project for Tiger while at Morgan Stanley. "It was like going through boot camp," Griffin said of his experience working with Robertson at Tiger.

Griffin tries to capture the old Tiger as he scours the securities markets for investment ideas for Blue Ridge Capital, he says, using the skills that Robertson and his experience at Tiger taught him. Things like risk management, not worrying about price, and never having enough information keep him occupied—as does the importance of understanding the quality of the management and how it could be expected to operate under various market conditions. "We look at any company, anywhere in the world," he said. "But we try to keep our positions small; on average we run 200 to 350 positions and try to keep things simple."

Griffin said that one of the things that Robertson taught him was that you need to have conviction when making investment decisions. Simply put—you have to be willing to go for it. If you believe in something, price should not be an issue. It needs to be made part of the portfolio. If you don't believe in it or don't have conviction in the position, you need to forget it and move on.

Many of Robertson's disciples left the firm in 1999 to strike out on their own, but a number of people remained through the end of the year and through the end of Tiger. These folks found that by the middle of 2000, as the business was wound down, they needed a new job. So what does an analyst at Tiger do when he no longer has things to analyze? The answer is simple—go out on your own. In the late summer and early fall of 2000, many Tigers set off on their own. They were people like Patrick Earle and Mark Bader, who had managed the telecom and media operation, set up KiCap Management. Martin Hughes and Johnny de la Hey launched Toscafund and Robert Ellis launched Catequil Asset Management. In an article in *The Orange County Register*, Earle was quoted as saying that Robertson recruited people who "are entrepreneurially driven at heart" and so it made sense that many of the former employees had started their own businesses.[3]

Most of the former Tigers went into the hedge fund business, but a number took different paths. One former Tiger, after leaving the firm, went first into public service and then into the venture capital business. Jonathan Silver, a former chief operating officer at Tiger, became a senior policy advisor in the first Clinton administration and currently runs Core Capital. He launched the firm in Washington in 1999 to focus on early-stage investment in technology companies.

Silver reflected on his time at Tiger as a place of "great energy and spirit" and said that a real key to the success of the operation was that Robertson hired aggressive self-starters. "Working at Tiger gave each of us at a relatively young age a significant responsibility for parts of the overall portfolio," he said. "Julian pushed us to defend our investment theses with fact-based analysis. [Being] a Tiger was helpful in ferreting out information while we were there and remained an important badge after leaving the firm." Silver's comments echo Robertson's comments about his time in the Navy, when as a young man he was given great responsibility and put into a position of leadership with very little experience.

Besides teaching his employees about the markets and how to manage money, Robertson also instilled in all his employees a commitment to philanthropy. "When we went to work there, none of us had an idea about giving back to the community or making a difference. We were all concerned about making money and winning the game," said one ex-Tiger. "However, Julian taught us all that there is more to it than just making money."

12

LESSONS LEARNED
FROM THE TIGER

R ETIREMENT HAS NOT SLOWED ROBERTSON'S COMPETI-
tive edge. He has been and continues to be a perfec-
tionist; he is extremely competitive, and just because he
doesn't manage money for investors does not mean he has lost
his interest in winning. He's still involved in the markets, and
he's still "kicking ass and taking names" as he has done for more
than 20 years. His peers and former colleagues call him probably the best long/short manager who ever lived, and all believe
that he still has a lot of living to do.

Robertson still focuses on the global equity markets because
he feels they offer an opportunity to "go places where prices are
very reasonable." He is currently buying companies with very
high free cash flow—once a value investor always a value investor. The companies that are attractive to him are those that
do not have regular growth but do have free cash flow. He is
particularly interested in companies that have 16 to 20 percent
average free cash flow. This indicates a company's ability to
build outward.

When we last met, he had turned his sights onto opportunities in Asia, in particular South Korea. One of the country's top

banks was particularly attractive to him. His research showed that it was selling at about four times operating earnings and was growing at a rate of 25 percent annually. The company, whose American Depository Receipts traded on the New York Stock Exchange, was very liquid, very cheap, and was growing rapidly, three things that in his eyes made for a good investment.

When he first discovered the bank in South Korea, the company was growing at about two times earnings, and by the time he started investing, his research showed that it was capable of growing very rapidly to a point of probably around 10 times earnings. He believed that even at a growth rate of 10 times earnings, the company would still be awfully cheap and that it made sense to get into the name. Robertson believed that an opportunity like this was something that many other investors would be able to uncover if they did even the most basic of research. However, because of the political uncertainty in the region, which translated into a perceived but legitimate risk in investing in Korea, a lot of people are not willing to put in the work to find these overseas bargains. To him, this is even more of a reason to get into the stock—he is able to profit from their inability to move into these regions.

But while Asia and Europe offer a number of interesting opportunities, Robertson is finding most of his investment opportunities in what he calls the fifty-first state—Mexico. In Mexico, Robertson is able to find very reasonable stocks that trade at five times free cash flow and offer significant upside potential, as the economy is in a constant state growth and rebuilding.

One of the stocks Robertson had liked was Cemex. It's a worldwide cement company that he thought was very well managed and very well priced, but because it is based in Mexico, investors were unwilling to focus on it. He also liked the Mexican Coca-Cola company, saying it was very well priced compared to other stocks but was also overlooked because of its location. Robertson is happy to go into stocks in countries and regions of the world that others overlook because to him this represents opportunities. By going where others refuse or are afraid to go, Robertson is often able to extract significant profits, prior to things settling down or becoming more in vogue–it is like shopping at the store the day before they advertise everything is on sale and getting all of the merchandise you want at discount before anyone else even knows it's available.

While many people believe Robertson has shifted his focus to other things, such as his New Zealand projects and working with the community (see Chapter 13), he still remains very active in the market. A number of former Tigers have said that they believe that since he closed the funds, Robertson has earned more than 20 percent on his own assets over the last few years. They believe that he continues to trade actively and look for and is able exploit value in all corners of the globe. And while many believe the numbers are quite high, he would not comment on how well he's done since Tiger folded.

"Nobody knows how much he is managing, except that it is north of a billion, or how much he is up," said one ex-Tiger. "But all of us know that when he asks us how we have done and we tell him, he just gives that smile and says, 'Oh, really, 'cause I did this.' Make no mistake, he is still in the markets and is still ferociously competitive."

So what can we learn from Robertson? What made him so successful? What caused Tiger to collapse? What lessons did other hedge funds take away from Tiger's history? Robertson has been accused of being gruff–a hard taskmaster sometimes–but the real problem behind Tiger's demise was not Robertson's character or ability to manage or hire employees, or for that matter, to get along with and retain his investors. It rested in his inability to adapt his investment philosophy: finding value in the markets. That, coupled with the enormous growth that Tiger experienced over its 20 years of existence, was the recipe for his destruction. Remember, the market never spoke to him, and he does not subscribe to the idea that the market *speaks* to anyone.

"I hate that term, *learn the market*," he said. "You hear these people on television saying the market this, the market that, and the market is a *collection of stocks* which represents certain companies, and these people who say that the market has told them this and that—well, the market has never spoken to me."

Peter Lynch once told Robertson that the only thing for sure was that whenever he got a promotion, the market would go down. As such Robertson does not believe that anybody really makes any money playing the *markets*. He believes that the only way to make money is to buy stocks that are cheap and watch them go up—or short stocks that are overpriced and watch them tumble.

In his pitch, Robertson told potential investors that the way to search for value is to use fundamental research like that described by Graham and Dodd. He and his team knew of no substitute for careful and comprehensive analysis of investment situations. Their research process included not only rigorous financial analysis, but interviews with senior members of a company's management team and discussions with important customers, suppliers, and competitors. The aim was to understand how management thinks about their businesses and at the same time develop a clear understanding of the industries in which they compete.

To do this, Robertson understood the two most important aspects of reliable research: first, hire a staff with strong qualitative and quantitative skills, grounding in their specific area and relationships with knowledgeable and important people in that area. Second, separate the wheat from the chaff. Tiger's size and trading activities around the globe allowed it to take advantage of "the best research available" to do just that.

But his research entailed more then simply looking at reports or checking with customers. To a Tiger analyst, this was only the tip of the iceberg. In many ways, the work that Tiger analysts and Robertson himself performed to get a name in the portfolio or trade put on set the standard for how research is conducted at hedge funds around the globe. His was the model, not only for many of the industry's best and brightest managers who are former Tigers, but for the countless numbers of existing and potential managers who are emulating Robertson or his Cubs.

A key part of the research model was the firm's Friday lunch meetings, where ideas were presented. The analysts would gather around the table and go through ideas one story at a time, picking apart every little aspect and reviewing every angle of a potential investment opportunity to determine if it was worthy of being in the portfolio. "It was quite an exchange," said one former analyst. "It was the type of thing that you had to be prepared for and one that if you were not, you would surely get caught."

The Friday lunch was not a place to be unprepared *or* long-winded. Robertson likes hearing stories quickly and efficiently. "Get to the point or don't bother," was the way one former analyst put it. And the time limit was short–five minutes or so, sum it up, get it out, and move on. That was the nature of the meetings, and they worked. If something was too complicated, he would not like the idea.

Analysts were expected to sum up their investment ideas in four sentences. The four sentences may have consisted of six months of work, but that was all the time they were given to make their case and get the information in front of Robertson.

Besides using its domestic office for idea generation and creation, the firm relied heavily on its trading offices in London and Tokyo. They focused on providing research for the funds, along with harnessing Tiger's network of investors and contacts around the globe for market intelligence. The firm was able to take advantage of these extensive market contacts as part of an enhanced larger network of Tiger investors, many of whom offered valuable and unique perspectives on investment ideas in their own business sectors, regions, or countries.

Tiger had achieved significant strength in the ability to gather and process information but the backbone to its success and ultimate downfall was Robertson's conviction to his investment philosophy. In order for something to have a perceived value and be worthy of being in the portfolio, Robertson had to understand the idea's story. If the story was built on solid research, Robertson would stick with it, riding out a storm and maybe even adding to the position as it was going against him. Often, he eventually reaped the benefits of his convictions.

As long as the story was simple, logical, and it made sense, he would stay with it. However, once things became complicated, or the underlying story changed, he would lose his faith and conviction, admit that he was wrong, and get out.

It was all about winning. Robertson simply wanted to be the best money manager around, and the only way to do that was to put up the best performance numbers. What allowed him to be so successful was that his research was so thorough that even when other very smart, well respected managers were trying to get out of a trade, he would sit there and tell the trader to "buy em!"

There were many times, when people watching what was going on would say he was crazy and that they needed to get out of the position, and he would just sit there and buy up as much as the market would let him. For Robertson, as long as he had faith in his research in the idea, he did not care how the market was reacting. He would believe that everybody else had not done the work and did not understand the opportunity. A great example of this was when he stuck with his short copper positions when the market was rising, and everyone else seemed to be covering and taking the losses. He knew the story; he had done the math and knew he was right.

The firm also perfected the art of shorting. It was an integral part of Tiger's investment strategy, and it was one of the ways that Tiger truly set itself apart from other investment vehicles. Shorting allowed Robertson to enlarge his universe of profit opportunities and at the same time reduce the firm's exposure to losses when the market turned against them. This is the defining characteristic of hedge funds in general and of the Tiger investment approach in particular. The reduction in market risk made possible by investments in shorts allowed him to take on greater amounts of individual company risk—a very desirable tradeoff, from his perspective.

Tiger "shunned" *market risk* because it believed that it had "no particular ability" to forecast or determine the overall direction of the market. However, the team was active in finding *company-specific risk*, because it believed its ability to analyze those risks was one of the firm's greatest strengths.

Robertson really pushed the use of leverage in hedge funds, as well. The investment strategy was such that at any given time it would not be unusual for the gross value of the firm's stock positions to be two or three times its underlying investment capital. During these periods, it would not have been unusual for its net long position (longs minus shorts) to have been only a fraction of its underlying investment capital.[1]

This is not something uncommon in the investment world, but for some lay people the following example should explain how this would work. The manager would be long 10,000 shares of stock X at $10.00 per share, which equaled a position of value of $100,000 and would be long 10,000 shares of stock Y at $5.00 per share, which equaled a position value of $50,000. The fund's long exposure would be $150,000. At the same time, the manager would short 10,000 shares of stock Z at $7.50 per share, resulting in a short position of $75,000. Adding the longs and the shorts together, the fund would have a net long position of $75,000.

Through the use of leverage, Tiger was able to commit capital aggressively to the best long and short investment situations. Leverage allowed the firm to increase exposure to the best opportunities available while reducing overall market directional exposure.

While the use of leverage contributed significantly to the firm's success over the years, Robertson's ability to understand risk was what allowed it to post such significant profits. It was not unusual for him to OK an investment decision based on an analyst's recommendation and then go behind the analyst's back and double or triple up on the position.

"He would constantly challenge your ideas and question how much could really be put to work in an idea," one analyst said. "In the end, I don't know what he used to determine what level he was comfortable to go to. All I know is that in more cases than I can remember, he always went north of my recommendations. And for the most part, he was right."

Robertson's conviction led him to take risks that analysts may not have approved, but his conviction also forced him to look to people outside of his inner circle for advice in areas in which he or Tigers did not have expertise. While he relied on his people for their strength and judgment to see a position, he often questioned it.

Once a trade was put on, there was a constant fight on the life and size of the position between Robertson and his analysts. Sometimes, he would want to make it bigger even though the analyst would tell him that it was not a good idea, and there were times when the analysts thought they should commit more capital, and he would refuse. There was a constant back and forth between Robertson and his analysts as to how big or how small a position would be, and it all came down a profit and loss statement. The P&L became a weird notional thing, because analysts would look at positions and figure out what they would have lost or made had Robertson put the trade on the way they had *recommended*, versus what he had done. It was a relationship that worked out great sometimes. At other times it didn't, and there was nothing an analyst could do about it.

Robertson pushed his analysts to look for the trades that went beyond the obvious choices (buy Wal-Mart, sell Kmart), to find the hidden treasures. Throughout his career at the helm of the Tiger funds, Robertson prided himself for knowing as much as he could about as many companies as he could. His ability to retain information is legendary and was sometimes the source of friction with his colleagues.

It was this constant learning process and searching for value that allowed Tiger over the years to increase its assets under management significantly. With this increasing amount of money, Robertson's investment style began to evolve from focusing on straight equity-based value plays to more of a global macro style that employed many different strategies. As he developed Tiger's analytical staffs, growth stocks also became a very good investment. If the analyst was right on the growth, the growth stocks would be tremendous performers. There may have been a year or two when they suffered, but if they were true growth stocks, then they would continue to grow and build out over time.

Most people do not understand investing or investment strategy. However, with the proliferation of technology and, more importantly, the rise of the Internet era, many believe the investment playing field has been leveled. Over the last six or seven years, investing has become a national pastime of sorts in the United States as men, women, and children, tune in, log on, and buy or sell. And while most people think this is good, there are many who believe it is amusing and in some cases, downright sad.

One of the hardest questions to answer on Wall Street–or any street, for that matter–is, what makes a good portfolio manager? Tens of thousands of people try to answer that question every day behind desks and in cubicles in almost every city in the world. The simplest answer lies in the performance numbers, but how do you get the performance numbers? You have to come up with a methodology and a time period to look at and then answer an even harder question: Does past performance predict future results?

The answer is unequivocally no. The reason is simple: No two markets are ever the same. History, for the most part, does *not* repeat itself, so the idea that you can look at something that has already happened to see what is going to happen tomorrow is absolutely ludicrous. Skill sets, not systems, is what allows one money manager to perform better than the next over time. And that is why Robertson and his colleagues at Tiger did so well regardless of market conditions. They understood how to search out and find value and, more importantly, understand the value. Robertson and his Tigers looked past the trends and truly saw the forest through the trees because they knew what to look for and how to find it.

However, this style of investing has fallen out of favor over the last few years. During the bull market, everyone was a star. It seemed no matter what they did or how they did it, managers of all shapes and sizes made the right decisions and made a lot of money for their investors. But after the bull left the building and the technology bubble burst, extracting profits from equity markets became so hard that most people failed. Managers could no longer just buy this technology stock or invest in that initial public offering and earn 20 percent before lunchtime.

During the late 1990s, it was easy to get into a position in a stock that everyone liked and make some money. Today, things are much more difficult. Today, the hardest part is figuring out what to get into before everyone else gets into it and make money without following someone else's lead. That being the case—follow the leader is and will forever be a very important game. It is alive, well, and quite active on Wall Street. And while some schoolchildren grow out of it, Wall Streeters play it all day long, regardless of market conditions, sentiments, or situations.

Picking winners is very hard. No one can possibly do it all the time; most can't do it half the time. So what managers have to do is get information from this source or that source, speak to this friend or that friend, and sometimes basically follow one person's leads and then another's. The key is the flow and access of information. Careers are made and lost on one manager's ability to access, gather, and process information. Robertson throughout his life has understood this and used it to his advantage, and it is something that all of the Cubs use as well. They understand the value of information and, more importantly, how to use what they get to extract profits from the markets.

When it comes down to it, there are very few original thoughts on Wall Street. And most people are afraid to come up with one, let alone put capital at risk if they haven't heard about it from someone who is already in or had it checked out with a bunch of people before taking a position. Sure, most people do their own research, but even the best managers don't commit capital unless the information is checked and rechecked. The market and performance are too important, and the simple research is too risky to just throw capital at an idea that they *think* is going to work. Successful managers want to commit capital to trades that they have a pretty good idea *are* going to work.

There are tens of thousands of individuals who call themselves money managers. These are people who manage money at hedge funds, mutual funds, proprietary trading desks, and other places with pools of capital. On Wall Street, there are many ways to skin a cat; when it comes to managing money, there has never been a more accurate statement. Everybody has an idea and a system for picking stocks or forecasting rates that they think will allow them to extract a little bit more from the markets.

"To think that all money managers can simply be put in this bucket or that bucket based on what they do or how do it is totally ridiculous," said Paul Wong, manager of Edgehill Capital, a hedge fund in Greenwich, Connecticut. "Two value guys may have similar ideas and look at things in a similar way, but because each of them is human, their decision-making process is completely different, and what they do with the information and how they come to conclusions is not the same at all."

Robertson describes himself as a classic A-type person, incredibly gracious, extremely pleasant, but willing to do whatever it takes to win. When David Saunders of K2 Advisors first joined the Tiger, one of his predecessors, told him that joining Tiger was like getting on a roller coaster. Initially, he would be put on a pedestal and be considered one of the firm's great assets, but slowly, after about three to six months working at the firm, he inevitably would become "a dog," and whether or not he could rebound from that point would determine where he stood with Robertson—and that, in turn, would determine how long he would be able to stay at Tiger. "This guy told me that it was inevitable that I would go from being great to being the worst guy on earth," he said. "But he also told me that it would not only happen to me but that it would happen to everyone, it was just the type of place it was, and it was how the firm was operated."

People who did not come out of the tailspin got the picture

that it was time to leave and moved on to other opportunities. Those who didn't—well, Robertson was keen to identify their weak spot and exploit it until they had no choice but to leave the firm. It was kind of like if you have a sore, and you keep picking it, and it gets bigger and bigger until finally it gets infected, and you can't take it anymore. Eventually, you want to get some medical attention and get it treated. The treatment was to leave the firm.

Although the ribbing might have gotten out of hand sometimes, Saunders said one of the hardest parts about leaving the firm was leaving the people. He said that most people really felt like they were part of a team and that all of them, regardless of how bad it was, admired and worshiped the coach. Robertson was running a very successful hedge fund, and after all, hedge funds have been and remain the place to be on Wall Street.

Indeed, for the last fifty-odd years, hedge funds *have* played a big role in the marketplace but, in my opinion, they will never replace the top guns of the investment world as the most important investment vehicles on Wall Street. It is clear that the best and brightest minds are the people behind the hedge fund industry, but that does not make them the most important. When it comes down to it, size matters, and hedge funds, no matter how mainstream they become, will never gather as much assets as the large mutual funds. This, too, is a lesson we can take away from Tiger Management.

Hedge funds have two weaknesses that limit their appeal to the public. First, because hedge funds do not have any standardized (read *regulatory*) reporting requirements like those placed on the mutual fund industry, no one, regardless of how thorough they tell you their database is, is able to really track hedge fund performance and assets. And while recently Morningstar, the famed mutual-fund tracking service, announced it will begin tracking hedge funds, until it has mandatory reporting requirements, the database is not going to be worth much. Second, no matter how much product is pushed down the throats of retail and institutional clients, no matter how much or how little Congress and the Securities and Exchange Commission tighten the rules, and no matter how badly retail investors want to invest in hedge funds, they will never eclipse mutual funds, pension plans, and plain-vanilla savings accounts because the masses are not willing to look at them and are not willing to spend the time to learn about how they work in order to invest in them. These weaknesses mean that hedge funds will never be able to match mutual funds in size and scope.

The largest equity-based mutual fund at this writing is Vanguard's S&P 500 index fund, with more than $94 billion under management, while the largest fixed income-based mutual fund is the Pacific Investment Management Company's Total Return Fund, which had assets of $73 billion under management at year end 2003. The second-largest equity fund was Fidelity's Magellan, with just under $68 billion in assets under management. In comparison, the largest hedge fund complex (complex means more than one fund) managed somewhere just south of $20 billion in early 2003, with the largest equity fund being approximately $2.5 billion and the largest fixed-income fund at $4 billion in assets under management.

Vanguard and Fidelity manage nearly $675 billion and $955 billion, respectively; the largest hedge fund is barely more than a rounding error on these firms' balance sheets. And in my opinion, no amount of regulation or marketing will ever change that.

"What Jones did with hedge funds is clearly important and it has had a significant impact on the financial services marketplace, but it is nowhere near as important as what [John] Bogle [of the Vanguard Group] did when he created the index fund,"

Bob Burch said. "He single-handedly changed the way people are able to invest in America and lowered the bar of investment so that everyone from nearly all walks of life can actually invest in and own part of what is great about America and capitalism."

Some will argue that as laws change and regulations become more user-friendly, the hedge fund industry will grow. However, the funds that grow, many industry observers believe, will not truly be hedge funds; what they will be are alternative investment vehicles that may represent one segment of the hedge fund industry. As they do this—as hedge funds have become more and more popular and mainstreamed—some believe that they are losing their edge.

Alternative rock was not an alternative any longer when Nirvana and REM reached number one on the *Billboard* chart and made their way onto Casey Kasem's Top-40 Countdown. And that is what has happened to some "hedge funds." They have gone mainstream.

Over the last 10 years, Wall Street has been abuzz about hedge funds. Whether at a cocktail party, a birthday party, a market event, or an investment conference, everybody always talks about these so-called alternative investment vehicles.

Hedge funds are the forbidden fruit in the investment Garden of Eden. People of all backgrounds, from all walks of life, are interested in hedge funds—what they do and how they do it. I find it quite thought provoking. Why do people care, and what is so important about these investments, that people have so much interest in them?

This insatiable appetite is traced back to two events in the mid-1990s. The first was the Asian flu and the ensuing collapse of the Asian economy being blamed on George Soros, and the second was the Russian default and the role that it played in the near collapse and subsequent bailout of Long-Term Capital Management LP.

Hedge funds, and Soros in particular, became the scapegoat of Asia's poor economic policy in the summer of 1997 when Malaysian Prime Minister Mahathir Mohamad said "that a foreign financier was upsetting currencies to pursue his own political agenda." Although the prime minister never mentioned Soros by name, it was clear that Mahathir believed that he was "responsible for attacking the currencies" because he opposed Burma's joining the Association of Southeast Asia Nations (ASEAN).[2]

"We ask ourselves," said the prime minister while traveling in Japan, "is it just speculation to make money, or is it something else? We feel that there is some other agenda, especially by this particular person."

"If they want to attack the British pound, by all means do so. Britain is rich," he continued. "Malaysia is [a] poor country, and it is not right for people like these to play and speculate in our currency."[3]

Then and now, the Soros Foundation and the Open Society Institute, both philanthropic organizations, sought to promote democratic government in Burma and elsewhere. Soros had spoken publicly against unnecessary travel to Burma because he believed the military government there, called the State Law and Order Restoration Council, had used forced labor to build tourist attractions and hotels.[4]

During the summer of 1997, Shawn Pattison said there was "absolutely no connection" between the philanthropies and Soros Fund Management, the hedge fund operation, refuting Mahathir.

"I can see how the misunderstanding may have arisen here, as Mr. Soros has been quite vocal in his urging the governments of Thailand and Malaysia not to admit Burma into ASEAN," Pattison said. "He continues to consider totalitarian repressive regimes threats to the region's prosperity and stability."[5]

Despite Soros's views, Burma had recently been admitted to ASEAN. He believed that the government was running an economic regime that is a disaster for Burma. It had practically no currency reserves and had a totally artificial value for the currency, which gave it a chance to favor its own people within the government's inner circle, so to speak, to the detriment of the general population. For example, anybody who had permission to, let's say, buy gasoline at the official price could resell it to those who did not have the same right or permission and make a living on it. Soros believed that it was a totally corrupt regime.[6] Because Soros voiced his opinion about what was going on, he was blamed for the Asian flu that swept the region. It is unclear if he went short the currency or took other action to take advantage of this situation.

This was not the first time the Hungarian-born investor was on the front page because of his global macro investing. In September of 1992, Soros had made headlines as the man who broke the Bank of England (refer back to Chapter 2), and now he was at it again. What Mr. Mahathir failed to realize is that by going after Soros and hedge funds, he helped fuel interest in the industry.

For the three years from 1995 to 1998, it seemed as if everyone and her brother were starting hedge funds. During this time, the bull market began to show signs that it was going to break out and brokers, traders, mutual fund managers, and market participants of all shapes and sizes could smell the money. The time of the hedge fund was upon us. One of the fastest and easiest ways to make it on Wall Street is to start a hedge fund. One of the overriding facts about Wall Street is that nobody thinks they get paid enough. Everybody wants more and is always looking for ways to get it. Hedge funds are one place people look when they are fed up with their boss, their bonus, or their job. During the mid-1990s, this was clearly the case. (The same, by the way, can be said of the industry today.)

"It was a strange time. For a while in the early part of the decade, hedge funds were not important but were something that people thought of after the fact," said Peter Testaverde, a partner at Goldstein Golub Kessler, an accounting firm in New York. "Then all of a sudden people started to get excited about hedge funds, and before we knew it, it seemed like everybody was trying to get into the business in one way or the other."

Unlike mutual funds and individual stocks, there are no formal reporting guidelines or exchanges that keep track of how many hedge funds are in the marketplace. A number of database services and consultants do offer advice of varying quality on the number of hedge funds and comment on performance and assets under management, but for the most part, the information is guesswork. "It is impossible to track the industry because nobody really knows how many funds exist and how many there are in operation at any given time," said Testaverde.

In May of 2003, at the Securities and Exchange Commission's Hedge Fund Roundtable, Chairman William Donaldson said in his opening remarks that there were more than 5,700 hedge funds operating in the United States, with approximately $650 million in assets under management.[7] However, many who follow the industry closely believe that there are somewhere between 2,500 and 3,500 *true* hedge funds operating at any given time, and that they manage collectively somewhere between $250 billion and $750 billion around the world.

In the late summer and early fall of 1998, as the effects of the Russian and Asian crises became clear, the market for hedge funds all but dried up. News of the losses and potential losses of Long-Term Capital Management rocked the world's financial markets to their core. John Meriwether and his team of Nobel laureates and rocket scientists ran into a brick wall—or, rather, crashed into it like a meteorite. Roger Lowenstein wrote a must-read book about the rise and fall of LTCM in *When Genius Failed.*

The interesting thing about the collapse, from a hedge fund manager's viewpoint, is not that it threatened to devastate the world's economy, but that it put hedge funds back on the map. And it wasn't a good part of the map, either. Before the near-meltdown, hedge funds were an anomaly. The press covered them rarely and talked only about the three big boys, Soros, Steinhardt, and Robertson.

Michael Steinhardt, of Steinhardt Partners, had suffered his first significant losses in 1994 (close to a billion dollars) and ended the year down, the first time in the history of his operation. The losses came from a bad trade in the European bond market. But in 1995, Steinhardt decided to close his fund, so the press had one less subject to cover. Steinhardt Parthners finished 1995 up over 20 percent. An investor who had put one dollar with Steinhardt at the birth of his fund and kept it there until he closed it 27 years later would have seen that investment grow to $462.24. That dollar invested in the S&P 500 for the same period of time would have been worth $17.06.[8]

People were still interested in Soros because of his run-in with the powers-that-be in Asia. The interest in Robertson came from the unbelievable performance numbers he was putting up (up 56.1 percent in 1997 versus an S&P gain of 33.4 percent and an MSCI increase of 15.8 percent).[9] By 1998, though, only two big boys were left. Steinhardt had retired in 1995, and the pickings for the press were slim. The only time the press bothered to write about hedge funds was in the annual stories about how much money was being made by the managers.

But thanks to LTCM, September 1998 became the month that put hedge funds above the fold in newspapers around the globe. The stories started after someone leaked a letter that John Meriwether had sent investors asking for new capital to "take full advantage of this unusually attractive environment" in the marketplace. He also asked for investors' patience and cash.

Meriwether needed money to meet margin calls and was experiencing a classic cash squeeze. He believed that the new capital would buy enough time for the fund to keep going until the markets turned. This was no different than when a homeowner looks to borrow some money from a friend or relative in order to make a mortgage payment.

Meriwether believed that lack of free cash was the only thing that kept it from performing and presented it with a financial crisis. The people at LTCM thought that if they could plug all the holes in the dam, they would be able to buy time and the trades would work in favor of them instead of against them. All they needed was cash.

The firm basically needed a rich uncle to help them get through the hard times. In time, Meriwether proved to be right, and all of the parties that helped in the bailout not only earned back their money but also got a return on their investment. It seems that the only people who did not get anything out of the fund were the initial investors whose stake was severely reduced after the bailout.

In Meriwether's case, his rich uncle was not Uncle Sam but Uncle Wall Street. In September, after exhausting all efforts to secure financing and help on his own, Meriwether turned to the Federal Reserve Bank of New York. David Mullins, then president, summoned the street's "poobahs" to discuss the fate of the massive hedge fund. Not since the days of J.P. Morgan nearly 100 years earlier had Wall Street's biggest and brightest gotten together in one room to save a financial institution—and themselves.

These were desperate times and, as we all know, desperate times call for desperate measures. The word at the time was that

Goldman Sachs and Merrill Lynch had made such big margin loans to LTCM that the Fed was worried that two of Wall Street's most powerful players might go belly-up should the fund be liquidated. If a hedge fund can't meet its margin calls, all its positions are sold immediately—in most cases at fire sale prices. However, in most cases, the meltdown ends with the fund. If LTCM went down, though, the New York Fed apparently feared that the final scene would look more like the end of Sodom and Gomorrah, and everybody would get burned.

Many are still uneasy that the Fed orchestrated a bailout. Of course, the question is, why did LTCM receive this special treatment? I, for one, don't believe this has been explored thoroughly enough by the press. Fourteen companies committed sums ranging from $100 million to $350 million to a fund of more than $3.5 billion so LCTM could meet margin calls and cover operating expenses. There is still a question as to why the bailout was needed and if in fact it was because the fund was too big to fail or because too many people "in the know" had too much invested in the fund and did not want to lose their investments.

While no one knows for sure, some have estimated that the liquidation of LTCM might have wiped out more than $1 trillion in value from the global markets.

By the start of 1999, LTCM's fortunes had begun to turn. The fund reported profits and announced that it would buy out its saviors, or at least give them back their capital. Less than a year after the bailout, Meriwether announced that he would wind down LTCM and start a new investment vehicle. By the early fall of 1999, LTCM had returned close to 75 percent of the bailout capital. The consortium announced "the portfolio is in excellent shape" and that the risk profile of the fund had been reduced by nearly 90 percent.

As part of the deal, LTCM's partners were allowed to operate a new fund only after they had repaid 90 percent of the loans.

By the end of March 2000, most of the money had been repaid, and by the end the year, Meriwether was again operating at a new hedge fund called JWM Partners. His goal was to reach assets of more than $1 billion, but his reach again exceeded his grasp.

In February 2001, Meriwether spoke at the Managed Funds Association annual Network conference in Miami's South Beach. He discussed the need for transparency and the need for investors to understand what they were doing when they bought a fund. I believe it was the first time he had spoken publicly since the bailout, and it was truly amusing. The idea that one of the most-secretive money managers of all time was talking about the need for transparency was quite a hoot. Since LTCM's inception, Meriwether and his team of brain surgeons had shrouded their operation in secrecy. The idea that this Midas trader was now advocating transparency—well, it was clearly different. LTCM's demise had caused the growth in the hedge fund industry to come to a screeching halt; now it seemed Meriwether's calls for transparency were going to usher in a new era.

Still, some in the audience thought something else. The *New York Post* quoted one person as saying "Maybe he was out in the sun too long," noting that it was 85 degrees in Miami that week. Another called Meriwether's speech nothing more than "a desperate act by a desperate man longing to get back into the limelight of an industry that wishes to forget him."[10]

In time, however, Meriwether's call for transparency and openness proved to be correct. In the post-LTCM hoopla, the hedge fund industry suffered a couple of setbacks. First, because of all the bad press, many institutional investors decided that to protect their jobs they should move assets from hedge funds to more conservative vehicles, like mutual funds. Then the dot-com bubble burst, and many hedge-fund superstars found they were little more than overpaid stockbrokers who couldn't handle a volatile market.

Remember, the key to a successful hedge fund operation is to "keep your clients wealthy, not to make them wealthy." This is very hard to do if all you are doing is evaluating stocks based on the news of the day, because once the news goes south, stocks will go with it. You need more to your investment strategy than just buying what everyone else is buying. Many of the hedge funds that expanded in this go-go era were not able to deal with the market when it turned from bull to bear and took a real hiding.

"The problem with being in the money management business is everybody expects you to do well, regardless of market conditions. When you exceed the market and beat your benchmarks, tons of money comes in. When all you do is beat the benchmark by a few hundred basis points, investors look at you and say, 'So what?' " said William Michaelcheck. He's chairman of Mariner Investment Group, a New York hedge fund complex that manages more than $4.5 billion in assets.

Hedge funds face another tough job in collecting fees once they've had a bad year or two. Most hedge funds have a *high-water mark*, stipulating that the fund will collect incentive fees only after investors are made whole on their original investment. So, if the fund loses money in year one, the manager cannot collect incentive fees until the investors get all the original investment back. The problem with this, from a manager's standpoint, is that if the fund loses 20 percent in year one and earns 20 percent in year two (a good recovery by any standard), the manager still won't earn any fees. In this case, it would take a return of 25 percent to make the investors whole. That's why some managers take uncharacteristic—and sometimes fatal—risks.

But Robertson had left his Tiger Cubs better prepared. As the markets rose and plunged in the early 2000s, funds of all shapes and sizes and strategies and styles were launching. Once again, it seemed like everyone wanted to get into the hedge fund game. Several of the funds were run by the Tiger Cubs who had taken over 101 Park Avenue. When they entered the game, the markets were starting to rebound from the dot-com crash. A year later, though, the industry was in a tailspin. Once again, many managers were battered by big losses. While the S&P finished down nearly 23 percent for 2002, some hedge funds lost as much as 30 percent or 35 percent! The question that many investors and third-party marketers asked as the numbers rolled in was, "How were these guys hedged?" The answer was they weren't. They had not mastered the hedging strategies Robertson had drummed into his Cubs. Many funds consolidated, many funds closed, and many managers ran for cover.

During the early days of 2003, the press and some financial institutions estimated that close to 6,500 hedge funds were gathering assets from institutions and rich individuals. By the middle of the year, some of the same people were saying that more than 1,000 funds had closed, were closing, or were on the verge of going out of business. The market had weeded out the bad apples. Not everyone can be or should be a hedge fund manager.

After the LTCM collapse and subsequent recovery, lots of managers and investors wanted to be in hedge funds. The problem was, there are only so many positions on the field at any one time, so there is room for only so many players. In 2001 and 2002, the hedge fund industry became overcrowded, overbought, and eventually oversold. Many of the fine men and women who started their own funds found that even though they built it, the investors never came.

"The only thing my lawyer, accountant, and prime broker forget to tell me when I was launching my fund was that it was going to be very hard to raise assets," said one start-up fund manager who requested anonymity. "Besides being the chief cook and bottle washer on the money management side of the business, I am also the chief cook and bottle washer on the money-raising side of the business. It is very tough, very tough. It seems like we are all competing for the same investment dollars. In this environment, nobody wants to take a chance with a new kid on the block."

However, those with the right pedigree seemed to have little if anything to worry about. For those sprinkled with a bit of Tiger magic, the money just seems to appear in their coffers. Most of the Tiger Cubs weathered the stormy markets well, and most have seen their assets balloon as investors look for what they believe is quality. This has helped maintain Robertson's legacy over the last few years.

In 2003 and 2004, the hedge fund landscape was still undergoing changes. Recently there have been more calls for regulation for hedge fund managers, and the industry as a whole seems to be waiting to see what, if any, regulations will be put in place. Also, over the last few years, many of Wall Street's most familiar firms have gotten into the hedge fund game. For a while, it seemed as if the brokerages were interested only in providing execution and clearing services to hedge funds. As the market for stocks dried up and investors found bonds too complicated, both wire-houses and regional brokerages looked to hedge funds as something they could sell regardless of market conditions.

Hedge funds had traditionally been open only to the high net worth investors and institutions, but the big brokerage firms started rolling out hedge funds for both their merely affluent as well as their rich clients to battle the malaise affecting Wall Street. Their financial advisors needed to have products to sell to clients, and traditional products don't work when the markets are down three years in a row. Hedge funds offered clients something new, something different—and something that had been forbidden since they were invented in the late 1940s.

Most wire-houses and regional firms now have some sort of hedge fund or fund of hedge funds—either under development or already on the market. In 2004, the average investor with as little as $25,000 could get into a hedge fund or, more likely, a fund of hedge funds. The problem is that many hedge fund managers have forgotten the most important thing—how to hedge. "The idea of a hedge fund is to protect assets in bad markets and profit in good markets," said Dale Jacobs, president and manager of Financial Investors LLC, a New York hedge fund complex.[11]

If used properly, however, many believe that hedge funds can be a way for the average investor to tap into investment expertise that they otherwise would only be able to read about. This democratization of hedge funds allows the average investor to diversify away from traditional equity and bond portfolios and into strategies that, in theory, aren't correlated to major market movements. That should limit losses in down markets and permit gains, if smaller gains, in up markets. However, with the recent rally in the major markets, hedge funds may come off the front burner and go back to the back burner as financial planners, brokers, and the like can once again sell traditional long-only products.

It is unthinkable that anyone can have year after year of stellar performance without a hiccup now and again. After all, these people are just a bunch of humans, and humans make mistakes.

Robertson commented on the recent interest in hedge funds: "The great advantage of hedge funds is: (a) You can make money on both sides of the market, and you are not just sitting there when the market goes down; and (b) You should feel some comfort in that almost all of these things are run by people who have put most of their equity into there, so not only do they have the most to gain from the 20 percent, but they also have the most to lose through their participation.

"I also think that the money that the hedge fund industry will offer will attract people away from those old-line types of business like the banks and mutual funds."[12]

The problem of late, however, is supply versus demand. Most of the funds with good track records have closed to new investors, and many of the funds that are open are not big enough to take money from institutional investors.

"It is very hard to get money placed with really good hedge funds," Robertson said. "To put a billion dollars into good hedge funds is literally almost impossible. And what I think can happen is that you will get a law of adverse selection: You won't get any of the ones that are great and who have closed up, and you will get the guys with no real talent who nobody is interested in investing with."

In the end, Robertson's tenure at Tiger Management taught the industry much about hedge funds—not only through his philosophy of value investing and his history of stellar returns, but also through his tactical errors that led to Tiger's downfall. Over the years, it has become more and more apparent that the good funds that remain nimble and can bob and weave through the markets are more apt to find success and keep it than are those who simply chase assets.

"Today, all of my people have left, and they have realized the mistake that we made was that we got too big," Robertson said. "I always had the feeling that if you got the talent to keep up with assets, then it did not make any difference how big you got. The trouble was, and I sort of overlooked this, the buffet table got smaller and there wasn't as much to choose from, because to make it meaningful we had to buy a huge amount of a company's stock, and there were only a few companies we could buy a huge amount and be liquid." Robertson believes that many good hedge fund managers realize this, which is why they have closed their funds to new investors. That knowledge is yet another part of Robertson's legacy, which for the most part he has created by building the most successful hedge fund in history. Moreover, he has used the profits from Tiger to build major philanthropic organizations and, most recently, resorts in New Zealand. This part of his story is discussed in the next chapter.

Robertson believes that his legacy to the industry is the record that he established at Tiger and the people who helped him establish it.

"A reporter came to me and told me about a story he was working on about the 25 best managers, and that 8 of them were ex-Tigers," he said. "We have all of these great people out in the industry, and we have a cadre of new ones here at Tiger who are beginning to find their way very well in the markets, and they have fantastic records and that together is a legacy."

13

NOBLESSE OBLIGE

G IVING BACK TO THE COMMUNITY IS A COMMON THEME on Wall Street. For as long as people have been making money and buying or selling securities in lower Manhattan, it seems that they have also, spent a fair amount of time trying to make the world a little better by giving back to those less fortunate.

Robertson and his colleagues are no strangers to making the world a better place. Giving back to community both through their time and their money is something that seems be as natural to them as managing money. Over the years, he and his family and his former colleagues have contributed tens of millions of dollars to causes and organizations around the world. Unlike some of his hedge fund contemporaries, Robertson seems to give to organizations and groups that draw little if any attention. There have been namings and articles written about his generosity, but his acts of kindness seem to be more of an invisible hand of sorts than ones made on the idea of getting ink.

In the hedge fund community, getting involved and doing good with the riches that these investment vehicles provide is rooted in the work of Alfred Winslow Jones. Jones, who with his wife Mary was very committed to the city of New York and a

233

number of charitable organizations, played a significant role in helping the city become a better place.

Jones looked at his hedge fund business as way to make money to do other things. As a businessman, he was not particularly interested in the markets or individual stocks but was more interested in using his hedge fund profits as a way to provide for his family and to give back to the community and to explore his interests outside of Wall Street. Many of the former Jones' people are still quite actively involved in community and arts programs as a result of his work in the community. And while his legacy to many is the creation of hedge funds, there are a few people who believe that his true legacy should be the fact that he gave so much of his time and money to charity based on his success as a hedge fund operator.

One of the programs that was very close to Jones and his wife was the Henry Street Settlement. Jones was drawn to the work of Henry Street through his travels abroad. During a number of these trips, he heard criticism from people who said the people of United States were eager to help those in other countries but did little to help those inside its own borders. The Henry Street Settlement was founded in 1893 by Lillian Wald to help people build better lives. Henry Street provides programs that range from transitional residences for homeless families and a mental health clinic to a senior services center and a community arts center.

Tony Jones (Alfred's son) is on the organization's board of directors, and his sister, Dale Burch, is the president of Henry Street. Together, they have worked very hard to educate hedge fund managers about the organization and its programs in hopes of raising awareness for Henry Street and to tap into some of the money that hedge funds are giving back to the community.

Philanthropy is found in almost every corner of the money management and investment business. Some of the world's greatest and most influential philanthropists are former and present Wall Street Titans. People like Ace Greenberg, Sandy Weil, and John Mulheren have made giving back a significant part of their respective operations.

Over the years, Wall Street has been very active in helping the community. There are many legendary stories of the firms' forcing their employees to contribute to everything from the arts to education. Companies like Bear Stearns have made it such a significant part of their operation that some employees have said they often think they get compensated based on their generosity.

At Bear Stearns, many employees have no choice but to allocate a specific amount of their annual earnings to some charitable organizations. Giving back is so important to the people at the top that if employees don't make a decision where their money should go, the powers that be at the firm make the decision for them and may potentially penalize them for their lack of interest.

Some say this "forced giving" is not so altruistic and has become more a function of working at the firm, rather than a function of the heart. It has become the stuff of legend, and many former Bear Stearns partners and employees make it a part of their new organizations. Along with training new investment bankers, money managers, brokers, and traders, Bear Stearns and some of the other great Wall Street firms have also trained the philanthropists as well.

The idea behind this kind of generosity seems to be that because the Street has been so good to so many, there needs to be a sharing of the wealth. And while many give purely as a function of trying to do good things with the riches that the Street has given them, there are many who believe that a significant portion of the money that gets donated to medicine, the arts, and community programs is a function of ego and oneupsmanship.

Many believe that the competition that exists on the floor of the exchanges, on the desks of investment bankers, and at the trading turrets has been transferred to the world of philanthropy. These masters of the universe have gone from being the biggest and brightest trader, broker, or investment banker to the most important givers to places like Carnegie Hall, Lincoln Center, the Metropolitan Museum of Art, and of course the hospitals and universities. Giving to charities in New York City, and probably all of the world's major financial centers and cities, has become a way of keeping score and of telling the world just how well someone is doing.

"Look, there are very few ways that people can show just how successful they are that is so public and out there than by naming a building or program after themselves," said one planned giving officer at large New York-based charity. "By giving money to put a name on a building or program, everybody immediately knows how much was donated, who it came from, and just how well that person is doing. When it comes down to it, it is great for us because we get the money and can do great things with it, and at the same time, we can use the gift as a tool to go after other people in the same industry and really play the gifts off each other in order to get even more money for our programs."

To be fair, there are many people who give money to programs not simply because they like to see their names in light. Many do it because they truly do want to make the world a better place. One of these people is George Soros. For the better part of the last decade, Soros has made a more than significant commitment to rebuilding Eastern Europe and funding various programs to make the world a better place. He has literally given hundreds of millions of dollars to educate individuals to help those "societies" where there are reformers who want to make the society more open through supporting independent media, restructuring educational programs, and supporting democracy through the Open Society Institute. According to tax records, in 2001 alone, Soros, contributed more than $150,000,000 to the Open Society Institute, which gave grants out totaling more the $139,000,000 to individuals and organizations around the world.[1]

George Soros has clearly taken the concept of Wall Street giving back to a new level: There is almost no one in the Wall Street community and any other community for that matter who has done so much to help so many people in the name of teaching and learning and creating democracy around the world. It is truly a remarkable thing that he has chosen to do. In doing so, he has once again set the bar extremely high for those in the hedge fund world who aspire to build an organization like his, both professionally and privately. Soros has chosen not to stand by idly when it comes to politics as well. During the 2003-2004 presidential campaign season, Soros gave more than $10 million to defeat George Bush. It was his personal mission to defeat the "Bush doctrine" in 2004.[2]

And while there is truly no one who can compare to the level of giving of Soros, the hedge fund community has been active in supporting and working with their communities—men like Paul Tudor Jones and Rob Davis have put giving back at the forefront of the industry. Jones created the Robin Hood Foundation, while Davis was the driving force behind Hedge Fund Cares. Together the two have raised millions of dollars to help people around the world. Robertson and his Tiger Cubs are actively involved in both groups. Many of these people are often thought of as ruthless traders, brokers, and investors, but they have made giving back a significant part of their lives.

Over the years, Robertson and many of the folks at Tiger have given generously to the arts, education, homeless, and health care. Robertson, like his contemporaries at Bear Stearns, made giving back a cornerstone of the ideals that were at the heart of the Tiger organization. Indeed, there are very few causes that someone from the Tiger team has not contributed to over the last 20 years, both in and outside of New York.

Robertson believes that he learned this generosity from watching his parents' commitment to their community over the years. One of his philanthropic tools is The Tiger Foundation, launched with a number of colleagues in 1990. Its purpose is to "provide financial support to top nonprofit organizations serving New York City's neediest families and to encourage active, informed philanthropy among the firm." During Tiger's reign, Robertson encouraged many of his colleagues not only to give money but also to give time, by taking part in the grant process and by serving on the foundation's board. It supports organizations that "work to break the cycle of poverty" and tries to avoid working with programs that "merely alleviate its symptoms" in favor of programs that provide families with the tools they need to "attain self-sufficiency and in turn build protective lives."[3]

The people at Tiger were encouraged to look at programs and organizations with the same keen eye that they looked at potential investment opportunities and, in turn, make educated, calculated decisions on where their money would go, no different than when they made investment decisions. Over the years, Robertson and his team would dissect many potential programs to ensure that their money was going to be put to use properly and was actually going to get to the people that the program promised it would get to. The idea was to truly understand the programs and evaluate how they worked, what their impact was, and what benefits the programs offered. Robertson encouraged his team to go out into the field, meet with executive directors, look at the books of the organization, meet with its employees, it clients or participants, and really try to learn about them in order to make an educated decision about supporting the effort. As Tiger thrived, the Tiger Foundation thrived. Over the years, Robertson and his team gave millions of dollars to programs in and around New York City.

Today, the foundation is still working to complete its mission of helping disadvantaged children and their families, including working on preventive programs. Although the money management firm is closed, the foundation is active, and many former employees contribute generously to its coffers on a regular basis. According to an Internal Revenue Service filing in November 2002, the foundation had just under $12 million in assets.[4] Its contributors included many of the firm's former employees who have now gone on to run their own hedge fund shops and, in turn, their own foundations. According to Internal Revenue Service records in 2001, the Tiger Foundation gave more than $3.4 million to groups in and around New York City.[5]

The Tiger Foundation supports a number of educational, vocational, social service, and youth development programs in an effort to reach people before they fall into a cycle of poverty and welfare. In 2001, the foundation provided grants to a number of programs in and around the five boroughs. They included the Boy's Club of New York, Bronx Preparatory Charter School, The Henry Street Settlement House, The Doe Fund, Child Care Inc., Project Reach Youth, and CityKids Foundation. Because the money was earned in New York City, the money is supposed to stay in New York City. Robertson believes that it is fine to help out other areas of the world, but when it comes to the Tiger Foundation, the money goes right back into the City in which the profits were created.

"Julian is very interested in having us learn about various programs and having us understand where the money is going and how it is going to be used," said David Saunders, the managing partner and founder of K2 Advisors, a billion-dollar-plus fund of funds, and a former trader at Tiger. "He wants us to see how we are impacting others so that we continue to give. He has meetings with various people who come in, and over the course of an evening explain to us how our money is being spent, what it is being used for, and how the programs are being benefited by our contributions."

Saunders and a number of former Tigers believe that Julian's philanthropic ways have severely impacted them and the way they look at the world and their role in it. Robertson has taught them that by supporting the Tiger Foundation and others like it, they can really help people who need it and not simply give money or be involved simply to show off to other colleagues or competitors.

In 1998, Robertson went a step farther in his efforts to be involved in the community by establishing The Robertson Foundation. This foundation has a much broader mandate than the Tiger Foundation as it works to support programs and issues around the world. According to documents filed with the Internal Revenue Service in October 2002, it had more than $352 million in assets. Through the foundation, Robertson and his wife Josie give to organizations that include education initiatives, church and religious groups, the arts, and medicine. In the 12 months ending November 30, 2001, the foundation distributed more than $18.9 million, according to documents filed with the Internal Revenue Service.[6]

"Julian is someone who tries to help everyone he can," said Dale Burch, a longtime friend. "I am sure over the years he has probably said no to somebody, but I don't know of anyone that he has turned down. He really wants to help people and make the place a little bit better."

In the early summer of 2004, The Robertson Foundation had more than $500 million in assets that was being used to make the world a better place. According to Bill Goodell, the president of the foundation and general counsel of the current Tiger organization, when Julian and his family decide to support a charity or organization, they look for specific results from their gift—no different than when Robertson makes an investment in a security. There is a high expectation, and when the foundation gives out the money, they expect to see a return. They feel obliged to get a return for the money.

"He and the family view what we are doing with the foundation's [assets] in the same way in which he invested in the stock market," Goodell said. "They are looking for ideas and opportunities that will have an impact; he wants to see a return on those monies."

And while Robertson knows that he will not see the returns on a financial ledger, he does use a performance ledger to determine if the money was spent and used appropriately.

The family and some close friends set priorities as to where the money will be given out and Julian and Goodell work tacitly alongside Josie and his sons throughout the year to make the gifts.

One such effort is an investment the foundation made in the New York City public school system. Robertson joined with Eli Broad of Sun America and funded some of early School's Chancellor Joel Klein's strategic planning exercise on reconfiguring the school department. An outcome of that work was the charter school initiative, which will start approximately fifty charter schools in the city over the next few years.

"If it works, Joel will be able to use the schools as laboratories for pushing the public school system to emulate the best practices and hopefully raise the bar on education in the city," Goodell said. "Our success will be their success."

Robertson has been an active supporter of the Robin Hood Foundation. The Robin Hood Foundation's single objective is to end poverty in New York City and the hedge fund community—people like Lee S. Ainslie III, managing partner of Maverick Capital Management; Stanley Druckenmiller, chairman and CEO of Duquesne Capital Management, and Dirk Ziff, vice chairman of Ziff Brothers Investments—digs deep.

The organization is known for their lavish annual galas, which in the past have featured Jerry Seinfeld and Led Zeppelin's Robert Plant. At the foundation's 2001 gala, one bidder paid $420,000 for a yoga package that included a session led by Madonna and Gwyneth Paltrow. Another anonymous bidder paid $54,000 each for "A Year with the Titans," ten lunches with some of the most prominent figures in business, including George Soros, Jack Welch, Warren Buffett, and Rupert Murdoch.[7] In its annual report filed with the Internal Revenue service for the year 2002, the foundation gave out more than $42 million to programs in and around New York City.[8] The auction in June of 2004 saw one hedge fund executive pay $300,000 for a round of golf with former president Bill Clinton and Mike Weir the left-handed Canadian who won the Masters in 2003.

Most of Robertson's philanthropic endeavors remain private, but one of his best-known gifts is probably the surprise $25 million gift he gave to Lincoln Center in honor of his wife. One of the single largest gifts ever given to the arts center, $10 million, has been used to create the Josie Robertson Fund for Lincoln Center. It supports a number of programs, including a "Midsummer Night Swing" and the "Live from Lincoln Center Festival" television series. In return for his generosity, the center's board named its fountain plaza in Josie's honor.

Beverly Sills, chairwoman of Lincoln Center, said the gift was notable not only because it was the largest in the center's history, but also because it was unrestricted, which meant that the organization could decide where the money was spent and how it was to be used.

Over the years, Robertson has also given sizable gifts to the University of North Carolina, as well as supporting legislation to limit automotive exhaust emissions and working to improve the educational system in Florida.

"Now that it is just my money that I am managing," he said, "it really does not matter how I spend my time. It would have not been right for me to spend so much time working on these types of projects when I was managing my partner's money."

One of the less conventional things he has done is to give $24 million to set up joint scholarships at the University of North Carolina and Duke University. The 30 Robertson Scholars, 15 from each school, are required to take classes at both universities and to live for at least a semester at each.

Robertson decided to set up this program because these two schools are about nine miles apart, and there has really not been much interaction between the two schools except for a legendary sports rivalry. He believes that by encouraging interaction between the two schools, a community between the institutions will emerge that is based on something more than who wins or loses a basketball game. Over the last few years, the program has become very desirable to students because it allows them to attend one of the best state schools in the country and one of the nation's top private schools. Established in 2000, it's the first joint scholarship program with the two universities. Each school received $12 million; a spokesperson at the University of North Carolina said it was the single largest gift by a living person in school history.

Robertson said at the time that the reason he established the program was because he realized from meeting a number of his son's friends who went to UNC that he missed a lot by not knowing the people at Duke, and he thought that many people who went to Duke missed a lot by not knowing the people at Carolina.

Robertson Scholars take some classes together. Their scholarships are valued at $100,000 over four years. They also provide the scholars with transportation between Chapel Hill and Durham, a laptop computer, and paid summer internships.

According to Mike McFarland, director of university communications at University of North Carolina, the schools will evaluate the program's effectiveness and its financial requirements during its fourth year of operation.

Robertson scholars are chosen on the basis of academic performance, commitment to public service, and leadership skills. Winners enroll in one campus and earn a degree from one university but are given a certificate showing that they have studied on both campuses.

In the winter of 2003, 30 freshmen and 30 sophomores were in the program, equally divided between Duke and UNC. Dr. Eric Mlyn, director of the program, said that the program will top out at 120 students in the next two to three years.

Chris Paul, Duke Class of 2005, said it has been "truly amazing" being Robertson Scholar. "This is more than just a merit scholarship where they give you a check and send you on your way," he said. "It is really a program that has brought the two communities together and really brings together people who want to not only make a difference in the university community but also do something to change the world."

Paul said a highlight of the program for him was the summer internship experience. In 2002, he worked at the Wilderness Society in Atlanta, and in 2003, he expected to go to South Africa and work in Cape Town on projects including environmental land reform and international development.

University of North Carolina sophomore Johanna Rankin said that the experience is unlike anything she could have ever imagined. In February 2003, the double major in French and international studies had just moved into her dorm at Duke and was beginning to experience life outside UNC. She spent the first semester of the 2002–2003 school year in South Africa, so adjusting to life at Duke was relatively easy.

"Being a Robertson scholar has given access to so many opportunities that I don't know where to start," she said. "Think about it, I am a UNC student with all the benefits of being a Duke student, right down to my university email account."

Rankin said that the current group of scholars is the program's guinea pigs and that as the program continues it will grow and "become even better than it currently is."

There is both an academic and sports rivalry that exists between both schools, and things really heat up around basketball season. As a Robertson scholars, the students are asked to talk to people, be ambassadors on campus, and to get people thinking about both schools, apart from which has a better team or which has higher academic standards. They work to foster community.

Along with supporting education, Robertson is also working hard to help the environment. One project that he worked on was California legislation requiring tougher auto emissions standards.

Governor Gray Davis signed the bill in July 2002 that mandates that the California Air Resources Board develop a plan for the "maximum feasible reduction" in tailpipe emissions, especially of carbon dioxide, from cars and light trucks, to go into effect in 2009. California is the only state not bound by the federal Clean Air Act because its laws predate the federal statute. Thus, California can set tougher standards than Congress.

"The technology is available. It's affordable. And it's widely utilized in other countries," Governor Davis said in a statement. "We're merely asking business to do what business does best: innovate, compete, find solutions to problems, and do it in a way that strengthens the economy."

Charles Territo, speaking for the Alliance of Automobile Manufacturers, which opposed the bill, said "This is an effort by California to put a finger in the eyes of Congress. Our belief is that we should issue tax credits for vehicles that reduce fuel consumption and get better miles to the gallon."

Robertson said he believes it is time we all stop polluting the environment and starting making it better so that we can all breathe a little easier. He thinks the time has come to stop throwing all these poisons into the air and changing the atmosphere. In Robertson's opinion, pollutants are flowing into the air only because automobile companies have big lobbies with self-interested people who are looking to make a buck while poisoning the atmosphere.

Besides working with former Tigers to give through the Tiger Foundation, Roberston also works with a number of former colleagues on initiatives and charitable programs. John Griffin was instrumental in Robertson's work with the University of Virginia's McIntire School of Commerce. In November 2000, the school dedicated a state-of-the-art trading floor in honor of Robertson after Griffin, along with a number of other former Tiger employees, raised close to a million dollars to honor their mentor. The Julian H. Robertson Jr. Capital Markets room resembles the trading floor found in any brokerage firm, complete with flat screen monitors, tickers, and trading and information software. The room serves as a classroom for students and a virtual research laboratory for teachers.

Students and faculty say that the room and all its technology is the equivalent of learning how to play baseball at Yankee Stadium.

Another of Robertson's favorite pursuits is art. He calls himself a late bloomer when it comes to many things, including art. Today, he prides himself on a collection that includes paintings by Matisse, Cezanne, Bonnard, Picasso, and Diebenkorn. His love for paintings came to him in his forties when he realized that he was missing out on "something spectacular."

"I got married late in life and on my honeymoon, I remember my wife took me by the Jeu de Paume [in Paris], and I said, 'Let's get out of here, I don't like this place,' because I really had not grown up yet," he said. "Now I love art, and I can't believe it took me such a long time to grow up."

His offices at 101 Park Avenue are hung with pictures that

any student of art would recognize. His collection has been the focus of a number of exhibitions, including one at the North Carolina Museum of Art where he displayed five paintings. Unlike other exhibitions where visitors are often worn out at the end, this exhibition, "filled you up without wearing you out" and allowed the visitor to give each work the time it deserved. The exhibition's three Picassos were *Woman with Hairnet (Femme a la resille)*, 1938; *Seated Woman, Red and Yellow Background (Femme assisse, fond rouge et jaune)*, 1952; and *Head of a Woman (Tete de femme)*, 1943. The exhibit also included Braque's *The Pedestal Table (Gray Vase and Artist's Palette) [Le gueridon (Vase gris et palette)]*, 1938, and Leger's *Pistons (Les Pistons)*.[9]

Visitors for years have admired a number the paintings in Robertson's collection that are hung at his apartment in New York and his other homes. One such admirer was Lawrence Wheeler, director of the North Carolina Museum of Art. Wheeler, after visiting with Julian and Josie, thought he could set up a small exhibition of a number of the important pieces in their collection. So he stripped the walls of the couple's living room of its pictures and put on a very fine exhibit.

In his so-called retirement, Robertson has found time to work on a number of projects outside of his endeavors in the hedge fund world. For example, he is involved in the development of parts of New Zealand. Robertson's love affair with New Zealand began when he chose it for his family's sabbatical in 1979. In a TV interview with Charlie Rose in July 1998, Robertson says, "I went to New Zealand because I thought it had the greatest geography in a small area of anyplace in the English-speaking world. I subsequently found out the island of Kauai in Hawaii has a bit more, but nevertheless, it was a fabulous experience. It was one of the great events of my life; we loved it."

"Josie was a saint to go with me and put up with me. We had

one great time down there. It was a splendid experience because nobody really has the material things that we have in the U.S. down there."[10]

Over the years Robertson's love for New Zealand has grown. Today he and Josie spend quite a bit of time there as he works on a number of projects. One of them is The Lodge and Golf Course at Kauri Cliffs, near Cape Brett. The 4,800-acre resort is near Matauri Bay, on North Island, 3 hours and 45 minutes north of the capital of Auckland, with a 180-degree view of the Pacific. Visitors have said that the best way to get to the property is by "going to the end of the earth and then going two stops further." Robertson said that the property derives its name from the giant old kauri trees on the estate (which he and Josie have given to the Queen Elizabeth II Trust for Conservation), and the 500 young kauri that have been planted on the property in an effort to return the land to its original forested state.

Robertson bought the property in 1997 as an investment, but then he realized the land needed to be developed. In an article in *Town & Country* in June 2001, he said that the deal was like "buying Pebble Beach for the price of a modest New York apartment."[11]

His first goal was to build a golf course. Robertson teamed up with designer David Harman, who is known for his work with Arnold Palmer and Jack Nicklaus, to create the par-72 Kauri Cliffs course. The course, which *Golfweek* has called one of the five best in the world, includes six ocean-side holes. "It is the most spectacular course I have ever played," said one friend of Robertson, who visited the property in Spring 2002. "Every hole is prettier than the next. It is just amazing; the views are just unbelievable."[12]

The course has four sets of tees, ranging from 4,940 yards for the yellow ladies' tees to 7,125 yards for the championship (what else?) Tiger tees.

"The whole course is distracting," said Dale Burch. "Everything is so pretty that every time you go up to a tee you don't know if you should take a swing or take a picture."

There's no waiting for tee times. The lodge is open to only 40 visitors at a time, and the course is so far from civilization there's no other place to stay. Robertson and his wife worked with architects both from the States and New Zealand to build it, completing it in just ten months.

The plantation-like main house includes the Tiger room, just off the main hall, decorated with an enormous Iranian tiger carpet that once was in Robertson's offices in Manhattan. In addition to the main house, guests can stay in eight two-suite cottages nestled down the hill from the lodge.

The staff consists mainly of people picked by the Robertsons, including some from the Deepdale, their golf course in Locust Valley, New York, and from the fly-fishing resort Huka Lodge, also on North Island.

Robertson is also developing another golf course and lodge on Hawke Bay, 200 miles southeast of Auckland on the Pacific, and had recently purchased a 30,000-case-a-year winery called Te Awa.

His friend and longtime investor, Bob Burch of A.W. Jones & Company, summed up Robertson's efforts in New Zealand: "Julian is using the same energy now that he had in the mid-1980s and 1990s and focusing it on building great golf courses, and really creating a tourist industry for New Zealand. He is full of energy and full of imagination, and it is really wonderful to see him in action."

Kauri Cliffs is just the first of a number of projects Robertson plans over the next few years, forever etching his name on the island nation as he has around the world.

Working with the new Cubs, developing interesting real estate projects, and working on various charitable activities has come easy to Robertson in his "retirement." This work remains extremely rewarding to Robertson and is something that he takes very seriously. Like Jones, Robertson has found great pleasure in using his wealth to help others. "He has a great lust for life; this is a fun guy," said Aaron Stern. "He is a person who–once you experience him–has an effect on your life. He is contagious–in the sense that he brings out some of the most positive qualities in human nature."

APPENDIX

TIGER MANAGEMENT GREW FROM A SINGLE ONSHORE hedge fund to a hedge fund complex that consisted of both onshore and offshore investment vehicles over its lifetime. Robertson created products that were marketed to both qualified purchasers and accredited investors. *Qualified purchasers* are defined as individuals or family vehicles with at least $5 million in investments and other entities with at least $25 million in investments. *Accredited investors* are defined as individuals with a minimum net worth or a joint net worth with spouse in excess of $1 million or having an income of $200,000 per year or $300,000 per year, respectively. The product offerings for the firm were as follows. This list was taken directly from the marketing piece titled *Tiger The Record . . . The Reasons:*

Tiger Fund. The first fund that Robertson and McKenzie launched in 1980 was organized as a New York limited partnership that was open only to qualified taxable U.S. investors. The minimum investment was $5 million.

Jaguar Fund. This fund was launched in 1980 as the offshore version of the Tiger Fund for qualified U.S. tax-exempt and non–U.S. investors. The minimum investment in Jaguar was $5 million.

Puma Fund. Launched in October 1986 as a New York limited

partnership for U.S. qualified taxable U.S. investors, Puma employed the same strategy as all of the Tiger funds but also used leverage and took advantage of less-liquid private placement opportunities. The fund had a four-year lock, and the minimum investment was $3 million.

Lion. Launched in July 1997 as a New York limited partnership, Lion was open to accredited investors. It employed the same strategy ats the Tiger Fund. The minimum investment was $5 million.

Ocelot Fund L.P. This fund was launched in July of 1997 and modeled after the Puma Fund. Tiger worked with Donaldson Lufkin and Jenrette, who acted as marketing and distribution agents for the fund to qualified investors.

Ocelot Offshore Fund L.P. This was launched in August of 1997 and modeled after the Puma Fund. This was the offshore version of the Ocelot Fund, which was marketed by Donaldson Lufkin and Jenrette to qualified U.S. tax-exempt and non–U.S. investors.

Tiger Growth of $1.00 (1980–1999)

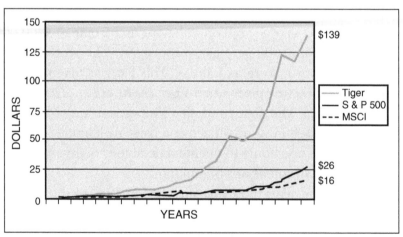

Source: "Tiger: The Record . . . The Reasons," *The Wall Street Journal,* www.standardandpoors.com and www.MSCI.com

The Tiger Record

Year	Tiger	S&P 500	MSCI
1980	54.9	28.9	21.8
1981	19.4	−4.9	−4.8
1982	42.4	21.5	9.7
1983	46.7	22.6	21.9
1984	20.2	6.3	4.7
1985	51.4	31.7	40.6
1986	16.2	18.7	41.9
1987	−1.4	5.3	16.2
1988	21.6	16.6	23.3
1989	49.9	31.7	16.6
1990	20.5	−3.1	−17.0
1991	45.6	30.5	18.3
1992	26.9	7.6	−5.2
1993	64.4	10.1	22.5
1994	−9.3	1.3	5.1
1995	16.0	37.6	20.7
1996	37.7	23.0	13.5
1997	56.1	33.4	15.8
1998	−3.9	28.6	24.3
1999	19.0	21.04	24.93

Source: "Tiger: The Record . . . The Reasons," *The Wall Street Journal*, www.standardandpoors.com and www.MSCI.com

NOTES

Introduction
Information for this chapter was gathered through interviews and meetings with former Tiger employees and colleagues of Julian Robertson's as well as members of the Burch and Jones family.

Chapter 1–Making Money in Metals
1. Tsukasa Furukawa, "Sumitomo calls Hamanaka actions criminal; copper trading losses increase to $2.6 billion," *American Metals Market* (September 20, 1996), 1.
2. "Copper scandal won't go away," *Purchasing* (December 12, 1995), 32.
3. This event was told to me by an analyst who listened to the call between Robertson and Druckenmiller.

Many of the events depicted in this chapter are based on conversations and meetings with former traders, analysts, and market participants who asked not to be named. The sources are from highly respected organizations and who, in some cases, acted as executing brokers for Tiger and its affiliates and worked closely with Sumitomo during and after the copper scandal hit the company.

Chapter 2–The Birth of a Tiger
1. Martin Donsky, "When a Tiger Is King of the Jungle, "*Business North Carolina* (August 1990).
2. "Julian Robertson dies at 95," *Salisbury Post* (February 22, 1995), 1.

3. Ibid.
4. Ibid.
5. "Julian Robertson dies at 95," p. 1.
6. Ibid.
7. Mary "Holtie" Woodsen is Mrs. Robertson's niece and still resides in Salisbury, North Carolina.
8. This information was gathered from I.R.S. Form 990, filed on behalf of the Blanche and Julian Robertson Family Foundation on March 16, 2003.
9. "City Loses an 'Angel,'" *Salisbury Post* (December 29, 1993), 1B.
10. Ibid.
11. Robertson provided a copy of the eulogy he read at his mother's funeral.

To research and write this chapter, interviews were conducted with friends and colleagues of Robertson and his parents, as well as individuals at local media outlets, the Navy's office of public information, members of Historic Salisbury, and other sources who observed and were part of Robertson's days in Salisbury.

Chapter 3–A Southerner on Wall Street

1. Gary Weiss, "The World's Best Money Manager–What You Can Learn From Julian Robertson," *Business Week Assets* (November/December 1990).
2. Sidney Cottle, Roger F. Murray, and Frank E. Block, *Graham and Dodd's Securities Analysis,* 5th edition. (New York: McGraw-Hill Trade, 1988) p. 4.
3. Conversations with Bob Burch, fall of 2002.
4. Reprinted by permission of *Fortune* magazine–All rights reserved.
5. Investors short a stock when they believe its price will fall. They borrow the stock from a broker, hoping to pay back with lower-priced stock. For example, if the stock sold for $20 a share when the short-seller borrowed it, and she replaced it at $10, the profit would be $10 a share, minus fees and commissions. If the stock rises by the repayment date, of course, the short seller loses. By using a series of short positions, savvy investors are able to profit in both good markets and bad markets.
6. Today, A.W. Jones & Company exists as a fund of funds that is managed by Burch. He would not comment on how much the firm has under management.

The information from this chapter was researched through interviews of former colleagues and associates of Robertson's during this period of his life.

Chapter 4–The Tiger Finds New Hunting Grounds
The information from this chapter was researched through interviews with former Tiger employees and investors.

Chapter 5–The Tiger Begins to Growl
1. Performance numbers for this chapter were provided by Julian H. Robertson Jr. through a document titled *Tiger The Record . . . The Reasons*, 1999 version.
2. Memo to Limited Partners from Julian H. Robertson Jr., January 17, 1985.
3. Memo to Limited Partners from Julian H. Robertson Jr., March 5, 1985.
4. Ibid.
5. Conversation with Julian H. Robertson Jr. in June 2002.
6. Memo to Limited Partners from Julian H. Robertson Jr., April 4, 1985.
7. Ibid.
8. Memo to Limited Partners from Julian H. Robertson Jr., May 24, 1985.
9. Ibid.
10. Ibid.
11. Memo to Limited Partners from Julian H. Robertson Jr., July 1, 1985.
12. Ibid.
13. Memo to Limited Partners from Julian H. Robertson Jr., July 29, 1985.
14. Ibid.
15. Memo to Limited Partners from Julian H. Robertson Jr., October 18, 1985.
16. Performance numbers for this chapter were provided by Julian H. Robertson Jr., through a document titled *Tiger The Record . . . The Reasons*, 1999 version.
17. Memo to Limited Partners from Julian H. Robertson Jr., December 13, 1985.

18. Memo to Limited Partners from Julian H. Robertson Jr., February 10, 1986.
19. Ibid.
20. Ibid.
21. Ibid.
22. Memo to Limited Partners from Julian H. Robertson Jr., May 20, 1986.
23. Ibid.
24. Memo to Limited Partners from Julian H. Robertson Jr., June 24, 1986.
25. Memo to Limited Partners from Julian H. Robertson Jr., July 25, 1986.
26. *Overhanging the market* is a term used in the context of the general markets. It is when a sizable block of securities or commodities contracts that, if released on the market, would put downward pressure on prices and prohibit buying activity that would otherwise translate into upward price movement. Examples include shares held in a dealer's inventory, a large institutional holding, a secondary distribution till in registration, and a large commodity position about to be liquidated.
27. Memo to Limited Partners from Julian H. Robertson Jr., December 18, 1986.
28. Ibid.

The information from this chapter was gathered from Robertson's correspondence with investors during this time in Tiger's operation, as well as through meetings with investors and former Tiger employees and colleagues.

Chapter 6–The Crash of 1987

1. Memo to Limited Partners from Julian H. Robertson Jr., January 21, 1987.
2. Memo to Limited Partners from Julian H. Robertson, Jr. March 6, 1987.
3. Ibid.
4. Ibid.
5. Ibid; and James Stewart, *Den of Thieves* (New York: Simon & Schuster, 1991). Siegel was sentenced to two months in prison and five months' probation and agreed to pay a $9 million fine. He received leniency from Judge Robert Ward in light of his cooperation in prosecuting others involved in the insider-trading scandals.

6. Memo to Limited Partners from Julian H. Robertson, Jr., March 6, 1987.

7. Ibid.

8. Memo to Limited Partners from Julian H. Robertson Jr., May 5, 1987.

9. Memo to Limited Partners from Julian H. Robertson Jr., June 23, 1987.

10. Memo to Limited Partners from Julian H. Robertson Jr., July 13, 1987.

11. Memo to Limited Partners from Julian H. Robertson Jr., August 12, 1987.

12. Memo to Limited Partners from Julian H. Robertson Jr., August 12, 1987.

13. Memo to Limited Partners from Julian H. Robertson Jr., October 2, 1987.

14. *Wall Street Journal* Staff, "The Crash of '87: Stocks Plummet 508.32 Amid Panicky Selling," *Wall Street Journal* (October 20, 1987).

15. Memo to Limited Partners from Julian H. Robertson Jr., November 10, 1987.

16. Kathryn M. Welling "Buy American and short Japan is Julian Robertson's strategy," *Barron's* (December 21, 1987).

17. Memo to Limited Partners from Julian H. Robertson Jr., November 10, 1987.

18. Ibid.

19. Ibid.

20. Ibid.

21. Ibid.

22. Memo to Limited Partners from Julian H. Robertson Jr., November 19, 1987.

23. Memo to Limited Partners from Julian H. Robertson Jr., December 24, 1987.

24. Ibid.

The information for this chapter was gathered through interviews and meetings with Robertson, former Tiger employees and colleagues, and investors.

Chapter 7—The Dawn of a New Era

1. Memo to Limited Partners from Julian H. Robertson Jr., March 21, 1988.

2. Memo to Limited Partners from Tim Schilt, April 5, 1988.

3. Ibid.

4. Ibid.

5. Memo to Limited Partners from Julian H. Robertson Jr., May 17, 1988.

6. Letter to William Clay Ford from Julian H. Robertson Jr., July 1, 1988.

7. Memo to Limited Partners from Julian H. Robertson Jr., July 20, 1988.

8. Memo to Limited Partners from Julian H. Robertson Jr., August 26, 1988.

9. Memo to Limited Partners from Julian H. Robertson Jr., September 23, 1988.

10. Memo to Limited Partners from Julian H. Robertson Jr., November 18, 1988.

11. Memo to Limited Partners from Julian H. Robertson Jr., January 6, 1989.

12. Memo to Partners from Julian H. Robertson Jr., May 9, 1989.

13. Ibid.

14. Memo to Limited Partners from Julian H. Robertson Jr., January 6, 1989.

15. Ibid

16. Ibid. At the time of the buyout, RJR was trading at $55 a share. KKR eventually bought the company at $108, at the time the largest leveraged buyout in history.

17. Memo to Limited Partners from Julian H. Robertson Jr., November 3, 1989.

18. *Tiger: The Record . . . The Reasons*, 1999 version.

Chapter 8–The Tiger Tangles with the Press

1. Gary Weiss, "The World's Best Money Manager–What You Can Learn from Julian Robertson," *BusinessWeek Assets* (November/December 1990).

2. Ibid.

3. Ibid.

4. *Tiger: The Record . . . The Reasons*, 1999 version.

5. Ibid.

6. Memo to Limited Partners from Julian H. Robertson Jr., January 7, 1992.

7. *Tiger: The Record . . . The Reasons*, 1999 version.

8. Memo to Limited Partners from Julian H. Robertson Jr., January 7, 1993.

9. A 13(d) is a report to the Securities and Exchange Commission by persons who acquire more than 5 percent of a certain class of securities in a corporation or entity.

10. Frederick E. Rowe, Jr., "The Best Instincts in the Jungle," *Forbes* (September 16, 1991), 78.

11. Memo to Limited Partners from Julian H. Robertson Jr., January 5, 1995.

12. Kevin Muehring, "Tale of the Tiger: Julian Robertson's Returns," *Institutional Investor* (February 1, 1997), 11.

13. Ibid.

14. Gary Weiss, "The World's Best Money Manager–What You Can Learn from Julian Robertson," *BusinessWeek Assets* (November/December 1990).

15. Ibid.

16. *Julian H. Robertson Jr. versus the McGraw-Hill Companies, Inc., Gary Weiss, and Stephen B. Shepard.* Amended complaint, September 12, 1997.

17. Ibid.

18. *Julian H. Robertson Jr. versus The McGraw-Hill Companies, Inc., Gary Weiss, and Stephen B. Shepard.* Defendant's answer, October 28, 1997.

19. Ibid.

20. "Julian Robertson and BusinessWeek announce settlement," *Business Wire* (December 17, 1997).

21. Ibid.

22. "BusinessWeek Agrees to Settle Libel Suit Brought By Investor," *The Wall Street Journal,* December 18, 1997.

23. Interview with Stephen B. Shepard, January 22, 2003.

24. Memo to Limited Partners from Julian H. Robertson Jr., January 6, 1998.

25. Ibid.

26. Ibid.

Information was gathered for this chapter from multiple sources, including former Tiger employees, brokers, and investors, as well as people involved with and party to the lawsuit between Robertson and McGraw-Hill. The performance numbers were gathered from Tiger documents and deemed to be true.

Chapter 9–The Peak and the Fall

1. Frederick E. Rowe, Jr., "The Best Instincts in the Jungle," *Forbes* (September 16, 1991), 78.
2. Robert Slater, *Soros: The Life, Times, and Trading Secrets of the World's Greatest Investor* (New York: McGraw-Hill Trade, 1995).
3. An interesting aspect of the situation is that had the trade gone the other way, Soros would have suffered enormous losses, which also would have made him famous.
4. This information was provided by Tiger and deemed to be accurate.
5. Interview with Hunt Taylor, Spring 2004.
6. Memo to Limited Partners from Julian H. Robertson Jr., January 6, 1998
7. *Tiger: The Record . . . The Reasons,* 1999 version.
8. Memo to Partners from Julian H. Robertson Jr., May 9, 1989.
9. Memo to Limited Partners from Julian H. Robertson Jr., March 30, 2000.
10. Ibid.
11. Ibid.

Chapter 10–The Press Dissects the Tiger

1. *All Things Considered,* National Public Radio, March 30, 2000.
2. Peter Siris, "Long-Time Star Calls It Quits; Good Strategy, Bad Results," *New York Daily News* (April 1, 2000), 41.
3. Gary Weiss, "What Really Killed Tiger," *BusinessWeek* (April 17, 2000), 166.
4. Ibid.
5. Ibid.
6. Ibid.
7. Gary Weiss, "The Buck Stops with Julian Robertson, Not the Market," *BusinessWeek* (April 17, 2000), 168.
8. Paul Krugman, "Reckonings; A Hedge Fund Pruned," *The New York Times* (April 2, 2000), Section 4, p. 15.
9. Ibid.
10. Alan Abelson, "Macro Trouble," *Barron's* (April 3, 2000), 3.
11. Ibid.

The information for this chapter was gathered through interviews with former Tiger employees, colleagues, and associates of the firm, as well as other individuals who were part of or knowledgeable about this period in Tiger's existence.

Chapter 11–The Tiger Cubs

1. This information was provided by TigerShark and is deemed to be accurate.
2. This information was provided by Tiger Technology Fund and is deemed to be accurate.
3. Gavin Serkin for Bloomberg News, "Hedge Fund Managers to Create Own Venture," *The Orange County Register* (September 17, 2000).

As a matter of disclosure, Tom Facciola has helped me in my class on hedge funds at the New York Society of Security Analysts.

The information for this chapter was gathered through interviews with current and former Tiger employees and associates.

Chapter 12–Lessons Learned from the Tiger

1. *Tiger: The Record . . . The Reasons,* 1999 version.
2. Staff and wire reports, "Malaysia Leader Makes Thinly Veiled Attack on Soros for Currency Crisis," *The Katmandu Post* (July 22, 1997).
3. Ibid.
4. Ibid.
5. AP-Dow Jones, "Soros Denies Currency 'Retaliation,'" July 24, 1997.
6. Dan Robinson, "Soros Denial," *Voice of America* (July 23, 1997).
7. Speech by S.E.C. Chairman William Donaldson: "Opening Statement at Hedge Fund Roundtable," May 14, 2003.
8. Stephanie Strom, "Top Manager to Close Shop on Hedge Funds," *The New York Times* (October 12, 1995), D1.
9. These numbers are net of all of Tiger's fees.
10. Beth Piskora, "Meriwether's History Lesson," *New York Post* (February 19, 2001), 37.
11. Interview with Dale Jacobs, Spring 2002.
12. Conversation with Julian H. Robertson Jr., June 2002.

The material for this chapter was gathered through interviews with market participants, hedge fund industry service providers, and former Tiger employees and colleagues.

Chapter 13–Noblesse Oblige

1. Open Society Institute–Form 990 filed with Internal Revenue Service; November 19, 2002.
2. Agence France Presse, "Soros Puts Money Where Mouth Is to Defeat Bush," Europe Intelligence Wire, January 12, 2004.
3. Information was taken from www.tigerfoundation.org
4. Tiger Foundation–Form 990 filed with Internal Revenue Service; November 20, 2002.
5. Ibid.
6. The Robertson Family Foundation–Form 990 filed with Internal Revenue Service Document; October 18, 2002.
7. Suzanne Wooley, "Ultimate Lunch Club," *Money* magazine (August 2001), 27.
8. The Robin Hood Foundation–Form 990 filed with Internal Revenue Service; September 7, 2003.
9. Kate Dobbs Ariail, "Small Wonders–An Exhibition at NCMA of Only Five Modernist Paintings Gives Viewers Time to Absorb Each Work," *The Independent Weekly* (July 11, 2001).
10. *The Charlie Rose Show,* July 17, 1998, Charlie Rose, Inc.
11. Melissa Biggs Bradley, "Betting on New Zealand," *Town & Country* (June 2001), 105.
12. Larry Olmstead, "Golf Insider's Resort Close-Up" *Golf Insider* (October/November 2002).

INDEX

INDEX

CPSIA information can be obtained
at www.ICGtesting.com
Printed in the USA
BVHW04s0125290618
520388BV00020B/189/P